THE EVERYTHING® Enneagram Book

Dear Reader,

I fell in love with the Enneagram when I learned that modern-day psychologists, psychiatrists, and theologians—respected, intelligent psychologists, psychiatrists, and theologians—utilized it as a counseling tool. With a background in psychology and an ongoing quest for continuing education in the field, I put a great deal of credence on the fact that generations of original thinkers in the field found the Enneagram a legitimate theoretical system for understanding human behavior.

Unlike the horoscope or other similar typing methodologies, the Enneagram is based on what happens to you in this life, on this planet. I found the Enneagram fascinating, and I integrated extensive research with my prior knowledge of psychology to find a way to present the material in an easy-to-understand manner—offering a broad overview that you can easily assimilate and use right off the bat.

I hope you enjoy this exploration into the hidden aspects of personality and come away with a glimpse into your light side, your dark side, and everything in between. If you're lucky, you'll also experience how it feels to crawl behind someone else's eyes and see what it feels like to see the world the way they do—a feat that is destined to improve your relationships. By the way, I'm a Four with a heavy Five wing. What's your type?

Susan Reynolds

Welcome to the EVERYTHING® Series!

These handy, accessible books give you all you need to tackle a difficult project, gain a new hobby, comprehend a fascinating topic, prepare for an exam, or even brush up on something you learned back in school but have since forgotten.

You can choose to read an *Everything®* book from cover to cover or just pick out the information you want from our four useful boxes: e-questions, e-facts, e-alerts, and e-essentials.

We give you everything you need to know on the subject, but throw in a lot of fun stuff along the way, too.

We now have more than 400 *Everything®* books in print, spanning such wide-ranging categories as weddings, pregnancy, cooking, music instruction, foreign language, crafts, pets, New Age, and so much more. When you're done reading them all, you can finally say you know *Everything®*!

Answers to common questions

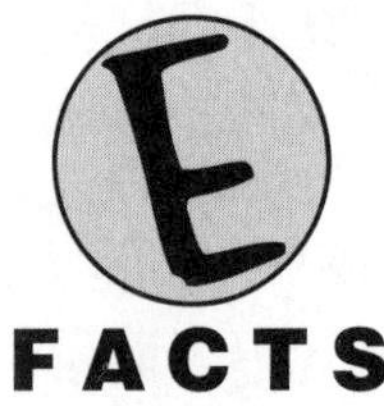

Important snippets of information

Urgent warnings

Quick handy tips

PUBLISHER Karen Cooper

DIRECTOR OF ACQUISITIONS AND INNOVATION Paula Munier

MANAGING EDITOR, EVERYTHING SERIES Lisa Laing

COPY CHIEF Casey Ebert

ACQUISITIONS EDITOR Lisa Laing

DEVELOPMENT EDITOR Elizabeth Kassab

EDITORIAL ASSISTANT Hillary Thompson

Visit the entire Everything® series at *www.everything.com*

THE EVERYTHING® ENNEAGRAM BOOK

Identify your type, gain insight into your personality, and find success in life, love, and business

Susan Reynolds

Adams Media
Avon, Massachusetts

With gratitude and great affection, I dedicate this book to Marjorie Sue Myers, one of my dearest friends, who was in the final stages of valiantly battling ovarian cancer while I was writing this book. She brought love, joy, and inspiration into many lives, and those lucky enough to have shared a portion of our journey with Margie miss her daily.

Published by Adams Media, a division of F+W Media, Inc.
57 Littlefield Street, Avon, MA 02322 U.S.A.
www.adamsmedia.com

ISBN-10: 1-59869-276-3
ISBN-13: 978-1-59869-276-1

Printed in the United States of America.

J I H G F E D

Library of Congress Cataloging-in-Publication Data
available from the publisher.

Interior illustrations by Jennifer Oliveira

Contents

Acknowledgments

Many kudos and thanks to the scholars and theorists who have written books about the Enneagram. Their interpretations and explanations of this system were invaluable in understanding and then forging a way to communicate its basic principles. This book uses Jungian terminology and concepts to explain the Enneagram. In deference to all the aforementioned Enneagram scholars, theorists, and authors, please understand that this book is not in any way attempting to create a new theory or seeking in any way to diminish the unique and valuable contributions of others.

The purpose of this book is to offer *Everything*® readers an easily understandable overview of the Enneagram—where it originated, how it works, why it's gaining favor as a personality typology tool, and how they can use it to further understand themselves and their loved ones and, hopefully, evolve. Each of the chapters has a Jungian overview, and this book does not purport to subvert, reconceptualize, or in any way refute or detract from previous Enneagram books. It is highly recommended that anyone interested in an in-depth, comprehensive understanding of this system read experts on the subject (see Appendix A). This book makes every effort to credit direct references to unique theorists, but, in deference to them, it primarily relies upon deductions formed after extensive research, input from working Enneagram coaches, and the use of Jungian concepts to assimilate and reconfigure descriptions of each of the nine types and behaviors that characterize enneatypes.

The author also thanks Acquisitions Editor Lisa Laing for the opportunity to work on this book, Development Editor Brett Palana-Shanahan for editing assistance, Paula Munier and John Waters for sharing their knowledge, and especially Clarence Thomson for his substantial input, careful review, and many clarifying insights. I also thank my friends: Emma Gordon, Kenny Harris, Darlene Torrence, Eddie Parker, Ann Masters, Evelyn Myers, Kika Rosenthal, Ken Silverberg, Margaret and Jaime Juntwait, Jane and Mike Rudes, Lori and Brian Zaslow, Mara McGinnis, Nancy Jaslow Bader, Brian Ballerini, Arlene Corsello, Sheila Ryan, Stanley Keith, Gale Giorgi, Wanda Whalen, Jan Berry Kadrie, Terra Mizwa, and many others; my siblings Roy, Jim, Rozanne, and their families; and especially my beloved children Brooke and Brett Aved for tolerating long periods of silence and limited opportunities to visit throughout the long course of writing this book.

Top Ten Things You Need to Know about the Enneagram

1. The Enneagram is believed to be derived from an extensive body of secret and sacred knowledge, possibly dating back to Sufi mysticism.
2. In the hands of contemporary interpreters it has evolved into a powerful system for personal, spiritual, and professional understanding of human personality.
3. The Enneagram symbol is a two-dimensional, nine-pointed figure enclosed in a circle, consisting of crisscrossing lines that connect nine points, or enneatypes.
4. Each enneatype is infinitely nuanced, and the types all overlap so descriptive qualifiers can be too limiting.
5. The numbers are neutral markers. For example, a Seven isn't healthier, more evolved, or somehow inherently better than a Two.
6. Everyone possesses qualities and characteristic behaviors of each enneatype, but everyone only has one enneatype.
7. Your enneatype is not who you are; it is what you habitually and consistently do.
8. Your enneatype does not change. You evolve or devolve within its parameters.
9. All the enneatypes are gender neutral.
10. You have a secondary energy (a wing, located on either side of your type on the Enneagram circle) and two connecting points (a security point and a stress point) that influence your behavior.

Introduction

▶ WELCOME TO THE ENNEAGRAM! Welcome to a cohesive personality typing system that is based on what you experience in early childhood and how it—in concert with your biological and genetic heritage—affects your future development.

No matter how well you're doing in life, the truth is that each and every person began life affected in some way by who or what they experienced. And each one, consciously or unconsciously, covered over or clouded their true self—that fragrant *essence* that is them devoid of all the clutter they picked up along the way. Lest you protest that you had perfect parents and a perfect childhood, the fact is you might not have been properly mirrored or validated, you might have been punished for being a certain way, you might have received mixed messages, your parents might have suffered a crisis that separated them from you, you might have responded to excessive restrictions, or your parents might have had vastly different sensibilities than you.

Here's the gist: Even with the most healthy, supportive parents on the planet, you veil, suppress, deny, or cloud parts of your true self, or essence, and then spend the rest of your life feeling as if you are missing important pieces of the puzzle you have become. In fact, it becomes your lifelong task, or quest, to unveil your essence and become whom you were meant to be. And the Enneagram is a marvelous road map to the treasures that lie inside you—unexpressed or expressed, conscious or unconscious, underutilized or unclaimed—and deliciously ripe with essence.

The veil becomes your personality and consists of what you think, what you feel, and how you act or react to various life situations. The way you process information, as well as the way you characteristically behave, creates an amalgam of personality traits that define who you are. The Enneagram delineates nine core personality types (enneatypes) and elucidates their primary fixations, motivations, and patterns of behavior. Because everyone is born with certain affinities, and everyone is greatly affected by their formative years, variations within each type can be wide ranging. Alterations in personality are also affected by adult life experiences, accounting for swings in one direction or another. The Enneagram types identify nine core personalities based on the basic or predominant way each type emotionally experiences, looks at, and interacts with the world around them.

The Enneagram is an extremely complicated system, and this book can admittedly only explore the basic concepts as they relate to the formation of personality (called the Enneagram of Personality). This book has been designed to offer enough substantial information to engage you, and to inspire you to study further. If your interest is limited to wanting to know what the Enneagram of Personality is all about and being able to use it to deepen your understanding of yourself and others, this book will definitely fill the bill. If you're a serious student of the Enneagram, or wish to become one, this book is a solid starting ground. You'll find a list of resources in Appendix A that will take you to the next level and beyond.

Meanwhile, this book will get you in the know when it comes to the Enneagram, offer you incredible insights into your own—and others'—personality, and give you a lot of food for thought about ways you can expand your own consciousness and lift the veil that shrouds your true self or essence.

1

Chapter 1

What's Your Type?

This is the burning question! If you're reading this chapter first, no worries; but if you've read through all of the descriptions in this book and selected whom you'd really like to be, or whom you definitely don't want to be, you may have a problem. Remember, it's important to answer as truthfully as possible. And if this test results in an answer you question, you'll find a multitude of tests you can purchase and take on the Internet. (See Appendix A for several sites.) Luckily, this book has an Enneagram expert as an editor, and he's providing his popular test, which is also available on his Web site for free!

Why This Test Works

Clarence Thomson, M.A. is the author of *Parables and the Enneagram* and coauthor of *Out of the Box: Coaching with the Enneagram* and *Enneagram Applications*. Thomson has been teaching the Enneagram internationally for over fifteen years and was a featured speaker at three International Enneagram Conferences. He has two master's degrees: one in theology and one in social communications, from the University of Ottawa and Université de St. Paul.

Thomson developed a test to identify enneatypes that he offers free on his Web site: *www.enneagramcentral.com*. For the past five years, Thomson estimates that he has received more than 5,000 hits a month, and his feedback is that 90 percent of those who take the test feel as if the test definitely nailed their enneatype.

The only fairly consistent complaints come from Nines, who report that they don't tend to recognize themselves using his test when other tests have revealed them to be a Nine. Also Sixes and Fours occasionally report that they showed up as a Nine. According to Thomson, "Nines don't recognize themselves in daily life; it's one of their primary issues. When Sixes are stressed, they feel overwhelmed and feel like Nines; and Fours, already a withdrawn type, confuse their melancholy with Nine's sense of hopelessness."

Thomson based his test on psychologist Karen Horney's book, *Our Inner Conflicts*. According to Thomson, it is Horney's theory that people generally react to life challenges in one of three consistent, neurotic patterns:

- Moving against others
- Moving toward others
- Moving away from others

Thomson connected these psychological patterns to the following enneatypes:

- **Types Three, Seven, and Eight** are more egoistic and tend to react to life in an active and aggressive way—they move against others.
- **Types One, Two, and Six** are more subject to their own internalized superego and tend to play by the rules—they compliantly move toward others.

- **Types Four, Five, and Nine** all tend to cope with life or strife by withdrawing from life—they move away from others.

The test has been designed to uncover your primary pattern and link it to the appropriate enneatype. It is important when taking this test, or any of the other Enneagram tests, to answer based on who you really feel you are rather than on who you would like to be. For older people, take the test thinking of the way you were when you were twenty. It is also helpful to consider how you react under pressure.

If you take the test and don't feel as if the results are accurate, you may have identified your wing or you may not be seeing yourself clearly. You could ask a few people who really know you well to take the test and choose what they think is true about you, and then compare the results. But please keep in mind that these tests aren't totally accurate by themselves. Nor are you totally bound by the parameters of one enneatype. You not only have fluctuating behavior within each enneatype, but you have an influential wing, as well as a security point and a stress point.

If you don't feel like the test has pegged you, it may be helpful to read the Emotional Origins section in the chapters that describe each enneatype. And reread the enneatype descriptions until you begin to see patterns of behavior. You can also find Enneagram seminars in many major cities throughout the world. (See Appendix A for Web sites that list classes.)

If you still aren't fairly sure you've identified your enneatype, you may have identified your wing, in which case you're close! Take heart; the more you study the Enneagram, the more you will figure out which type you are.

Enneagram Questionnaire Part 1

Part 1 consists of three groups of twenty questions each. Answer each question by checking the box next to the response that best describes your personality. It might make your response clearer if you think of *Seldom* as false, *Sometimes* as maybe, and *Often* as true. Please remember that the results depend on you—the better you depict your true feelings the more accurate the outcome!

Group A1

1. I seem to know what should be done in most situations.

- ☐ Seldom
- ☐ Sometimes
- ☐ Often

2. I find it easy to make moral decisions.

- ☐ Seldom
- ☐ Sometimes
- ☐ Often

3. Compromise is wrong when making moral decisions.

- ☐ Seldom
- ☐ Sometimes
- ☐ Often

4. I am good at getting along with people.

- ☐ Seldom
- ☐ Sometimes
- ☐ Often

5. I am a natural facilitator.

- ☐ Seldom
- ☐ Sometimes
- ☐ Often

6. I work well within systems.

- ☐ Seldom
- ☐ Sometimes
- ☐ Often

7. I have some trouble with a lot of "shoulds" in my life.

- ☐ Seldom
- ☐ Sometimes
- ☐ Often

8. What I should do is often more important than what I may feel.

- ☐ Seldom
- ☐ Sometimes
- ☐ Often

9. Life is difficult.

- ☐ Seldom
- ☐ Sometimes
- ☐ Often

10. Authority is important to me. We need to pay more attention to it than we usually do.

- ☐ Seldom
- ☐ Sometimes
- ☐ Often

11. I have a keen sense of what people need.

- ☐ Seldom
- ☐ Sometimes
- ☐ Often

12. I love to hear people's life stories.

- ☐ Seldom
- ☐ Sometimes
- ☐ Often

13. Whom I'm with is more important than where we go.

- ☐ Seldom
- ☐ Sometimes
- ☐ Often

14. I am good at making people feel special.

- ☐ Seldom
- ☐ Sometimes
- ☐ Often

15. Sometimes I feel I do more for others than I do for myself.

- ☐ Seldom
- ☐ Sometimes
- ☐ Often

16. Sometimes I play the devil's advocate.

- ☐ Seldom
- ☐ Sometimes
- ☐ Often

17. Friends can always count on me.

- ☐ Seldom
- ☐ Sometimes
- ☐ Often

18. I stick with a job until it is finished.

- ☐ Seldom
- ☐ Sometimes
- ☐ Often

19. People need to earn my trust.

- ☐ Seldom
- ☐ Sometimes
- ☐ Often

20. I like the motto, "Be prepared."

- ☐ Seldom
- ☐ Sometimes
- ☐ Often

Scoring

Each selection has a value: Seldom (False) = 0, Sometimes (Maybe) = 1, and Often (True) = 2. Add up your scores and fill in the following to find your total for this group of twenty questions.

_____	Seldom	×	0	=	_____
_____	Sometimes	×	1	=	_____
_____	Often	×	2	=	_____

GROUP A1 TOTAL: _____

Group A2

1. I hate conflict.

- ☐ Seldom
- ☐ Sometimes
- ☐ Often

2. At a social gathering I usually wait for someone to choose me to talk to.

- ☐ Seldom
- ☐ Sometimes
- ☐ Often

3. I like to have more information than most before I act.

- ☐ Seldom
- ☐ Sometimes
- ☐ Often

4. My emotions seem more intense than others'.

- ☐ Seldom
- ☐ Sometimes
- ☐ Often

5. I have a hard time making decisions. I procrastinate.

- ☐ Seldom
- ☐ Sometimes
- ☐ Often

6. I love to watch things at distance. I am a natural observer.

- ☐ Seldom
- ☐ Sometimes
- ☐ Often

7. I don't mind being a little different from the crowd.

- ☐ Seldom
- ☐ Sometimes
- ☐ Often

8. I'm more sensitive than most people and I suffer because of it.

- ☐ Seldom
- ☐ Sometimes
- ☐ Often

9. Solitude is important for me.

- ☐ Seldom
- ☐ Sometimes
- ☐ Often

10. I can get by on less than most people can.

- ☐ Seldom
- ☐ Sometimes
- ☐ Often

11. I can see all sides of every situation.

- ☐ Seldom
- ☐ Sometimes
- ☐ Often

12. I am modest. I find it hard to self-promote.

- ☐ Seldom
- ☐ Sometimes
- ☐ Often

13. I'm more patient than many of my friends.

- ☐ Seldom
- ☐ Sometimes
- ☐ Often

14. People tell me their troubles.

- ☐ Seldom
- ☐ Sometimes
- ☐ Often

15. I love bookstores and libraries.

- ☐ Seldom
- ☐ Sometimes
- ☐ Often

16. Others' needs seem more important than my own.

- ☐ Seldom
- ☐ Sometimes
- ☐ Often

17. I think my subjective opinions are often more important than surveys.

- ☐ Seldom
- ☐ Sometimes
- ☐ Often

18. Aesthetic development is crucial for a full life.

- ☐ Seldom
- ☐ Sometimes
- ☐ Often

19. I love privacy.

- ☐ Seldom
- ☐ Sometimes
- ☐ Often

20. Sometimes I have the feeling I am somehow defective.

- ☐ Seldom
- ☐ Sometimes
- ☐ Often

Scoring

Each selection has a value: Seldom (False) = 0, Sometimes (Maybe) = 1, and Often (True) = 2. Add up your scores and fill in the following to find your total for this group of twenty questions.

______	Seldom	×	0	=	______
______	Sometimes	×	1	=	______
______	Often	×	2	=	______

GROUP A2 TOTAL: ______

Group A3

1. I like to put a little pressure on people to see what they're made of.

- ☐ Seldom
- ☐ Sometimes
- ☐ Often

2. There's always room at the top—for me.

- ☐ Seldom
- ☐ Sometimes
- ☐ Often

3. I like the phrase, "Just do it."

- ☐ Seldom
- ☐ Sometimes
- ☐ Often

4. I'm a natural leader.

- ☐ Seldom
- ☐ Sometimes
- ☐ Often

5. Sometimes I tend to step on some toes to get things done.

- ☐ Seldom
- ☐ Sometimes
- ☐ Often

6. At a social gathering, I usually choose with whom I will talk.

- ☐ Seldom
- ☐ Sometimes
- ☐ Often

7. I'm a natural optimist.

- ☐ Seldom
- ☐ Sometimes
- ☐ Often

8. I tend to like a lot of variety in my life.

- ☐ Seldom
- ☐ Sometimes
- ☐ Often

9. Given a choice between excitement and peace, I often choose excitement.

- ☐ Seldom
- ☐ Sometimes
- ☐ Often

10. I have a low boredom threshold—I make things happen.

- ☐ Seldom
- ☐ Sometimes
- ☐ Often

11. I have a lot of energy.

- ☐ Seldom
- ☐ Sometimes
- ☐ Often

12. I enjoy work. Sometimes I can turn it into fun.

- ☐ Seldom
- ☐ Sometimes
- ☐ Often

13. I thrive on competition.

- ☐ Seldom
- ☐ Sometimes
- ☐ Often

14. I really know how to celebrate.

- ☐ Seldom
- ☐ Sometimes
- ☐ Often

15. I tell it like it is. I don't pussyfoot around.

- ☐ Seldom
- ☐ Sometimes
- ☐ Often

16. Justice is important to me. Sometimes so is revenge.

- ☐ Seldom
- ☐ Sometimes
- ☐ Often

17. I am a natural champion of the underdog.

- ☐ Seldom
- ☐ Sometimes
- ☐ Often

18. My least favorite word is wimp.

- ☐ Seldom
- ☐ Sometimes
- ☐ Often

19. I get a lot done, more than most people, and I like to be recognized for that.

- ☐ Seldom
- ☐ Sometimes
- ☐ Often

20. Clothes don't make the person, but one's image is important to me.

- ☐ Seldom
- ☐ Sometimes
- ☐ Often

Scoring

Each selection has a value: Seldom (False) = 0, Sometimes (Maybe) = 1, and Often (True) = 2. Add up your scores and fill in the following to find your total for this group of twenty questions.

_____ Seldom × 0 = _____
_____ Sometimes × 1 = _____
_____ Often × 2 = _____

GROUP A3 TOTAL: _____

Part 1 Scoring

Compare your scores from all three groups. If your highest score was in Group A1, see Part 2, Group B1. right here on page 9. If Group A2 shows your highest score, proceed to Part 2, Group B2 on page 14. And finally, if you scored highest on Group A3, go to Part 2, Group B3 page 18.

Enneagram Questionnaire Part 2

This part of the questionnaire consists of three groups, each consisting of three subgroups of sixteen questions each. You will only answer questions in one group, which is determined by your answers to Part 1. Answer each question by checking the box next to the response that best describes your personality. Again, be honest—your accurate score depends on it!

Answer the questions in Groups B1.1, B1.2, and B1.3 if your highest score in Part 1 was in Group A1.

Group B1.1

1. I have a knack for knowing the right way to do things.

- ☐ Seldom
- ☐ Sometimes
- ☐ Often

2. I don't like compromise.

- ☐ Seldom
- ☐ Sometimes
- ☐ Often

3. "There is always room for improvement" is my motto.

- ☐ Seldom
- ☐ Sometimes
- ☐ Often

4. Quality is more important than quantity—always.

- ☐ Seldom
- ☐ Sometimes
- ☐ Often

5. We should all develop our full potential.

- ☐ Seldom
- ☐ Sometimes
- ☐ Often

6. Life is difficult; we have to do our best.

- ☐ Seldom
- ☐ Sometimes
- ☐ Often

7. "God is in the details." People should know how the system works.

- ☐ Seldom
- ☐ Sometimes
- ☐ Often

8. I have a strong tendency to compare what is real with what would be perfect.

- ☐ Seldom
- ☐ Sometimes
- ☐ Often

9. I have a tendency to evaluate things closely.

- ☐ Seldom
- ☐ Sometimes
- ☐ Often

10. I think it is important to do good work in everything I do.

- ☐ Seldom
- ☐ Sometimes
- ☐ Often

11. I have high standards for myself and for others, too.

- ☐ Seldom
- ☐ Sometimes
- ☐ Often

12. I can get irritated when people don't meet or even have standards.

- ☐ Seldom
- ☐ Sometimes
- ☐ Often

13. People need some kind of moral compass.

- ☐ Seldom
- ☐ Sometimes
- ☐ Often

14. Sometimes I am clearer about what I ought to do than what I really want to do.

- ☐ Seldom
- ☐ Sometimes
- ☐ Often

15. I have a strong sense of social responsibility and social order.

- ☐ Seldom
- ☐ Sometimes
- ☐ Often

16. I always try to do my best, and the world would be a better place if everyone did their best.

- ☐ Seldom
- ☐ Sometimes
- ☐ Often

Scoring

Each selection has a value: Seldom (False) = 0, Sometimes (Maybe) = 1, and Often (True) = 2. Add up your scores and fill in the following to find your total for this group of twenty questions.

_____	Seldom	×	0	=	_____
_____	Sometimes	×	1	=	_____
_____	Often	×	2	=	_____

GROUP B1.1 TOTAL: _____

Group B1.2

1. I have a knack for knowing and meeting other people's needs.
   - ☐ Seldom
   - ☐ Sometimes
   - ☐ Often
2. I have a lot of fantastic friends.
   - ☐ Seldom
   - ☐ Sometimes
   - ☐ Often
3. I am modest and I help others get the spotlight.
   - ☐ Seldom
   - ☐ Sometimes
   - ☐ Often
4. I am naturally a nurturing person.
   - ☐ Seldom
   - ☐ Sometimes
   - ☐ Often
5. I'm good at giving people the perfect gift.
   - ☐ Seldom
   - ☐ Sometimes
   - ☐ Often
6. Love is the most important thing in the world.
   - ☐ Seldom
   - ☐ Sometimes
   - ☐ Often
7. I love to tell people their good points to encourage them.
   - ☐ Seldom
   - ☐ Sometimes
   - ☐ Often
8. I pride myself on being a people person.
   - ☐ Seldom
   - ☐ Sometimes
   - ☐ Often
9. I have this ability to see what people really need, sometimes even before they do themselves.
   - ☐ Seldom
   - ☐ Sometimes
   - ☐ Often
10. If I can, I try to meet those needs. I think it is important to be modest, so I don't flaunt my own needs.
    - ☐ Seldom
    - ☐ Sometimes
    - ☐ Often

11. I think relationships are the most important thing in the world and I have a lot of them.

- ☐ Seldom
- ☐ Sometimes
- ☐ Often

12. People just naturally come to me, especially to share in times of stress or sorrow.

- ☐ Seldom
- ☐ Sometimes
- ☐ Often

13. I am a good listener.

- ☐ Seldom
- ☐ Sometimes
- ☐ Often

14. I think we get ahead in this world by helping others get what they want.

- ☐ Seldom
- ☐ Sometimes
- ☐ Often

15. I don't need much recognition, but I do get warm feelings when I am appreciated.

- ☐ Seldom
- ☐ Sometimes
- ☐ Often

16. I try so hard.

- ☐ Seldom
- ☐ Sometimes
- ☐ Often

Scoring

Each selection has a value: Seldom (False) = 0, Sometimes (Maybe) = 1, and Often (True) = 2. Add up your scores and fill in the following to find your total for this group of twenty questions.

_____	Seldom	×	0	=	_____
_____	Sometimes	×	1	=	_____
_____	Often	×	2	=	_____

GROUP B1.2 TOTAL: _____

Group B1.3

1. I like to be the devil's advocate. It flushes out the whole truth.

- ☐ Seldom
- ☐ Sometimes
- ☐ Often

2. People need to earn my trust.

- ☐ Seldom
- ☐ Sometimes
- ☐ Often

3. I love family and community traditions. I do my share.

- ☐ Seldom
- ☐ Sometimes
- ☐ Often

4. I'm good at community functions.

- ☐ Seldom
- ☐ Sometimes
- ☐ Often

5. I'm my own worst enemy.

- ☐ Seldom
- ☐ Sometimes
- ☐ Often

6. I don't trust authority figures, even though I know they are important.

- ☐ Seldom
- ☐ Sometimes
- ☐ Often

7. I like jobs that have clearly assigned tasks. I'll do them well.

- ☐ Seldom
- ☐ Sometimes
- ☐ Often

8. I'm a loyal friend.

- ☐ Seldom
- ☐ Sometimes
- ☐ Often

9. My few trusted friends are really important to me.

- ☐ Seldom
- ☐ Sometimes
- ☐ Often

10. It's important to have friends you can trust, because you can't trust a lot of so-called authorities.

- ☐ Seldom
- ☐ Sometimes
- ☐ Often

11. The government, the media, and the medical profession—they all tell just their side of the story.

- ☐ Seldom
- ☐ Sometimes
- ☐ Often

12. Sometimes I have trouble making up my mind.

- ☐ Seldom
- ☐ Sometimes
- ☐ Often

13. It seems that any decision I make will bring trouble down on me.

- ☐ Seldom
- ☐ Sometimes
- ☐ Often

14. I think I just worry too much.

- ☐ Seldom
- ☐ Sometimes
- ☐ Often

15. You have to worry because you can't trust just anyone.

- ☐ Seldom
- ☐ Sometimes
- ☐ Often

16. Sometimes I go ahead and do what I worry most about, just to get rid of the tension.

- ☐ Seldom
- ☐ Sometimes
- ☐ Often

Scoring

Each selection has a value: Seldom (False) = 0, Sometimes (Maybe) = 1, and Often (True) = 2. Add up your scores and fill in the following to find your total for this group of twenty questions.

______	Seldom	×	0	=	______
______	Sometimes	×	1	=	______
______	Often	×	2	=	______

GROUP B1.3 TOTAL: ______

▶ **Answer the questions in Groups B2.1, B2.2, and B2.3 if your highest score in Part 1 was in Group A2.**

Group B2.1

1. I love drama. Life is dramatic when lived fully.

☐ Seldom
☐ Sometimes
☐ Often

2. It is important for me to be authentic.

☐ Seldom
☐ Sometimes
☐ Often

3. Taste in matters of art, music, clothes, and manners is important.

☐ Seldom
☐ Sometimes
☐ Often

4. I don't mind standing out in the crowd.

☐ Seldom
☐ Sometimes
☐ Often

5. Sometimes I have to share my melancholy feelings.

☐ Seldom
☐ Sometimes
☐ Often

6. I love being original. Creativity is important to me.

☐ Seldom
☐ Sometimes
☐ Often

7. I think my emotions are more intense than most people's.

☐ Seldom
☐ Sometimes
☐ Often

8. I am more sensitive than most people. I experience more pain than most.

☐ Seldom
☐ Sometimes
☐ Often

9. The pain may be worth it though, I enjoy beauty so much.

☐ Seldom
☐ Sometimes
☐ Often

10. It seems to me that a lot of people just skim over life.

- ☐ Seldom
- ☐ Sometimes
- ☐ Often

11. I can see beauty where others can't; this often sets me apart.

- ☐ Seldom
- ☐ Sometimes
- ☐ Often

12. I feel sort of different from ordinary people.

- ☐ Seldom
- ☐ Sometimes
- ☐ Often

13. My tastes seem more refined. I place a higher value on artistic sensitivity.

- ☐ Seldom
- ☐ Sometimes
- ☐ Often

14. I often have trouble in relationships because of my sensitivity.

- ☐ Seldom
- ☐ Sometimes
- ☐ Often

15. Relationships start out fine, but then little things go wrong.

- ☐ Seldom
- ☐ Sometimes
- ☐ Often

16. It seems like I can never have the perfect relationship I'm searching for.

- ☐ Seldom
- ☐ Sometimes
- ☐ Often

Scoring

Each selection has a value: Seldom (False) = 0, Sometimes (Maybe) = 1, and Often (True) = 2. Add up your scores and fill in the following to find your total for this group of twenty questions.

_____	Seldom	×	0	=	_____
_____	Sometimes	×	1	=	_____
_____	Often	×	2	=	_____

GROUP B2.1 TOTAL: _____

Group B2.2

1. I need my privacy. I relish solitude.

- ☐ Seldom
- ☐ Sometimes
- ☐ Often

2. Sometimes it feels like I'm invisible.

- ☐ Seldom
- ☐ Sometimes
- ☐ Often

3. I like lots of information before I act.

- ☐ Seldom
- ☐ Sometimes
- ☐ Often

4. I can get by on less than most people can.

- ☐ Seldom
- ☐ Sometimes
- ☐ Often

5. I'm more logical about life than most.

- ☐ Seldom
- ☐ Sometimes
- ☐ Often

6. I'd make a good reporter. I like to watch what's going on.

- ☐ Seldom
- ☐ Sometimes
- ☐ Often

7. I really like to share information.

- ☐ Seldom
- ☐ Sometimes
- ☐ Often

8. Descartes had it right: "I think, therefore I am."

- ☐ Seldom
- ☐ Sometimes
- ☐ Often

9. What I think is important to me.

- ☐ Seldom
- ☐ Sometimes
- ☐ Often

10. I need more privacy than others—time alone to think clearly about life.

- ☐ Seldom
- ☐ Sometimes
- ☐ Often

11. I'm a keen observer of life.

- ☐ Seldom
- ☐ Sometimes
- ☐ Often

12. I understand what is really going on.

- ☐ Seldom
- ☐ Sometimes
- ☐ Often

13. I think I'd rather watch than participate in a lot of things.

- ☐ Seldom
- ☐ Sometimes
- ☐ Often

14. When I'm alone I think more clearly and objectively than most people.

- ☐ Seldom
- ☐ Sometimes
- ☐ Often

15. I don't get emotional when I make my judgments and decisions.

- ☐ Seldom
- ☐ Sometimes
- ☐ Often

16. I like to plan things before they happen and then replay them in my mind.

- ☐ Seldom
- ☐ Sometimes
- ☐ Often

Scoring

Each selection has a value: Seldom (False) = 0, Sometimes (Maybe) = 1, and Often (True) = 2. Add up your scores and fill in the following to find your total for this group of twenty questions.

______	Seldom	×	0	=	______
______	Sometimes	×	1	=	______
______	Often	×	2	=	______

GROUP B2.2 TOTAL: ______

Group B2.3

1. I can see all sides of a question.

- ☐ Seldom
- ☐ Sometimes
- ☐ Often

2. I have some trouble asserting what I want.

- ☐ Seldom
- ☐ Sometimes
- ☐ Often

3. I don't decide my priorities very easily.

- ☐ Seldom
- ☐ Sometimes
- ☐ Often

4. I don't mind routine.

- ☐ Seldom
- ☐ Sometimes
- ☐ Often

5. I hate conflict.

- ☐ Seldom
- ☐ Sometimes
- ☐ Often

6. I have a little trouble with procrastination.

- ☐ Seldom
- ☐ Sometimes
- ☐ Often

7. I'm a natural peacemaker and negotiator.

- ☐ Seldom
- ☐ Sometimes
- ☐ Often

8. I'm sort of laid-back and mellow.

- ☐ Seldom
- ☐ Sometimes
- ☐ Often

9. I understand others' points of view. I don't push mine if theirs are good.

- ☐ Seldom
- ☐ Sometimes
- ☐ Often

10. I have some trouble taking initiative; I prefer to work with others.

- ☐ Seldom
- ☐ Sometimes
- ☐ Often

11. Sometimes I don't pay enough attention to what I want myself.

- ☐ Seldom
- ☐ Sometimes
- ☐ Often

12. I start out with good intentions, then end up doing something else.

- ☐ Seldom
- ☐ Sometimes
- ☐ Often

13. I don't get angry much, and even when I do, I don't show it.

- ☐ Seldom
- ☐ Sometimes
- ☐ Often

14. Occasionally I get a kind of sneaky revenge.

- ☐ Seldom
- ☐ Sometimes
- ☐ Often

15. People really like me because of my pleasant personality.

- ☐ Seldom
- ☐ Sometimes
- ☐ Often

16. I'm not threatening or pushy but I still get things done.

- ☐ Seldom
- ☐ Sometimes
- ☐ Often

Scoring

Each selection has a value: Seldom (False) = 0, Sometimes (Maybe) = 1, and Often (True) = 2. Add up your scores and fill in the following to find your total for this group of twenty questions.

_____	Seldom	×	0	=	_____
_____	Sometimes	×	1	=	_____
_____	Often	×	2	=	_____

GROUP B2.3 TOTAL: _____

▶ **Answer the questions in Groups B3.1, B3.2, and B3.3 if your highest score in Part 1 was in Group A3.**

Group B3.1

1. I love to succeed. I hate to fail. I don't fail much.

- ☐ Seldom
- ☐ Sometimes
- ☐ Often

2. Clothes don't make the person, but they might make the sale.

- ☐ Seldom
- ☐ Sometimes
- ☐ Often

3. I hate to waste time. I'm efficient.

- ☐ Seldom
- ☐ Sometimes
- ☐ Often

4. Most people can't keep up with me. I accomplish a lot.

- ☐ Seldom
- ☐ Sometimes
- ☐ Often

5. I believe in having goals and really working for them.

- ☐ Seldom
- ☐ Sometimes
- ☐ Often

6. I like recognition for my hard work. Money is good, too.

- ☐ Seldom
- ☐ Sometimes
- ☐ Often

7. Sometimes I have to set my emotions aside and get the job done.

- ☐ Seldom
- ☐ Sometimes
- ☐ Often

8. I like the Army slogan, "Be all you can be."

- ☐ Seldom
- ☐ Sometimes
- ☐ Often

9. I think it is important to succeed at what you try to do.

- ☐ Seldom
- ☐ Sometimes
- ☐ Often

10. I work hard, I play by the rules (unless they're unfair), and I love to compete.

- ☐ Seldom
- ☐ Sometimes
- ☐ Often

11. I think competition brings out the best in us and I love to be number one.

- ☐ Seldom
- ☐ Sometimes
- ☐ Often

12. I'm a positive, upbeat person with lots of energy.

- ☐ Seldom
- ☐ Sometimes
- ☐ Often

13. I may work a little too hard at times, but a little stress doesn't hurt anyone.

- ☐ Seldom
- ☐ Sometimes
- ☐ Often

14. Success doesn't always come cheap, and you have to be willing to pay the price.

- ☐ Seldom
- ☐ Sometimes
- ☐ Often

15. I don't make the rules of life, but I do make the most of them.

- ☐ Seldom
- ☐ Sometimes
- ☐ Often

16. I can make a system work.

- ☐ Seldom
- ☐ Sometimes
- ☐ Often

Scoring

Each selection has a value: Seldom (False) = 0, Sometimes (Maybe) = 1, and Often (True) = 2. Add up your scores and fill in the following to find your total for this group of twenty questions.

______	Seldom	×	0	=	______
______	Sometimes	×	1	=	______
______	Often	×	2	=	______

GROUP B3.1 TOTAL: ______

Group B3.2

1. I'm a natural storyteller. Polish improves truth.
   - ☐ Seldom
   - ☐ Sometimes
   - ☐ Often
2. I'm really resilient. I bounce back quickly.
   - ☐ Seldom
   - ☐ Sometimes
   - ☐ Often
3. I have a teensy problem with addictions: sweets, alcohol, drugs, or even new ideas. I like excitement and variety.
   - ☐ Seldom
   - ☐ Sometimes
   - ☐ Often
4. I can turn work into fun.
   - ☐ Seldom
   - ☐ Sometimes
   - ☐ Often
5. I'm better at starting things than finishing them.
   - ☐ Seldom
   - ☐ Sometimes
   - ☐ Often
6. Few have as much energy and enthusiasm as I do.
   - ☐ Seldom
   - ☐ Sometimes
   - ☐ Often
7. Humor is central in my life.
   - ☐ Seldom
   - ☐ Sometimes
   - ☐ Often
8. Most people aren't as happy as I am.
   - ☐ Seldom
   - ☐ Sometimes
   - ☐ Often
9. If you look at things right, you know they're going to work out.
   - ☐ Seldom
   - ☐ Sometimes
   - ☐ Often
10. People shouldn't dwell on the negative.
    - ☐ Seldom
    - ☐ Sometimes
    - ☐ Often

11. I always have lots of things to do that I like. Why do people sit around and complain?

- ☐ Seldom
- ☐ Sometimes
- ☐ Often

12. Oh sure, I have troubles, too, but I can usually think of a way to live life to the fullest.

- ☐ Seldom
- ☐ Sometimes
- ☐ Often

13. If something doesn't work, then stop doing it. Do something else; be creative.

- ☐ Seldom
- ☐ Sometimes
- ☐ Often

14. I appreciate the newness of things.

- ☐ Seldom
- ☐ Sometimes
- ☐ Often

15. I love to start new projects if the old ones get boring.

- ☐ Seldom
- ☐ Sometimes
- ☐ Often

16. I can't stand boredom. People who are bored or boring should do something about it.

- ☐ Seldom
- ☐ Sometimes
- ☐ Often

Scoring

Each selection has a value: Seldom (False) = 0, Sometimes (Maybe) = 1, and Often (True) = 2. Add up your scores and fill in the following to find your total for this group of twenty questions.

_____	Seldom	×	0	=	_____
_____	Sometimes	×	1	=	_____
_____	Often	×	2	=	_____

GROUP B3.2 TOTAL: _____

Group B3.3

1. Life is a war. I'm glad I'm strong.

- ☐ Seldom
- ☐ Sometimes
- ☐ Often

2. I put a little pressure on people to see how they respond.

- ☐ Seldom
- ☐ Sometimes
- ☐ Often

3. I tell it like it is. I don't pussyfoot around.

- ☐ Seldom
- ☐ Sometimes
- ☐ Often

4. I like to use my power to get things done.

- ☐ Seldom
- ☐ Sometimes
- ☐ Often

5. I'm a natural leader.

- ☐ Seldom
- ☐ Sometimes
- ☐ Often

6. Sometimes I offend people without meaning to.

- ☐ Seldom
- ☐ Sometimes
- ☐ Often

7. My least favorite word is "wimp."

- ☐ Seldom
- ☐ Sometimes
- ☐ Often

8. The shortest distance between two points is a straight line. I like that.

- ☐ Seldom
- ☐ Sometimes
- ☐ Often

9. People should be straight, honest, and clear—no mealy-mouthed excuses.

- ☐ Seldom
- ☐ Sometimes
- ☐ Often

10. Just do it.

- ☐ Seldom
- ☐ Sometimes
- ☐ Often

11. Sometimes you just have to take matters into your own hands to get things done.

- ☐ Seldom
- ☐ Sometimes
- ☐ Often

12. There's a lot of injustice. People of integrity just have to straighten things out.

- ☐ Seldom
- ☐ Sometimes
- ☐ Often

13. I like action, results, and a clear understanding of what needs to be done—then I do it!

- ☐ Seldom
- ☐ Sometimes
- ☐ Often

14. I don't mind a good fight to set things right, either.

- ☐ Seldom
- ☐ Sometimes
- ☐ Often

15. I don't back down when I know I'm right.

- ☐ Seldom
- ☐ Sometimes
- ☐ Often

16. People know they can count on me, no matter what.

- ☐ Seldom
- ☐ Sometimes
- ☐ Often

Scoring

Each selection has a value: Seldom (False) = 0, Sometimes (Maybe) = 1, and Often (True) = 2. Add up your scores and fill in the following to find your total for this group of twenty questions.

_____ Seldom × 0 = _____
_____ Sometimes × 1 = _____
_____ Often × 2 = _____

GROUP B3.3 TOTAL: _____

Part 2 Scoring

Fill in your Part 2 scores below. Remember that you should have only three scores for this part of the test. Match your highest score to one of the nine enneatypes listed below.

Group	Score	Enneatype
B1.1	_____	One: Evangelical Idealist
B1.2	_____	Two: People Pleaser
B1.3	_____	Six: Loyal Guardian
B2.1	_____	Four: Creative Seeker
B2.2	_____	Five: Masterful Hermit
B2.3	_____	Nine: Peaceful Lamb
B3.1	_____	Three: King of the Hill
B3.2	_____	Seven: Optimistic Dreamer
B3.3	_____	Eight: The Dominator

One: Evangelical Idealist

I have a strong tendency to compare what is real with what would be perfect. I have a tendency to evaluate things closely. I think it is important to do good work in everything I do. I have high standards for myself and for others, too. I can get irritated when people don't meet or even have standards. People need some kind of moral compass. Sometimes I am clearer about what I ought to do than what I really want to do. I have a strong sense of social responsibility and social order. I always try to do my best, and the world would be a better place if everyone did their best.

Two: People Pleaser

I pride myself on being a people person. I have this ability to see what people really need, sometimes even before they do themselves. If I can, I try to meet those needs. I think it is important to be modest, so I don't flaunt my own needs. I think relationships are the most important thing in the world and I have a lot of them. People just naturally come to me, especially to share in times of stress or sorrow. I am a good listener. I think we get ahead in this world by helping others get what they want. I don't need much recognition, but I do get warm feelings when I am appreciated. I try so hard.

Three: King of the Hill

I like the Army slogan, "Be all you can be." I think it is important to succeed at what you try to do. I work hard, I play by the rules, usually (unless they're unfair), and I love to compete. I think competition brings out the best in us and I love to be number one. I'm a positive, upbeat person with lots of energy. I make things happen and I don't mind if others recognize that. I may work a little too hard at times because it is hard to make life work on all fronts, but a little stress doesn't hurt anyone. Success doesn't always come cheap and you have to be willing to pay the price. I don't make the rules of life, but I make the most of them. I can make a system work.

Four: Creative Seeker

I am more sensitive than most people are, which is why I probably experience more pain than most. It seems to me that a lot of people just skim over life. The pain may be worth it, though, I enjoy beauty so much. It seems I can see beauty where others can't. This often sets me apart from others. I feel sort of different from ordinary people. My tastes seem more refined and I place a higher value on artistic sensitivity than many of my friends. I often have trouble in relationships because of my sensitivity. They start out fine, but then little things go wrong. It seems like I can never have the perfect relationship I'm always looking for.

Five: Masterful Hermit

Descartes had it right: "I think, therefore I am." What I think is important to me. I may require more privacy than others, but a person needs some time alone to think clearly about life. I'm a keen observer of life. I understand what is really going on. I think I'd sooner watch than participate in a lot of things. When I'm alone I think more clearly and objectively than most people. I don't get so emotional when I make my judgments and decisions. I like to plan things before they happen and then replay them in my mind. Then I know what I really think and feel about what happened.

Six: Loyal Guardian

I'm a loyal friend and my few trusted friends are really important to me. It's important to have friends you can trust, because you can't trust a lot of so-called authorities. The government, the media, and the medical profession—they all tell their side of the story and you have to listen with an inner ear to get the real message. Sometimes I have trouble making up my mind. It seems that any decision I make will bring trouble down on me. I think I just worry too much, but you do have to worry because you can't trust just anyone. Sometimes I just go ahead and do what I worry most about, just to get rid of the tension.

Seven: Optimistic Dreamer

Most people aren't as happy as I am. If you look at things right, you know they're going to work out all right. People shouldn't dwell on the negative. I always have lots of things to do that I like, and I don't see why so many people sit around and complain. Oh sure, I have troubles, too, but I can usually think of a way to live life to the fullest anyway. If something doesn't work, then stop doing it. Do something else; be creative. I have a little problem with some of my appetites but nothing to worry about. I appreciate the newness of things. I love to start new projects if the old ones get boring. I can't stand boredom. People who are bored or boring should do something about it.

Eight: The Dominator

The shortest distance between two points is a straight line. I like that. Straight, honest, clear, no mealy-mouthed excuses—just do it. John Wayne was right. Sometimes you just have to take matters into your own hands to get things done. There's a lot of injustice in the world and people of integrity just have to straighten things out. I like action and results. I like a clear understanding of what needs to be done and then I do it! I don't mind a good fight to set things right, either. I don't back down when I know I'm right. People know they can count on me, no matter what.

Nine: Peaceful Lamb

I'm sort of laid-back and mellow. I'm modest and can understand others' points of view. I don't push mine if theirs are good; I'll go along. I don't like conflict, I'd sooner get along and work together with people. I have some trouble taking initiative. I'd just as soon work with others. Sometimes I don't pay enough attention to what I want myself. I get distracted easily. I start out with good intentions, but then I end up doing something else. I don't angry much, and even when I do, I don't show it. I might do a slow burn once in a while and occasionally I get a kind of sneaky revenge. People really like me because of my pleasant personality. I'm not threatening or pushy, but I still get things done.

Chapter 2

An Introduction to the Enneagram

2

If you're reading these words, you've at least heard about the Enneagram. Maybe you overheard friends or coworkers describing people using numbers: "She's such a Four," or "You have to expect that from an Eight." You probably thought they were discussing numerology, astrology, the tarot, or, if you had a background in psychology, the Myers-Briggs Type Indicator. Whether you were irritated or intrigued—or both—this chapter will introduce you to an ancient system that has evolved into a modern tool for understanding human personality.

The Fundamental Questions

Nothing is more interesting, more confusing, or more frustrating to people than other people. Everyone's life is filled with questions about the true motives, core beliefs, and hidden fears of coworkers, friends, family members, and, perhaps most importantly, themselves. What is it that makes one person an optimist and another a pessimist? Why is one person status conscious and another oblivious to the opinions of others? Why does an argument seem to energize your brother but leave your sister exhausted? How can your daughter be so good at so many things but so bad at sticking to any one of them? Why does your husband judge other people so harshly, even the people he loves? Why do you find it so difficult to ask for what you want?

It shouldn't surprise you to learn that people have been delving into the mysteries of human personality for centuries, long before the advent of modern psychology. What may surprise you, however, is that the Enneagram is one of the most popular modern tools for understanding human personality and possibly one of the oldest.

It's human nature to be curious about what makes people tick. Once the basic needs for food, shelter, love, and security are met, people can't help wondering about the motives of others—who they are under their skin and why they do the things they do. It may even be a survival instinct. What could be more useful than the ability to figure out what makes people tick? Its value in daily life should be obvious: Knowing what really motivates your employees is bound to make you a better manager. Understanding the true fears behind your children's behavior is sure to make you a better parent. Recognizing your own core beliefs cannot help but improve your romantic relationships.

What Is the Enneagram?

The Enneagram is a personality typing system that most theorists believe has ancient roots that may go as far back as Islamic or Sufi mysticism. The origin of this extensive, complicated body of secret and sacred knowledge has remained obscure, but one can find parallels in Sufi, Christian, and Kabala sources. What we do know is that generations of spiritual teachers passed the Enneagram system down orally, and that around the same time that Freud and Jung were developing theories on human psychology at the turn of the twentieth century, George Ivanovich Gurdjieff, a spiritual teacher of some prominence during those times, began sharing his knowledge of the ancient Enneagram system to select students.

Current Enneagram teachers trace modern knowledge of the Enneagram to the 1960s and 1970s when psychologist Oscar Ichazo and psychiatrist Claudio Naranjo, M.D., who used their modern psychological knowledge to interpret the ancient spiritual teachings, began offering interpretative classes to select students. The Jesuits are also credited with interpreting and teaching the Enneagram through retreats and within the confines of their religious institutions for many years.

The word *Enneagram* is Greek, the diagram is of Sufi (Islamic) origin, and the personality designations are given in Latin, but scholars dispute the contributions and proportions of its three traditions. Mystics, priests, psychologists, and social scientists have all studied, taught, written about, and utilized it. In the hands of contemporary interpreters it has evolved into a powerful system for personal, spiritual, and professional understanding of human personality.

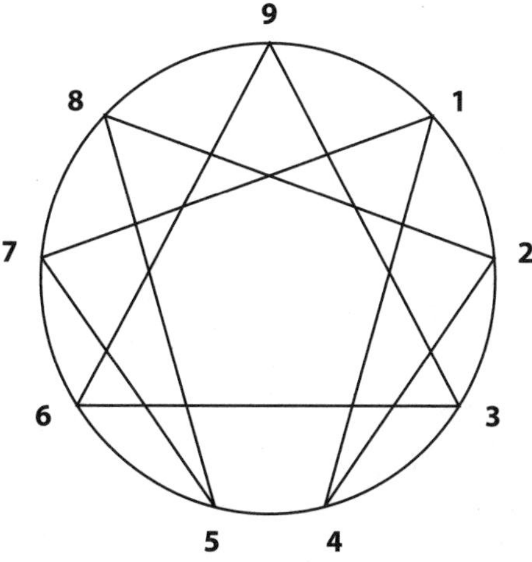

FIGURE 2-1 The Enneagram with Its Interconnecting Points

This system, which describes and organizes nine distinct but interconnected personality types, has evolved into a practical and accessible tool for those seeking a better understanding of their friends, their family, and especially themselves.

FACT

The Enneagram (pronounced *any-uh-gram*) is a two-dimensional, nine-pointed figure enclosed in a circle. The figure is made up of crisscrossing lines that connect the nine points, which are equally spaced around the circle according to the interaction that occurs between them. The name comes from the Greek *ennea*, which means "nine," and *grammos*, which means "something written or drawn."

There are several different Enneagram teaching systems, for example, the Enneagram of Personality and the Enneagram of Process. This book focuses on the Enneagram of Personality. Some writers have referred to this system as the Enneagram of Fixation, but you'll rarely see that designation in modern works on the topic. When most people talk about the Enneagram they mean the Enneagram of Personality, and for the sake of simplicity this book will use that shorthand, too.

The Enneagram symbol (including the star shape and the circle that surrounds it) diagrams the interrelationships of nine basic personality types, or *enneatypes*. Each type can be thought of as a bundle of related habits or deeply ingrained ways of thinking, relating, and reacting. The intersecting lines and the positions of the different types around the circle map the interrelationships and describe the tasks each person faces. The object of using the Enneagram as a tool for transformation is to use the knowledge it provides about the formation of ego limitations to weaken your particular fixation. Each of these nine points is identified by a number, which is used to refer to the core enneatype.

However, virtually all the teachers and interpreters of the Enneagram offer additional descriptive labels for the different types. Type One, for example, has been called the Reformer, the Perfectionist, the Critic, the Good Person, and, in this book, the Evangelical Idealist. Some theorists utilize these labels as a method of identifying the primary fixation for each type; however, don't get too caught up in the labels. Labels can be misleading, and most people who use the Enneagram as a tool refer only to the number of each type.

Rather than use the labels already in existence, each of the nine chapters that discuss the individual types uses a tagline that provides those just learning the system a way to visualize the type and identify it with someone they may already know—someone that embodies many of the type's characteristics. This will help you understand the depth and complexity of each type, rather than one aspect of each type.

No matter what tagline or identifier you use, attaching negative connotations interferes with figuring out which type you are. Unfortunately, most people are likely to recoil if asked to accept a tagline such as the Dominator but will jump at the chance to be called the Peaceful Lamb. These labels are meant to be helpful in terms of tagging or remembering distinctive qualities for each type, but it's very important to remember that each type is infinitely nuanced and that descriptive qualifiers can overlap.

QUESTION?

Do the Enneagram numbers (One through Nine) represent any kind of ranking, order, or hierarchy?

No, the numbers are meant to be neutral markers. In other words, a Seven isn't healthier, more evolved, or somehow inherently better than a Two, and a Nine's habits aren't any more or less desirable than an Eight's. Each type has its individual strengths and weaknesses.

Everyone possess characteristics, behaviors, and fixations of each of the nine types, but the theory of the Enneagram is that each person also has one primary way of navigating through life. This way of perceiving, interpreting, and interacting with your inner and outer world is your enneatype. But you also have a link to at least one other type, or wing, that greatly influences how your personality functions, as well as a connecting security point and a connecting stress point that also can play a significant role. There will be times in your life when you will behave exactly like all the other enneatypes, but most Enneagram theorists strongly believe that your enneatype does not change.

Also, bear in mind that the types are gender neutral. The fact that you are a man or a woman is likely to influence the way your type expresses itself, but the bundle of traits that make up a type are neither inherently masculine nor feminine. The roles of men and women in society come into play here, too. In the United States, for example, men tend to be rewarded for a certain type of competitiveness, which is apparent in Eights and Threes, while women are typically reinforced for the nurturing and supporting roles that are more natural to Twos and Sixes. But the world is home to plenty of female Eights and male Twos, and at a basic level they behave very much as their opposite-gender counterparts.

Personality by the Numbers

Modern psychologists define human personality as patterns of thinking, emotion, and behavior that are unique to an individual and consistent over time. The numbering system of the Enneagram identifies nine basic enneatypes that delineate core personality traits or behaviors that fit within specific patterns. Your enneatype, also referred to as your style or core personality, has four basic components:

- **Your focus.** The vast majority of Enneagram teachers agree that each type has a particular drive to focus on certain things, and that how you focus—and what you focus on—plays a crucial role in your personality formation. Attention for human beings functions as sunlight does for a plant. What do you focus on? How do you focus?
- **Your energy.** Your energy always follows whatever you focus your attention on. You invest your energy on what's important to you, and that same focus in turn juices you up. What floats your boat? What gets you excited or depressed? Where does your energy go?
- **Your worldview.** Everyone develops a way of seeing the world, or what the Germans call a *weltanschauung*. What's your life philosophy? How do you feel about your place in the wider world? Are you comfortable in the world?

- **A strategy.** A strategy is a structured response to an external situation that causes you to act or react quickly from an unconscious place inside. This fourth component is defined by therapists familiar with neurolinguistic programming as a series of strategies that can play an important role in how a personality functions. What's your modus operandi in the world? How do you typically react to a variety of experiences? How do you behave when stressed? How do you act when happy?

Your Enneagram style is not who you are; it is what you habitually and consistently do. Your enneatype or personality is both dynamic and structured, like water flowing downhill from a stream. Understanding this dynamic flow of energy—or your patterned ways of behaving—helps you delineate ways that you can make changes in your life.

When they intervene, therapists and coaches interrupt a client's primary patterns of doing, or being, as an effective way of weakening a person's fixations and helping that person break free of destructive or counterproductive behavior.

As noted Enneagram teacher and author Helen Palmer pointed out, the basic personality types of the Enneagram represent "how you are in normal circumstances; how you meet each other on the street." And once you have identified what is holding you back, you have the opportunity to make choices that can alter your characteristic, and often unconscious, ways of being in the world. The essential premise of the Enneagram is that at the core of these patterns lies a single energy, a dominant tendency, or a fundamental weakness that engenders the other elements of the pattern and is the primary driving force in everything a person does.

Clarence Thomson, author of *Out of the Box* and guru on the Enneagram Central Web site, describes this core driver as "a prevailing wind that bends a tree permanently, sculpts our interior geography, and shapes our entire life." Some believe that only a few, very enlightened people (the Buddha, Jesus Christ, Mohammed) have transcended the restrictions and limitations of their own personality in this life. But according to Thomson, "The Enneagram describes the inner box we are in and helps us realize the depth and contours of the problems we face. It is primarily a diagnostic tool, which is always the first step in dealing with any situation."

Studying the Enneagram can also be an invitation out of the confining, limited box of an unexamined personality. And if you are willing to take a cold, hard look at your pattern of behaviors, and then do the self-reflection and behavior modification work required—including adopting behaviors from your connecting points that will help you expand your behavioral choices—you can create opportunities to creak open the box and expand your own vision of yourself. Ultimately you will seek to become fully integrated, whole, and liberated from ego restraints.

The Enneagram system assigns nine distinctive personality patterns with numbers, which is a convention that some people find off-putting when they first hear about it. Identifying someone as a Seven or a Two sounds suspiciously like someone has arbitrarily decided to lump unique individuals into narrow, bland categories—pigeonholing people without taking their complexity into consideration. But far from reducing individuals to limiting lists of traits and habits, the Enneagram numbers are meant to provide foundations for explorations that can lead to a much deeper understanding of human personality. Remember: A basic tenet of this system is that each person, each manifestation of the type, is a unique kaleidoscope of interacting forces within the personality.

The dominant tendency alone does not define a personality. It's just one of many factors that combine to make people who they are. This dominant tendency is, in fact, both your best friend and your worst enemy. It's your primary way of coping with life's challenges, developed in childhood and hardened over time. And it does not always serve your best interests.

All of the leading teachers of this system theorize that a person's basic type never changes. They conjecture that core patterns are rooted so deeply they continue to color a person's experience throughout his or her life. A Five can't become a Two, for instance, or a One a Six. The idea is that a person's core, or go-to coping strategy—your back-against-the-wall default pattern—is, by definition, fixed. Look at it this way: If you are a Seven, you cannot help being future focused; it's second nature to you. If you're a One, it will simply be more natural to focus on putting out fires in the here and now.

If you think about this idea, there's an obvious logic to this notion. When you consider the people in your life, do you really know anyone who is, essentially, both status conscious and oblivious of the opinions of others? Passionate and diffident? Empathetic and egocentric? Generous and stingy? "(Enneagram) types are based on passions," Palmer says, "and passions are based on certain physiological responses. You can't be lustful and detached at the same time. The passions are expressions of energy, which rely on different neurological response systems."

This isn't to say that an essentially egocentric person can't grow and find a way to empathize with others, a means-to-an-end-motivated Three can't find genuine joy in doing something for its own sake or a flighty Seven can never persevere. In fact, from time to time, everybody can exhibit behaviors that are very much like those of the other types—potentially all of them—for a range of reasons that will be covered later.

Furthermore, the deeper you delve into the system, the subtler it becomes. This is no blunt instrument, but a sophisticated tool that can account for a fluid range of human behaviors. The system starts with the broad-stroke basic personality types but then refines the picture of each individual by taking into account the influence of other factors, such as these rather obvious examples:

- Your inherited characteristics
- Your living situation or physical environment
- The presence or absence of emotional trauma
- Your parents' enneatypes
- Your parents' degree of function, or pathology, within their enneatypes
- Your siblings' enneatypes
- Your wings and connecting points
- Your parents' and siblings' wings and connecting points

Also, most Enneagram theorists discuss at least three basic degrees of personality functioning—healthy, average, and unhealthy—within each enneatype. The types each also have connecting points, or alternate type behaviors, that they gravitate toward when under duress or when feeling happy or secure. How your enneatype style or personality functions can also be greatly affected by what's happening in your life—if your needs are being easily met, or if you have life and death issues of survival to address.

Again, it's important to recognize one of the most important principles of the Enneagram system: no person is his or her enneatype. The types represent overemphasized coping mechanisms, patterns developed in childhood and clung to in adulthood, but not the true self or essence of a person. All interpreters of the Enneagram agree that a fully integrated, whole self is far greater than the sum of the traits or behaviors that make up any single personality enneatype.

Also, numbers are not progressive. You don't evolve from a One to a Nine. Some types may be more evolved in certain ways, but all types can evolve within their personality range, reaching a point where they are essentially liberated from ego restrictions and able to live their lives from their essence, or truest self.

The placement of the numbers on the Enneagram circle by modern scholars made the concepts fall into place and made sense of Enneagram theory. If you follow the circle logically according to the interactions that take place between types, the circle consists of three triads that are grouped as follows:

- Two, Three, and Four
- Five, Six, and Seven
- Eight, Nine, and One

Other than Chapter 3, which provides a brief overview of each enneatype, this book follows the same organization in that the type descriptions and triad discussions start with type Two then proceed around the circle.

The Promise of the Enneagram

By identifying consistent patterns of thinking and feeling, and organizing them around motives that are rarely apparent, the Enneagram helps you to make sense of the often confusing, quirky, and contradictory things people do. One of the key promises of the system is that it can provide you with an opportunity to transcend the compulsions of your core personalities and help you understand the people around you.

Search for Deeper Meaning

Psychologists talk about this transcendence in terms of personal transformation. The more spiritually oriented might call it conversion. Palmer describes it this way: "The idea is that you discover the motivation within yourself that is the passion or negative tendency, and either through psychological insight understanding or spiritual methodology . . . you try to interrupt the automatic habit of the passion so that it doesn't express itself and cause damage to others in the environment."

Although it's a serious personality theory, often used as a serious assessment tool, the Enneagram can also prove something of a parlor game—providing quick and entertaining insights into the personal traits or habits of friends and family. It can help to explain why Rozanne, a Nine, always stays out of the fray at family events and rarely expresses preferences of her own making; or why Brett, a Five, retreats into a private world while he sorts out his feelings. Or you might finally recognize why two people in the same family who have similar characteristics are still undeniably different. For instance, Brooke may be a creative, artistic Four with an extroverted, ambitious Three wing who wants to be a rock star, while Chris may be a highly intellectual, creative Four with a Five wing who favors conceptual art created in the confines of a secluded studio. People are an endlessly fascinating mystery, and the Enneagram can serve as a treasure map to their buried strategies, motives, and values.

To get the most out of this system, Enneagram theorists and teachers encourage deeper study. Deeper study will help you more fully understand the nuances of personality and how the system can help you understand yourself and others, how it can help you evolve, and how it will help you live more fully as your best self.

On another level, the Enneagram provides a powerful tool for personal and professional growth. It can reveal the hidden things that are holding you back from advancing in your career, finding love, or making the most of your personal gifts. It can help you to plumb the depths of your own underlying fears and motives, taking you down into yourself beyond mere personality to reveal what's really going on in there. As prominent Enneagram author, scholar, and teacher Don Riso put it so eloquently yet simply, "It shows us what is standing in our way of a fuller and more graceful life." It can reveal, in a phrase, the central patterns that prevent you from being authentic, or achieving your true identity.

In the Corporate World

Increasingly, the Enneagram is being used as a practical, down-to-earth business tool. Companies all over the world are putting it to work to improve their employee interactions. Organizations as diverse as Boeing, Genentech, Motorola, and the Stanford MBA program have reportedly hired Enneagram consultants. It has been used in team building, sales, corporate communications, and conflict resolution.

The system can provide managers with insights into the work styles of their employees, give salespeople a better understanding of their customers' values, and allow venture capitalists to get a better sense of the people they're thinking of investing in. It's useful in the workplace in general because knowledge of the Enneagram's personality types improves communication among coworkers. If nothing else, simply introducing the idea that there are at least nine points of view can be incredibly useful in a work setting.

But don't fall into the trap of thinking that your personality type should determine your job or profession. Certain types may be uniquely suited to and drawn to certain professions, but individual differences, and all the nuances that come into play, even within the Enneagram, lead to a wide berth of possibilities and fluctuation. Statistically, you may see more Twos, who love helping others, in nursing, for example, than Sevens, who are attracted to more adventurous professions. You may see more Threes, who love having a prominent place in society, running for public office than Fives, who tend to be intellectual and reclusive; but you will also find plenty of Sevens working in hospitals and Fives serving on city councils.

In Your Love Life

The Enneagram is also increasingly popular as a tool for enhancing, managing, and even repairing romantic relationships. It's even used by modern-day matchmakers.

Because successful relationships require plenty of self-awareness, the Enneagram can be a powerful tool in the quest to find a compatible mate. It can help you understand your needs as well as the needs of a potential partner. If you are already in a relationship, the system can help you sort out the dynamics that cause painful misunderstandings, and you will learn about the quirks, needs, and expectations that hinder your relationship. People who have gone through Enneagram-based couples counseling report that the process allowed them to see themselves and their partners with real clarity for the first time. It often provides an opportunity to discover the hidden needs of your partner and ways to fulfill them.

It's tempting to think about relationship compatibility in terms of type compatibility—as in he's a Three and she's a One and that has disaster written all over it, or they're both Fives so they should get along fine. None of the leading Enneagram teachers believes that any two people are more or less likely to be compatible solely based on enneatypes. The beauty of the Enneagram is that it can help you see your and someone else's underlying motivations, expectations, fears, and misconceptions. It may well help you finally understand life from someone else's point of view.

The Enneagram and Psychology

Although enneatype behavioral patterns, particularly when they fall in the pathological stages, often correlate to psychological labels—manic-depressive, bipolar, narcissistic, obsessive-compulsive—each enneatype contains multiple elements of dysfunctional behavior. In other words, it's not accurate to imply there is a simple and direct correlation between enneatypes and psychological definitions of specific mental or emotional illnesses. The Enneagram is not a tool that should be substituted for diagnoses of psychological, emotional, or mental disease, but it does have validity when used as a tool for delineating, describing, and confronting the personal and professional limitations of the functioning personality. In other words, normal, mentally healthy, emotionally stable people can use the

Enneagram as a way to gain an image of their personality, how it functions, and how they can open it up to new possibility.

The Enneagram describes nine core personality styles that reflect a person's ego, or primary way of being in the world. When a person's life is not functioning and he enters therapy, the therapist helps that person confront, interrupt, and alter his ingrained ways of behaving or ego state. The more you are able to release your ego patterns, the better chance you have of becoming your fully integrated, highly functioning true self. Your Enneagram style or enneatype is equivalent to your ego state, and the usual consensual task of spiritual growth is to dismantle your ego state.

Schools of Thought

As of this writing, there is no single, unified school of the Enneagram—no strict Enneagram standard, so to speak. The modern Enneagram of Personality that is most common in the United States emerged in the 1960s from the work of psychologist Oscar Ichazo, who is widely considered its modern-day founding father. Ichazo's work is thought to have grown out of the writings of Petyr Ouspensky and G.I. Gurdjieff, prominent spiritual teachers and writers in the early twentieth century, and heavily influenced Claudio Naranjo, M.D., who spread the teachings during the 1970s through a select group of teachers, psychologists, and counselors.

It's fair to say, however, that Don Riso's book, *Personality Types: Using the Enneagram for Self-Discovery*, and Helen Palmer's book, *The Enneagram: Understanding Yourself and the Others In Your Life*, both published in the 1980s and reprinted many times since, have done more to popularize the system than any other works on the subject. They each have a distinct way of presenting Enneagram concepts that will help serious students of the Enneagram broaden their understanding of the system—how it works and the specifics of each enneatype.

As one of its earliest proponents, Palmer is considered a *grande dame* of the Enneagram. She writes about "spiritual passions" and type people based on fundamental sins: anger, pride, envy, avarice, gluttony, lust, sloth, fear, and deceit—sort of the seven deadly sins plus two. She has also called these sins or weaknesses "capital tendencies" and postulates that each personality is dominated by one of the nine capital tendencies.

Riso and his writing partner Russ Hudson—scholarly, widely published, and highly respected Enneagram theorists and teachers—emphasize the use of modern psychological tools and principles to interpret and work with the Enneagram. They favor terms like "motivations" and "compulsions." Any serious student of the Enneagram will gain a firmer understanding of each enneatype by reading Riso and Hudson's books on personality types, which you will find listed in the informational resources in Appendix A.

Most Enneagram teachers recognize at least three ranges of health within each type—healthy, average, and unhealthy—but Riso and Hudson codified a far more detailed and comprehensive concept of nine levels of development: three within each of the three primary ones (healthy, average, and unhealthy) within each enneatype. They consider the delineation of where a person is in terms of the nine levels a direct result of how strongly they have identified with their core personality types. The healthier you are emotionally and psychologically, the less attached you are to the limiting habits of your type; the more your mental and emotional health deteriorates, the more you cling to your fixations.

The Enneagram may have arisen from ancient concepts, but modern interpretations are evolving and many proponents are finding ways to apply the concepts in increasingly innovative and specialized ways in a wide range of fields, from business to personal relationships. As of this writing, more than forty books have been published on the Enneagram, and Enneagram-oriented Web sites are popping up all over the World Wide Web. A recent Google search revealed more than one million references to the Enneagram. You'll find a list of some of the most reputable Web sites, as well as the most informative books or sources of study on the subject, in Appendix A at the back of this book.

Chapter 3

Meet the Enneatypes

This chapter offers a brief overview of each of the nine personality types in the Enneagram. The purpose in having you meet all nine types at one time is that it will help you integrate the information quicker. Also, the Enneagram is a complicated and complex system that will be easier to learn if you have the same ideas reframed in succeeding chapters, delving each time a bit farther into the comprehensive theory. Succeeding chapters offer an in-depth analysis of each type as well as explain key concepts, such as security points and stress points, wings (how they affect each type), and instincts (how each type favors one primary instinct).

Sound Like Anyone You Know?

When it comes to creating a label that identifies each type, the scholars, teachers, and authors of the Enneagram have struggled to provide a name that succinctly captures the primary personality. First of all, if the label is somewhat generic, it could also easily apply to other types. The problem with labels—with words in general—is that they can unnecessarily restrict a definition, and they often mean different things to different people. No matter how hard each author has struggled, positive and negative connotations, as well as overlaps, are almost unavoidable. Identifying labels from some of the most respected authors are referenced below, but subsequent chapters will offer suggestions for catchy words or phrases that will assist in helping you identify and retain knowledge about each type's distinctive personality.

FACT

Don't be surprised if none of the type descriptions seem to fit. It's human nature to be somewhat oblivious to your own faults. Also, if you find that some of the things in the description of the type with which you identify don't fit you like a glove, it's important to remember that characteristic behaviors within each type fluctuate widely depending upon many factors, such as the degree of stress in your life or how well your life is going.

Just as a few select words cannot fully describe each personality, it's important to reiterate that no one is a pure personality type. Your enneatype or core personality type is enriched, deprived, supplemented, and nuanced according to your individual circumstances. All people are born with unique characteristics, into unique circumstances, and they all progress in unique ways. To help you get a clearer snapshot of each type, in each summary to follow, examples drawn from movies and literature are offered here, primarily derived from lists provided by Enneagram authors Thomas Condon and Judith Searle in their books (listed in Appendix A). Keep in mind that famous personalities mentioned throughout the book are also nuanced and are only being named to represent a primary, recognizable attribute.

It is important to reiterate that Enneagram scholars believe that everyone also possesses a wing, the energy and focus of the number to either side of their type, that adds dimension to their core personality. They also believe that people are capable of functioning different ways at different times—according to their degree of stress or sense of security—which allows for a surprising fluctuation in personality characteristics within each type. The latter influences arise from each enneatype connecting security and stress points on the Enneagram circle.

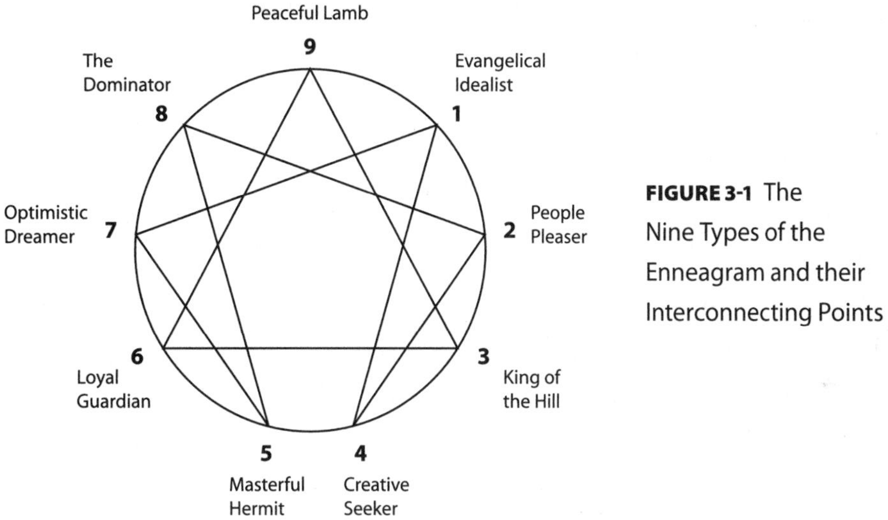

FIGURE 3-1 The Nine Types of the Enneagram and their Interconnecting Points

Type One

Prominent Enneagram scholars and authors Riso and Hudson dubbed the One personality the Reformer. Palmer and Daniels, also well respected Enneagram scholars and authors, preferred the Perfectionist. A One personality has also been called the Critic and the Good Person. This book uses the Evangelical Idealist because it seems to cover more thoroughly the central concern of the One personality, which is to internalize, live by, and promote moral principles. Ones are typically passionate defenders of what they perceive as the one, good, true, right way to live. Whether it's a religious precept or a philosophical ideology, Ones have a cause to trumpet. Their ideology or theology usually has rigid rules that Ones feel compelled to follow and that they vigorously desire others to follow as well. They are always aiming to be the best person they can be, which leads to an obsession with perfection. Ones can be overly critical, harshly judgmental, and punishing to themselves and others.

Ones are usually principled, disciplined, self-controlled types who keep society on its toes and the trains running on time. They want, above all, to do the right thing and live by a set of capital *R* rules. Ones take their responsibilities very seriously and generally think long and hard before they speak or act. If they breach their own rules, they tend to punish themselves. Pathological Ones are often self-righteous, intolerant, and cruel. Self-actualized Ones can be wise mentors, realistic advocates for worthwhile causes, dedicated public servants, healthy and effective coaches and teachers, and inspiring truth tellers.

Ones can be objective, balanced, moral, conscientious, repressive, critical, controlling, and perfectionist. They lie awake at night terrified that they are not sufficient and that they will be rightfully blamed for whatever goes wrong. They hide their tendency to feel like they are the only ones even trying to do things right. They harbor a nasty streak of resentment toward others and feel so compelled to be right at all costs that it frequently costs them their relationships and any real chance for a joyful life.

A few famous people commonly identified with the One enneatype include Ralph Nader, William Bennett, Martha Stewart, Hillary Clinton, Michael Medved, Dr. Jack Kevorkian, Confucius, Greta Van Sustern, and fictional characters such as Jack Webb's character in *Dragnet* and Dana Carvey's Church Lady from *Saturday Night Live.*

Type Two

Riso and Hudson chose as their label the Helper, while Palmer and Daniels preferred the Giver. This type has also been called the Caretaker and the Loving Person. This book selected People Pleaser because Twos are typically inclined to sacrifice their own desires for the sake of their family, coworkers, or society. Twos are the lovers of the Enneagram, those people who love you so much they'll do anything for you, even if they just met you. Twos need you to love them to feel secure in the world, so all their giving has massive strings attached.

While Twos can certainly be compassionate and empathetic, they are often helpful to a fault. On the plus side, Twos are the concerned, nurturing, warm-hearted types for whom service is the most noble—and natural—calling, which means they play very important roles in society.

Twos are very relationship focused, which means they tend to put personal connections first in their lives. Twos need to love and to be loved, which means they often have a hard time saying no. They sense your needs almost before you know you have them, and it drives them crazy that you can't do the same for them.

When they aren't emotionally healthy, Twos will use emotional manipulation in attempts to win your love. At their worst, they become flagrant self-serving martyrs and emotional vampires willing to suck you dry to get their emotional fix. However, when they are operating at peak capacity, Twos are genuinely altruistic caregivers, which explains why they are frequently doctors, nurses, and counselors. Their honest concern for others leads them to make the world a more loving place.

FACT

Common adjectives used to describe Twos include selfless, loving, empathetic, helpful, giving, codependent, possessive, manipulative, and prideful. They seek to hide the fact that they really don't feel worthy of love. Underneath that, however, they don't want you to know that they are pretty sure that you need them and cannot live without them. They struggle with a false sense of pride and shoot themselves in the foot by emotionally manipulating others at the expense of developing honest relationships—with themselves or anyone else.

As an insight into Two behavior, some famous Twos include Barbara Bush, Mia Farrow, Desmond Tutu, Tammy Faye Bakker, Kathie Lee Gifford,

Princess Diana, Monica Lewinsky, Florence Nightingale, Mother Teresa, Bill Cosby, and fictional characters such as the children's icon Mr. Rogers, Mary Poppins, and Counselor Troi from *Star Trek: The Next Generation*.

Type Three

Riso and Hudson labeled a Three personality as the Achiever. Palmer and Daniels preferred the Performer. Others have dubbed this type the Succeeder and the Effective Person. This book calls this personality type King of the Hill because Threes will claw their way to the top of their chosen professions; in fact, they feel compelled to clamor over anyone who gets in their way to achieving maximum success. They have a deep-seated need to be seen as the top dog—prestigious, powerful, rich, and highly enviable.

Energetic, focused, and often driven, Threes are also the Enneagram's chameleons. They will mold themselves to be whatever is going to get them what they want or whatever will earn them the most money, get the girl who will make them look the best, or rise to the top of a social group, be it the country club crowd or the local chapter of the Teamsters. Threes focus on work and material success and often identify so strongly with their accomplishments that they seem to feel that they are what they do. They want to do very well and look good while doing it, so they are attracted to high-profile jobs and lavish lifestyles. They are often drawn to politics, Hollywood, or other high-status professions.

Threes can be ambitious, accomplished, competitive, goal-oriented, charismatic, opportunistic, conniving, and false. Their secret fear is that there really is nothing under the mask they present to society. They struggle with being deceitful and selling themselves short when they make career, social status, money, and a manufactured image more important than their friends, family, and, ultimately, their own true selves.

Pathological Threes can become cold-hearted, devious opportunists willing to do whatever it takes to succeed. But at their best, Threes are gracious, self-assured, highly accomplished, and admirable people who embody our American cultural values—when they are balanced.

Some famous people who embody Three energy include David Bowie, Dick Clark, David Copperfield, Tom Cruise, Michael Jordan, Elvis Presley, Summer Redstone, Oprah Winfrey, Tiger Woods, O.J. Simpson, and fictional characters Jay Gatsby from *The Great Gatsby*, Scarlett O'Hara, and Macbeth.

Type Four

Riso and Hudson chose the Individualist for type Four. Palmer and Daniels selected the Romantic. Others have called this type the Artist and the Original Person. In this book, type Four is dubbed the Creative Seeker, primarily because Fours are typically creative artistic personalities who spend their lives seeking the real identity they suppressed as children. Fours are also constantly searching for ways to express their deepest feelings, particularly the bittersweet melancholy they secretly cherish.

Sensitive, idealist, and creative, Fours are the Enneagram's artists—if not literally then temperamentally. They seek the solutions to all of their problems within their own feelings and tend to be introspective types, drawn to both beauty and tragedy and the expression of beauty and tragedy through art. They possess a refined sense of the aesthetic and can be demanding and uncompromising about their personal vision of a project or pursuit. They are also easily wounded by criticism. Not surprisingly, they are drawn to the arts, but any creative endeavor has its appeal.`

A pathological Four turns her darkest feelings inward and is in danger of becoming highly self-destructive—even alarmingly masochistic. Unhealthy Fours may spend copious amounts of time wallowing in their self-created sense of hopelessness and acting as if they hate themselves. However, when the Four has a balanced personality, he is able to use his inner turmoil to face the world squarely and then contribute his creativity by completing beautiful art with an original point of view.

Famous personalities that reflect the Four enneatype include Diane Arbus, Charles Baudelaire, Leonard Cohen, Marlon Brando, Kurt Cobain, Eric Clapton, Judy Garland, Johnny Depp, Bob Dylan, Jack Kerouac, Billie

Holiday, John Malkovich, Edgar Allan Poe, Anne Rice, Vincent Van Gogh, and fictional characters such as Blanche DuBois and Hamlet.

Fours are artistic, expressive, discerning, unique, melancholy, self-absorbed, withdrawn, and elitist. Their secret fear is that they really aren't special after all, and they seek to hide their contempt for anyone who has less discerning sensibilities. Despite their elitist attitude, they struggle with envy, mostly in desiring things or people that are not interested in them or that gave up on them long ago.

Type Five

Riso and Hudson labeled type Five the Investigator. Palmer and Daniels preferred the Observer. Others have dubbed this type the Thinker and the Wise Person. In this book, type Five is the Masterful Hermit, because Fives love their solitude and they love to obtain a masterful knowledge of whatever most interests them. Fives retreat from the world in order to understand the world; and when healthy, they are not tragic hermits but self-contained and self-sustained people who enjoy their own company.

Curious, insightful, and highly analytical, Fives are often viewed as the Enneagram's brainiacs. While it's true that some become eccentric and increasingly secretive, they can also be introverted yet very attractive and desirable people. Fives possess a questing intelligence and are happiest when they are gathering knowledge. They usually develop a highly specialized and well-developed skill, often in technical areas. They are detail oriented and preferential to libraries, research, and delving deeply into the subjects that interest them. They tend to keep others at arm's length, and they can be arrogant about their pet theories.

Pathological Fives do, unfortunately, tend to lose their grip on reality, alienate their friends, and devolve into a swarm of fears and extreme eccentricities. Fives use their mastery, knowledge, and incredible perceptiveness to make discoveries in science, improve processes in a range of industries and disciplines, and share profound insights that change the world.

Fives are typically wise, farsighted, knowledgeable, perceptive, intense, disconnected, eccentric, secretive, and stingy. They are secretly afraid that others will literally engulf them, as in swallow them whole. They don't want you to know that they're smarter than you and are probably the only ones who really know what's really going on. They are greedy in the sense of withholding themselves and not sharing their energy, and they can become so self-absorbed that they retreat too far from the fold.

Famous personalities that are Fives include Bill Gates, Thomas Edison, Albert Einstein, George Stephanopoulos, Agatha Christie, Steve Wozniak, Georgia O'Keeffe, Phil Spector, Thelonious Monk, and fictional characters such as television's OCD sleuth Adrian Monk on *Monk*, Ebenezer Scrooge, and Sherlock Holmes.

Type Six

Riso and Hudson labeled a Six the Loyalist. Palmer and Daniels call this type the Trooper. Others label a Six the Team Player. In this book, the term Loyal Guardian is used for Sixes because they are typically the most loyal type in the Enneagram and because they guard themselves against fear by either finding something they can believe in or by fighting against something they perceive as dangerous. Sixes can serve an important role as guardians of our societal values, but it's important to note that Sixes flip from being phobic to counterphobic—ardently avoiding what they fear by doing something radical to prove they aren't afraid.

Once a Six challenges authority and determines the best course of action, she dedicates her life to following the rules and holding others to equally high standards. However, if she feels betrayed, she will attack the person, organization, or government that she believes failed her.

Sixes often deal with a fear of being in the world by either finding something or someone who makes them feel part of something larger than themselves that they can truly believe in, or by finding something or someone to rebel against. More than anything, Sixes want to feel secure, safe, and fully supported. Whichever route they take, they investigate and challenge new ventures until they know what they are dealing with. They can be endearing, lovable people, but they can also send very mixed signals.

When Sixes lose their sense of security and fall apart, they can become hysterical, violent fanatics who see conspiracies everywhere. However, when they are stable and evolved, Sixes find the courage that is within them, which frees them to trust others, help build communities, and share their inherently positive, cooperative spirit.

Sixes have been described as loyal, cooperative, engaging, likable, obedient and alternately contradictory, evasive, cowardly, and paranoid. Sixes are terrified that they will lose the support and guidance of others, but most of their relationships are little more than Band-Aids for their own insecurities, which leaves them feeling separate and resentful. They are the most susceptible type to fear, and they get in danger when their self-doubt and reactive impulses cause them to test others' commitments to them, which often destroys the relational security they crave.

Famous people who embody Six energy include Woody Allen, Warren Beatty, Richard Nixon, Penny Marshall, George Carlin, Ted Turner, Suzanne Somers, Jon Stewart, Spike Lee, J. Edgar Hoover, Andy Rooney, and fictional characters George Costanza from *Seinfeld*, Kate in *Taming of the Shrew*, and Ahab in *Moby Dick*.

Type Seven

Riso and Hudson named type Seven the Enthusiast; Palmer and Daniels preferred the Epicure. Others used the Materialist and the Joyful Person. This book uses the Optimistic Dreamer label for Sevens because they are the ultimate optimists, forever dreaming of a bright future and busy having a good time while awaiting it. Sevens typically possess marvelous, almost magical, energy and synergy that propels them and everyone around them toward enthusiastic adventure. Of course, Sevens have a host of nagging fears that ultimately drive them, but they cover it well, embodying the idea that a distracted mind is a happy one.

Sevens are often energetic, versatile, magnetic, and, by all appearances, perpetually happy. They are the Enneagram's renaissance people—talented and accomplished in many disparate fields and constantly reinventing themselves and their environments. They are generally adventurous, impulsive pleasure seekers with a boundless zest for life, but they often struggle with commitments and would rather move on to something new than complete something that now bores them. They've got quicksilver minds and are often restless and hyperactive. In truth, they use frenetic activity and the thrill of adventure to mask anxieties. A lot of comedians who harbor an unseen dark side are Sevens.

When their defenses fail them, Sevens become manic, impatient, hedonistic, and willing to run over anyone who gets in the way of their next plan. When healthy, Sevens are productive, deeply grateful, unfailingly generous people who fully assimilate their experiences and bring a deep and special joy to the world.

Sevens can range from enthusiastic, optimistic, multitalented, versatile, playful, and generous to hyperactive, scattered, impulsive, and irresponsible. They worry about others weighing them down or depriving them of eternal happiness. They don't want anyone—even themselves—to realize that their relentless search for the silver lining in every cloud is a fear-driven response to avoid pain at all costs. They can go overboard with gluttony, as in excessive in everything they do, and disintegrate when hyperactivity and escapist optimism keeps them separated from true intimacy and discovering their real potential.

Famous personalities that provide a glimpse into Sevens include Katie Couric, George Clooney, John F. Kennedy, Sr., Michael Caine, Robin Williams, Ray Bradbury, Magic Johnson, Regis Philbin, Richard Branson, Sarah Ferguson, Tom Robbins, and fictional characters Peter Pan and Isadora Wing of *Fear of Flying*.

Type Eight

Riso and Hudson labeled type Eight the Challenger. Palmer and Daniels selected the Boss, and others referred to this type as the Leader and the Powerful Person. In this book, the label for Eights is the Dominator for fairly clear reasons—their whole thing in life is to win every battle and dominate when it comes to money and power. Eights typically want to rule the world and will gleefully squash anyone who challenges them or blocks their way to the top. They usually have a massive lust for life that only the acquisition of power can fulfill.

Strong, decisive, and bracingly self-confident, Eights are often seen as the Enneagram's thousand-pound gorillas. They can be fiercely independent and honest, but they are energized by confrontation. They believe in going after what they want and often take on leadership roles at work and in social groups. They will protect their friends and are even capable of being surprisingly sensitive. When career driven, work provides a means to gain control over their lives and destinies, they become workaholics and power mongers.

When pathological, Eights can become hard hearted, lashing out at any attempt to control them, recklessly overestimating their own power, and mowing down anything and anyone who gets in their way. But when they are balanced, whole human beings, Eights use their strength and courage to champion worthwhile causes for the right reasons—to benefit society—rather than to reflect or fortify their own ambitions. Healthy Eights find the strength that lies just beneath the surface when one trusts others enough to allow oneself to be vulnerable.

Eights are powerful, protective, determined, confident, and forceful, but also defiant, intimidating, destructive, and sadistic. They don't want anyone to know that they are really afraid of being dominated by others. They do everything to prevent you from knowing that their boastfulness and bullying is a shield for weakness. Their lustfulness—for life, for power—is way over the top, and their downfall happens when their compulsive need to be strong and in control cuts off their ability to empathize.

Famous people who represent Eight energy include Humphrey Bogart, Lucille Ball, Napoleon Bonaparte, Fidel Castro, Alan Dershowitz, Indira Gandhi, Charles Barkley, John Gotti, Dennis Miller, Rush Limbaugh, Johnny Cash, Barbara Walters, Geronimo, the late Texas governor Ann Richards, and fictional characters Zorba the Greek and Petruchio in *The Taming of the Shrew*.

Type Nine

Riso and Hudson labeled Nines the Peacemaker. Palmer and Daniels preferred the Mediator, and others selected the Preservationist and the Peaceful Person. This book named Nines the Peaceful Lamb because this type often spends their lives avoiding conflict at all costs and loves being the sweethearts of the Enneagram. Nines cannot envision a world absent of peace and harmony and thus consider it their mission to impose it. Nines are willing to sacrifice everything for the sake of peace in the family, peace in the community, peace in the church, peace everywhere.

Nines are undeniably agreeable, peaceful, and extremely wary of conflict, making them equivalent to Zen masters in the Enneagram. Nines who have evolved to the highest rungs of their personality spectrum are truly spiritual leaders who practice divine detachment. They love, but they also release and allow everything and everyone to evolve according to their divine design.

The average, ego-driven Nine, however, practices detachment as a way to avoid anything that will create anxiety. They will repress anger and deny feelings for eons, even when their loved ones are literally feeling frozen out by unspoken resentment emanating from the peaceful Nine. Nines can make great diplomats and mediators, but their indecisiveness, neutrality, and foot dragging can also drive their family or coworkers nuts.

At their best, Nines are flexible, modest, and realistically optimistic, but Nines surrender their sense of self for the sake of relationship and can eventually become disconnected from their own lives. They essentially live their unfocused lives lost in a dense fog.

Pathological Nines are capable of actually harming the ones they profess to love so much through emotional neglect and passive-aggressive striking back. Nines can be deadly but silent. If they are balanced, however, Nines experience an emotional awakening and focus the right amount of attention on themselves and their loved ones. When in top form, Nines have a palpable, confident serenity that makes them incredibly effective communicators, calming mediators, and fully connected partners.

Nines are modest, trusting, easygoing, self-effacing, and patient, but also complacent, accommodating, repressed, passive-aggressive, apathetic, and numb. They cower in fear that if they rock the boat, everyone won't love them anymore. They try to hide the fact that their nothing-bothers-me exterior covers a core of anger and resentment, but it leaks out in stinky, silent, unexpected ways. They are lazy in the sense that they don't invest the energy required to reveal their true feelings, express their real desires, or take responsibility for their own spiritual growth.

Nines get into trouble when their habit of ignoring problems and dissociating to avoid conflicts allows neglected troubles in work and in relationships to fester, become serious, and present a real danger to themselves and others.

Famous people who are Nines include Ronald Reagan, Fran Leibowitz, Tony Bennett, Bill Clinton, Clint Eastwood, Jimmy Stewart, Walter Cronkite, Jerry Seinfeld, Grace Kelly, Sandra Bullock, Patty Hearst, the Dalai Lama, and fictional characters Dorothy in *The Wizard of Oz*, the bumbling detective Columbo, and Edith Bunker.

Chapter 4

Jung's Theory of Personality

Some concepts within Carl Jung's theory of personality can be useful for a layman in interpreting complex Enneagram theory. Some of Jung's concepts that correlate to Enneagram theory include psyche, self, ego, persona, shadow, complexes, libido, progression, regression, extroversion, introversion, individuation, and self-actualization. Once you have gained an understanding of these concepts, you will have another leg up on comprehending how the Enneagram of Personality works.

The Elements of Personality

Psyche is a Greek word meaning "soul," and psychology is basically a theory or method of understanding the science of the soul—what comprises your soul, how your soul functions, and what changes your soul. Carl Jung was a disciple of Sigmund Freud who then branched off and formulated his own theories. According to Jung, your psyche, or self, encompasses everything that is you—your genetic heritage including sensory, intuitive, cognitive, or emotional proclivities or tendencies; your physical or emotional components; your primary and secondary environments, that is, your family and your culture; and your dreams. Within your psyche, your unique qualities of, ego, shadow, persona, and complexes formulate a distinctive personality that arises out of all these various elements.

What Is My Self?

The basic concept is that *self* is your whole personality, including the conscious and unconscious aspects of a psyche. Jung believed that you were born with a true self, or essence, and that your unique ego, or personality, emerged as a result of your heredity traits and your early childhood development—your need to function in your primary environment and your culture—working in tandem with your hereditary, genetic, or unique inborn qualities. He believed the self's one true purpose was to transcend—rise above or resolve—all of the opposites contained within your personality and create a balanced, whole psyche that is far closer to your true self, or essence. Because your ego arises out of the self, you cannot have a healthy ego without a healthy self. Jung defined the self as transcendent and transpersonal and regarded it as the most important aspect of the psyche.

According to Enneagram theory, you can liberate your true self by weakening and dissolving the rigid patterns that keep your ego state (personality) fixated to known perceptions, beliefs, or behaviors within the parameters of your Enneatype. When you gradually free yourself from these rigid patterns, you are finally capable of being fully present to the moment and responsive to the demands of the present in accordance with your essence or true self. Your Enneagram style is actually a distortion of your true personality and is only a small portion of your true self. The more fully actualized you are, the less obvious and influential your Enneagram style becomes.

What Is My Ego?

Jung believed that your ego is the center of consciousness that creates your identity. The ego's primary purpose is to help you function in society by organizing and balancing the conscious and unconscious aspects of your psyche to form an integrated, stable personality. A balanced, healthy ego achieves equilibrium between the conscious and unconscious aspects of a person's psyche that integrates all the various qualities of self and results in a fully self-actualized personality. An inflated, or exaggerated, ego creates an imbalance that often results in a narrowly defined, rigid, and intolerant personality. At the far end of the spectrum, an overly inflated, deluded ego results in a psyche that feels godlike and can become increasingly dangerous to the self and to others (because a person with an overly inflated ego will project his or her negative unconscious onto others, such as Hitler, Osama bin Laden, and other radical fundamentalists). Jung defined the ego as the mediator and protector of the self whose purpose is to observe, receive, and interpret information about the self and others.

Like most crises, a midlife crisis results from an inflexible, entrenched ego or system of beliefs that has excluded large portions of a person's psyche. In a midlife crisis, people often make an abrupt turn, behave like a child, or simply change their beliefs and personality in an unconscious attempt to rebalance their ego. This crisis resolves itself when you break free of rigidity and redefine who and what you are and how you behave.

In regard to the Enneagram of Personality, your ego is a grouping of conscious and unconscious behaviors, opinions, truths, and thoughts that developed as a way for you to comprehend and live within your childhood environment. Your ego becomes a pattern of beliefs, habits, and behavior that you have, consciously or unconsciously, chosen to present to the world;

it's the personality you use to navigate life's challenges. Generally, a healthy ego not only functions well in society but allows for a relatively uncomplicated unveiling and blossoming of your essence. An unhealthy ego creates self-designed roadblocks or impediments that hinder your ability to grow or even begin to function anywhere near your peak potential within society.

Your Enneagram ego, or personality, is the way you have learned to express yourself in the world and the way you communicate who you are to others. These personality traits become your most enduring way of perceiving, relating to, and thinking about the world and your place in it. A healthy person develops and sustains a flexible ego. An ego-driven personality functions, but it is often too reliant on reactionary impulses or behaviors or too restrictive to express your true self. An unhealthy ego may become pathological—rigid, inflated, or deflated—and definitely does not serve its owner well.

What Is My Essence?

Your essence is you, stripped of your ego. It's your authentic, fully integrated true self. Moving toward your essence doesn't eliminate your personality or ego, it merely frees you to make choices rather than succumb to fixated behavior. It expands your vision of yourself.

When you regress, you move farther away from your true essence; when you progress, you move closer to your true essence. Your essence is more than the sum of everything in your psyche, of which your core personality is only a part. It's the point at which the restrictions imposed upon your core personality are truly liberated, allowing the other elements of your unencumbered true self to emerge. In other words, your core personality or Enneatype contains methods of coping or adaptive responses that allow you to function in the world. Your ego boundaries within your core personality determine the degree of compulsion or rote response that define your life. These behaviors are the fixations that shape your core personality. As you integrate, you free yourself from the fixations that have shaped your life and increasingly learn to live from your essence.

What Is a Persona?

A persona is the mask the ego creates to disguise itself or to adapt to circumstances. More tightly defined than your ego, your persona is typically an idealized image that you want others to see and believe is real. Healthy, functioning personalities develop a more realistic, flexible persona that helps them navigate in society but that does not collide with nor hide their true self. Unhealthy, dysfunctional personalities create an inflexible, false, often exaggerated persona designed to hide their true self, which they eventually begin to believe is their true self.

A persona is frequently adopted to help you identify with your profession, no matter if you are a doctor, a minister, a stripper, or a talk show personality. This becomes a problem if you lock into a persona and come to view it as the totality of your personality. In some cases, your persona develops into an alter ego that you come to consider more real than your ego. In the grips of pathological regression, for example, you may develop a potent alter ego to act out negative emotions. Occasionally your alter ego becomes so entrenched you believe it is real, similar to an evil twin.

What Is a Shadow?

Your shadow is that part of your psyche that contains unconscious, unexpressed aspects of your personality that you either strongly dislike (negative shadow) or don't know you possess (positive shadow). Shadows grow in intensity inversely proportional to your knowledge of it—the less you know the denser it becomes. If you have a weak or ineffective ego, the shadow may muscle its way into prominence. People often project their shadow material onto someone else—viewing your husband as controlling when in fact you are the controlling partner; or viewing your husband as brilliant when in fact you are brilliant but almost completely unaware of it. A large part of unveiling your essence, or true self, involves claiming your negative and your positive shadow and all of its projections. You have to first claim your shadow to change it. Oddly enough, particularly if you came from a dysfunctional, destructive family, you may have greater difficulty owning your positive shadow.

How does projection work?

Projection occurs when rather than acknowledge or accept negative traits or positive virtues, your ego projects these traits onto other people. Falling in love occurs when you project your hidden, positive qualities onto another person. And when you vehemently dislike someone, whatever it is that drives you crazy about another person is likely to be a quality you possess. Projection offers you opportunities to recognize messages from your unconscious about who you really are.

Shadows are generally seen as the dark side of your personality that your ego goes to great lengths to keep under control and safely hidden. The positive shadow harbors qualities of your idealized, or self-actualized, self that you have yet to discover and that you usually project onto loved objects. One must face the negative shadow and reclaim the positive shadow to find a healthy balance based on consciousness rather than repression. Repressing your negative shadow often leads to neurosis or psychosis, while failing to acknowledge your positive shadow dilutes full expression of your true self. Claiming and learning to live with your shadow is both empowering and crucial to progression toward the self. When you are in the grips of a shadow trait or behavior, you may say, "I am not feeling like myself," or "It was so unlike me to do such and such."

What Are Complexes?

According to Jung, some people develop complexes—related groups of emotionally charged ideas, thoughts, and images that exist in the personal unconscious and may be positive, negative, or somewhere in between—in reaction to their early childhood environment or experiences. For example, someone could have a healthy mother complex focused on nurturing, a negative mother complex focused on destruction, or for most people somewhere in between. Complexes can act as a subpersonality, and the more negatively charged complexes, or disruptive behaviors a person has, the more neurotic or psychotic that person becomes.

One goal of Jungian therapy is to bring any unconscious and disruptive complexes into consciousness so the patient can limit acting-out behaviors in favor of more balanced, expansive choices. Enneagram coaches or therapists using the Enneagram as a resource for understanding human psychology may opt to identify and disrupt a patient's ego patterns as a way to help a client become more aware of undiscovered resources that her limited or fixated ego boundaries have excluded from her awareness.

Jung's concept of a personality complex is a grouping of repressed or suppressed urges that correlate to an ongoing theme. You could have a father complex, a mother complex, an abandonment complex, a power complex, and so on. A complex creates convictions and impulses that usually appear in behaviors that consciously or unconsciously express the needs of the complex. Sometimes a complex may develop as a separate persona, or alter ego.

How Your Personality Functions

Various energies within your psyche, such as libido, progression and regression, and individuation, allow you to function. Jung theorized that your libido is the psychic energy that frequently flows between opposite forces within your ego and determines whether you are balanced or out of balance. Your personality also has a progression or regression that determines how you cope with, or adapt to, security and stress. Individuation is the process of separating your ego from your parents'. One must individuate to achieve self-actualization or the unveiling of your true self or essence.

Libido, or Balancing of the Opposites

Contrary to what most people think, and contrary to Freud, who linked people's most basic drives to sex, Jung did not equate the libido strictly to the sex drive. Jung defined the libido as the motivating psychic energy that reflects a natural instinct for preservation of the species and self-preservation. Unlike Freud, Jung suggested that libido encompasses different expressions of your basic drives. Jung believed the flow of libido, or psychic energy, flows between two opposite impulses within your psyche—the greater the tension, the stronger the libido. When your psyche is out of balance, the flow of the libido serves as a sort of pressure valve. Jung believed that a failure to achieve balance between opposite drives sends your libido flowing into the unconscious where it will eventually demand expression through neurotic (ego-driven) or psychotic behaviors (deeply pathological behaviors) within your enneatype.

Progression and Regression

Jung's theories on progression (movement within the psyche toward adaptation to the environment) and regression (movement backward) are similar to the Enneagram concepts of integration and disintegration. Within the Enneagram, the flow of your libidinous energy plays a central role in the loosening or tightening of your particular Enneagram style. When things in your life are going well, you are ripe for expansion and may integrate or progress toward individuation and self-actualization by adopting behaviors that support forward movement. Conversely, when you feel insecure or are under severe stress, you may disintegrate or regress away from individuation and self-actualization by lapsing into pathology. If you are not progressing or regressing, you are relying on ego-driven behaviors that allow you to cope but that do not help you progress toward the ultimate goal of self-actualization—becoming authentic, flexible, fully present, and able to access your current adult resources

Fixed, or childish, stages of consciousness result from a failure of the child to progress beyond the patterns she learned in order to deal with her early childhood experiences. For example, for survival, very young children are naturally enmeshed with their parents and siblings, but at some point a healthy child individuates, or separates. Some people never individuate, resulting in a fixed or immature personality.

Per Enneagram theory, each enneatype has a complementary security point and stress point, indicated by placement on the Enneagram circle. In times of stress you are more likely to adopt characteristics of the pathological side of your stress point, but you might also respond to the challenge and boldly experiment with its more desirable characteristics. In times of relaxation, when you are most receptive to expansion, you are more likely to nourish the desirable or more self-actualized characteristics of your security point, but you may also indulge in some of its less desirable characteristics.

These points may cause some confusion in that Enneagram theorists originally believed that a person under stress (consciously or unconsciously) adopted negative behaviors from their stress point, and that a person who felt secure (consciously or unconsciously) adopted positive behaviors from their security point. Under this theory, when a Seven felt secure, for example, she would have integrated or progressed toward the positive energies of Five; and, when a Seven felt stressed, she would have disintegrated, or regressed by assimilating some of the negative energies of One.

Today, however, most theorists believe that people adopt positive and negative behaviors from both their stress point and their security point. Thus, using the same example, when a Seven feels secure, she integrates, or progresses toward individuation, by adopting positive behaviors from both her security and her stress points—positive behaviors from both Five and One; and when a Seven feels stressed, she disintegrates, or regresses away from individuation, by adopting negative behaviors from One and Five. However, when stressed, you may also choose positive behaviors from your stress point that facilitate growth.

All theorists agree that our stress and security points are where our energies of growth and change frequently reside. In succeeding chapters when individual enneatypes are discussed, you'll see the Jungian terms of progression and regression used to identify each enneatype's movement between its connecting points as they relate to the process of individuation or self-actualization.

Individuation

Jung defined individuation as the process of forming an integrated personality, which allows you to self-actualize—become what or who you were born to be, what you were before you formed an ego based on what happened in your childhood. This individuation or self-actualization process is a lifelong, ongoing process or quest. Through therapy or active self-development using introspection and conscious choice, you can work toward unveiling your negative and positive shadow, unraveling your personality restrictions, broadening your ego, and integrating or self-actualizing your psyche. Your goal is to finally become your true self, or essence. Jung offered the analogy that most people have a self that is equivalent to a large, multistoried apartment building, but they consciously or unconsciously confine their personality to the first few floors.

Introversion and Extroversion

The concepts of *introversion* and *extroversion* are important components in understanding the Enneagram as a personality typology. Most people assume that introversion refers to people who are shy, withdrawn, and more comfortable living within the parameters of their internal world of thoughts, feelings, fantasies, and dreams and that extroversion refers to people who are outgoing, socially adept, and most comfortable living in the external world. However, Jung defined extroversion as an orientation in which your ego, or overall personality, was focused on your persona, or public face, and the external world. Jung defined introversion as an orientation in which your ego was focused on the internal world that encompassed the collective unconscious and its archetypes. Neither orientation is superior, but Jung may have considered an introverted type more evolved. Unfortunately, in our culture, and many others, the extroverted personality is often considered more desirable and is usually valued more than the introverted personality.

In terms of the Enneagram, which will be discussed in greater depth in Chapter 6, theorists have suggested triads within each group of types that prefer a primary instinct—the relationship triad (Twos, Threes, and Fours), the fear triad (Fives, Sixes, and Sevens), and the anger triad (Eights, Nines, and Ones). The idea is that each type within the triad would be either extroverted, introverted, or somewhere in the middle. For example, in *Your Secret*

Self, Fensin and George delineated three distinct personality styles within each triad, as follows:

- Central
- Extrovert
- Introvert

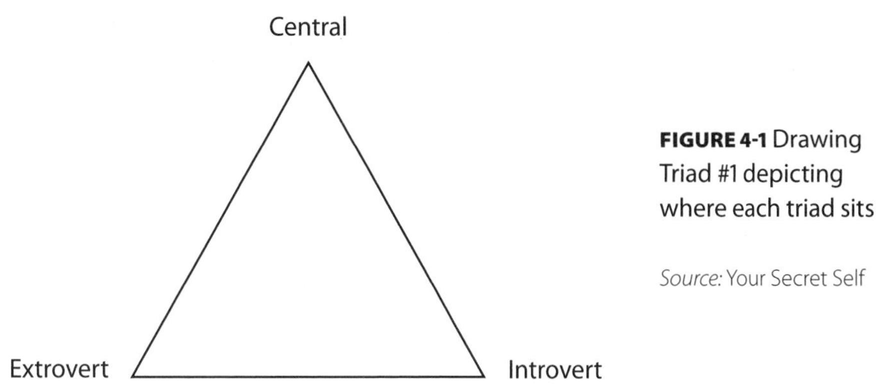

FIGURE 4-1 Drawing Triad #1 depicting where each triad sits

Source: Your Secret Self

One type on the corner of the triangle would be more outer-directed or extroverted, and the other corner more inner-directed, or introverted. The third or central type would be somewhere in the middle, or somewhat muddled in its orientation. In the anger group, type Nine would be central, type Eight would be extroverted, and type One would be introverted. In the fear group, type Six would be central, type Seven would be extroverted, and type Five would be introverted. The following table illustrates how Fensin and George viewed introversion, extroversion, and being somewhere in the middle and how it affects each personality type.

Group	Type	Personality Characteristic
Relationship	Two	Overrelates to People (extroverted)
Relationship	Three	Denies her own feelings; lets others define her (central)
Relationship	Four	Relates to her image of herself (introverted)
Fear	Seven	Creates plans to divert fear (extroverted)

Group	Type	Personality Characteristic
Fear	Six	Alternates between avoiding and confronting fear (central)
Fear	Five	Escapes fear by withdrawing from others (introverted)
Anger	Eight	Directs anger outward (extroverted)
Anger	Nine	Denies her own anger and avoids conflict (central)
Anger	One	Withholds or hides her anger (introverted)

Derived from The Secret Self

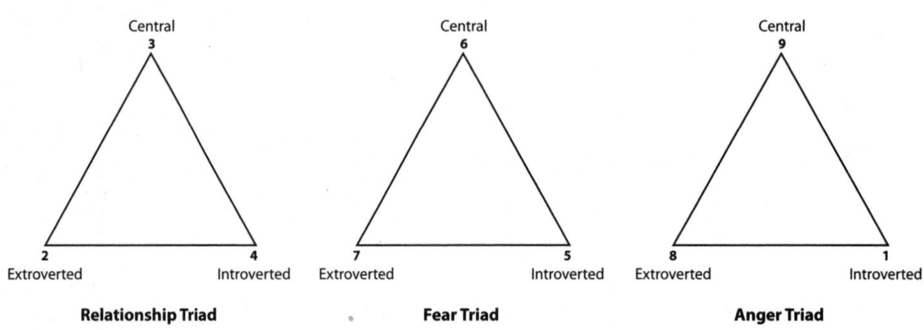

FIGURE 4-2 Triad 1 = relationship, triad 2 = fear, triad 3 = anger

Source: Your Secret Self

In *What's My Type?*, authors Hurley and Dobson also address the triad within each group of types but refer to the middle type as balancing points rather than central. They believe Threes, Sixes, and Nines reflect the inner contradiction, which is created by preferring and overusing one center, by idealizing or coveting balance between what is happening outside (extroverted) themselves with what is happening inside (introverted) themselves. As such, these types become too focused on how they are perceived and repress any creative energy generated by their primary instinct.

In other words, Threes sacrifice sensitivity to feelings and use their instincts to create an idealized image of success. Sixes sacrifice their ability to conceptualize or think through any challenges by relying on outside authority figures or institutions. Nines stifle their physical or regenerative energy and deny their feelings for the sake of serenity.

How It All Ties into the Enneagram

The succeeding chapters will employ these Jungian concepts to more fully explain and clarify the dynamics of the Enneagram—how each personality type develops, functions, progresses, regresses, and either achieves self-actualization or sinks into pathology.

To review, you are born with a true self that encompasses everything you possessed before your early childhood environment influenced your development. This true self is also known as your essence. When you are born, you are greatly influenced by whomever is there to nourish and support you. How these people treat you and how you react to their behavior, in concert with your physical, intellectual, instinctual, or emotional characteristics, determines what becomes your modus operandi, or way of being in the world. This equates to your enneatype style, ego state, or personality. Your parents, parental figures, and your siblings have a major effect on how you formulate a personality and your primary way of perceiving, interacting with, and responding to other people and to your environment, including your geographical region, country, and culture or religion.

Every ego state, personality, or enneatype style develops and harbors shadows, and most also contain complexes or fixations. It comes down to this: You began life affected in some way by who or what you experienced, and you, consciously or unconsciously, covered over or clouded your true self. You might not have been properly mirrored or validated, you might have been punished for being a certain way, you might have received mixed messages, your parents might have suffered a crisis that separated them from you, you might have responded to excessive restrictions, or you might have had parents that had vastly different sensibilities than you. Even with the most healthy, supportive parents on the planet, you still veiled parts of your essence, and it becomes your lifelong task, or quest, to unveil your true self and become whom you were meant to be.

Further, your libido is the psychic energy that flows between your opposing drives, and how you accelerate or depress your libido determines your progression toward or regression from individuation and self-actualization. Self-actualization means bringing all the parts of yourself into one whole, integrated self—your true self.

The Enneagram delineates nine enneatypes or core personalities. Within each enneatype, an individual is either functioning at maximum capacity (self-actualized), functioning fairly well but according to his or her ego needs (ego-driven), or not functioning well (pathological). You can be in between or at either ends of the spectrum (whole or crazy).

Chapter 5

The Dynamics of the Enneagram

Most scholars believe that a combination of your genetics and your early childhood environment determine your core personality or type. They also believe that you retain your core personality throughout your life, which leads some to consider the Enneagram inflexible or static. In actuality, other factors—such as your wing, your security point, and your stress point—create a dynamic system that describes either your ongoing growth and development toward self-actualization and unveiling your essence or your descent into dysfunction and pathological neurosis and psychosis.

How It Works

The Enneagram provides a framework to help you understand the patterns you developed for seeing and organizing the world. These patterns are formed from the interaction between your genetic disposition and the early childhood environment you grew up in. Your parents or caretakers played a primary role in how you came to see and interact in the world. Everyone develops an ego that eventually obstructs their essence. The Enneagram helps you understand how your ego formed, how neighboring types influenced you, and in which direction—and how—you can progress to achieve wholeness and live your life with integrity emanating from your true self.

Again, the Enneagram numbers are not reflective of superiority in any way and are placed on the Enneagram circle according to the compilation of characteristics that formed each personality. No one progresses from one number to another, and, in fact, Enneagram theorists believe that your enneatype does not change. However, you can progress in your own development or develop patterns of behavior within your enneatype that reflect the healthier aspects of your personality.

Most theorists agree that there are three major gradients of behavior within each type that this book has chosen to generally identify in Jungian terms as follows:

- **Self-actualized:** highly functioning personality
- **Ego-driven:** normally functioning personality
- **Pathological:** highly dysfunctional personality

In other words, depending on what is occurring in your present life and how you are coping with any challenges, you are capable of progressing upward or regressing backward within your individual type.

It's important to remember that your ego or Enneagram style is not the same as your essence or true self. You are born with an essence that gets suppressed, denied, or even lost by your efforts to respond to or cope with your childhood circumstances. Instead, you form an ego that allows you to function within your familial and larger world. If your family is healthy and nurturing, you are likely to form a healthy, functioning personality. If your family is dysfunctional and destructive, you are likely to form a pathological personality (filled with defense mechanisms and maladaptive behaviors) that will eventually veil your essence. If everything goes exceptionally well, you may develop a self-actualized personality that encompasses the full spectrum of your conscious and unconscious psyche; it expresses and reflects your true essence. However, most people are not that lucky and have to deal with all sorts of denial, personality distortions, and behavior malfunctions to unveil our essence. More on this later in the chapter.

Wings

Every enneatype has a wing—one of the types on either side of it that provides subtle, or not so subtle, nuances to its personality. In other words, your personality consists of one enneatype and a mixture of your enneatype with one of the two types adjacent to it on the circumference of the Enneagram. For example, Ones have either a Nine wing or Two wing; Fours have either a Three wing or Five wing; Sevens have either a Six wing or Eight wing.

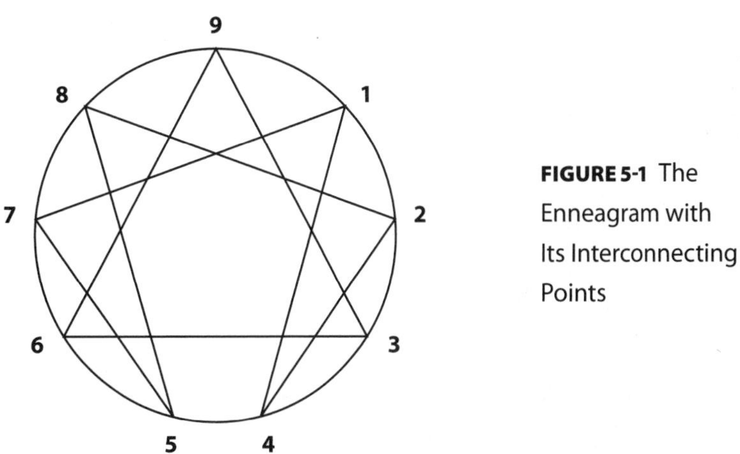

FIGURE 5-1 The Enneagram with Its Interconnecting Points

The wing both complements your basic personality and encompasses important and sometimes contradictory elements within your personality. It illustrates and defines another side to your personality that will increase your own and everyone else's ability to understand the totality of your personality. Like the positioning of each type on the Enneagram, the wings have also been positioned according to the same Enneagram concepts that define how your personality was formed. As such, they will be congruent with your core enneatype.

Does your wing change when you're stressed?
No, your wing remains constant. Even when stressed, the wing is always with you and is neither released nor clutched to your side. When stressed, you typically—consciously or unconsciously—lean toward your stress point when it comes to behavior shifts.

Once you have determined your enneatype, you'll want to read the two adjacent types to determine which one most seems to apply to you. As with determining your enneatype, reading through the basic traits and then delving into the complexities will help you identify your wing. A wing influence may also be obvious when you take the personality test and a certain number crops up repeatedly. The appropriate wing accounts for varying personalities in each core personality or enneatype. For example, a Six with a Five wing will be intrinsically different from a Six with a Seven wing.

Wings determine your secondary fears and desires, as well as the motivations that drive you and the traits or behaviors you develop to form your personality. The proportion of primary (core personality) and secondary (wing) influences can differ significantly. If a person's wing constructs a large portion of that person's personality, it's frequently called a *heavy* wing. If the wing is present but the personality is heavily influenced by the core personality, that person has a *moderate* wing. If the core personality completely dominates the secondary personality to the point that it is almost imperceptible, that person has a *light* wing. In each case, the core enneatype always dominates the overall personality. For example a Seven is always a Seven, but you may be a Seven with a light Eight wing, a Seven with a heavy Six wing, or a Seven with a moderate Eight wing.

As with your enneatype, your wing does not change. However, when you allow for gradations within your enneatype and your wing, as well as within your security point and stress point, you have an ever-widening set of variables.

Security Point and Stress Point

Because human beings fluctuate, evolving in a positive direction or devolving in a negative direction, the delineations of an Enneagram are far from static. Everyone progresses through life and either expands or contracts—integrates and grows or deteriorates and disintegrates. As discussed in Chapter 4, according to Enneagram theory, each enneatype has two connecting points on the Enneagram circle—a security point and a stress point. Most theorists believe you, consciously or unconsciously, adopt positive and negative behaviors from both points. This book interprets the movement between connecting points as a progression toward self-actualization, or a regression toward pathology, determined by the adoption of positive, or negative, behaviors or attitudes from your security point or your stress point.

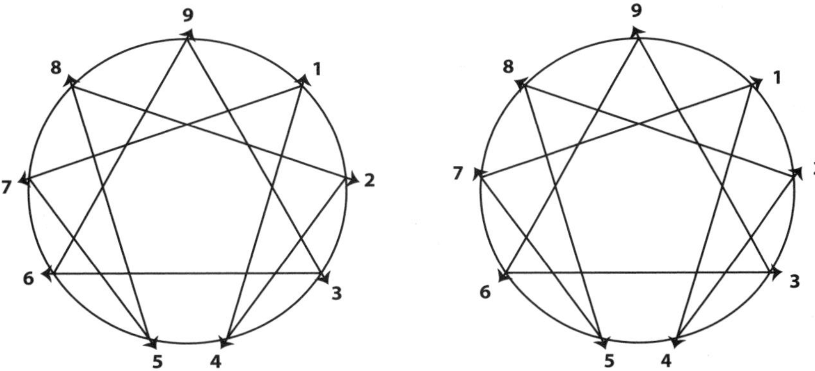

FIGURE 5-2 Circle 1 = The Connecting Security Points. Circle 2 = The Connecting Stress Points.

These points are determined by connecting enneatypes, all of which were intentionally aligned by their placement on the circle. These points explain behavior fluctuations, as well as emerging or reactive characteristics that are unexpectedly revealed or purposefully mined as you grow into a mature adult. Basically, you consciously or unconsciously adopt positive or negative behaviors or characteristics from two other enneatypes—as determined by your security point and your stress point—that can become part of your overall personality. Thus, your overall personality typology consists of four aspects:

- Your core personality or enneatype
- Your wing
- Your security point
- Your stress point

Together, these four elements construct your personality. Where you are currently functioning also plays a crucial role in deciphering the current state of your personality's fixations or complexes. For example, if you are ego-driven, as you regress, you are more likely to manifest qualities in the low range of your enneatype. In other words, you may not be neurotic or fully pathological but simply exhibiting behaviors that indicate you are on the path to basic personality meltdown.

Is it possible to achieve the pinnacle of self-actualization?
The pinnacle of self-actualization is an inspiring yet elusive goal that implores humans to reach the ultimate state of being—joyfully whole and detached from worldly concerns. The process of actualization is ongoing and consistently incomplete. Humans are always in state of flux, spiraling upward or downward in their quest for transformation. Perfection is a useful concept in terms of setting goals, and although humans can never fully attain absolute perfection, striving to become your best self is a worthy pursuit.

To determine where you are on the personality continuum, you can read your enneatype and your wing descriptions to locate the traits or behaviors that apply. For example, if you have a highly functioning, healthy personality, you will likely find yourself in the self-actualizing aspects of the appropriate type and wing; if you have a dysfunctional personality on the skids, you will likely find yourself in the pathological aspects of the appropriate type and wing. You can also read descriptions of your security and stress points in the appropriate stage, but keep in mind that integrating or disintegrating personalities do not develop all aspects, or only one aspect, of the security or stress points. Even though you may be clearly in one stage of development, you may adopt positive (high side) or negative (low side) influences from either your security or your stress point. These are nuances that appear as you grow, often in reaction to what is occurring in your life, that help you evolve or that hasten your slide into dysfunction.

For example, if you are caught in a downward spiral, you might adopt the corresponding pathological characteristics of your stress or security point—a reclusive Five might become aggressive and sociopathic like a pathological Eight, which would reflect regression. But this same Five might also adopt a positive behavior from its stress point and learn to take creative action in the external world like a dynamic healthy Eight, which would reflect progression. The common denominator is that external energy from your stress point can work both ways.

Integration or Progression Toward Self-Actualization

Unlike disintegration, progression toward integration frequently involves a conscious decision to seek growth and development. You may decide it's time to seek ways to let go of restrictive behaviors and open up to your full potential. You may experience the sort of grace that occurs when everything in your life is going exceptionally well and you simply blossom. Or you may opt to set the process in motion by purposefully addressing issues that you know have held you back. Potent clues for a progression toward self-actualization can be found in your security point, as indicated by your placement on the Enneagram, or in the high side of your stress point. For example, a Nine seeking to progress toward self-actualization can choose to adopt behaviors consistent with a self-actualized Three or a self-actualizing Six; a progressing Five can opt to act like a self-actualizing Eight or a self-actualizing Seven. The positive qualities inherent in the progression toward self-actualization will help you fully see the limitations created by remaining fixated in your type and will give you an inkling of the behaviors, attitudes, beliefs, and actions that will help expand your personality toward your true self, or essence.

Disintegration or Regression Toward Pathology

When feeling under duress, defeated, or repressed (when you overextended yourself and feel as if you are close to a breakdown, have been doing everything you know to achieve a desired result and nothing is working, or have been consistently repressing your feelings), you might regress or move further away from your essence. This downward slide is usually unconscious and compulsive. Often people will adopt motivating attitudes and behaviors inconsistent with their usual personality, but these motivating attitudes and behaviors are usually consistent with where they are currently functioning personality wise. In other words, if you are an ego-driven Four experiencing extreme frustration, you may unconsciously act like an ego-driven Two experiencing extreme frustration or an ego-driven One; if you are a pathological Six, you may regress toward a pathological Three or a pathological Nine. This regression may allow you the opportunity to cope in difficult situations, or it may simply reflect your current state of instability.

People who have regressed to the lowest rungs of pathology become increasingly dangerous to themselves and to others. As they spiral downward, they relinquish their fragile hold on reality until they reach a psychotic break, becoming schizophrenic, clinically depressed, or hysterical. Unless rescued, psychotics remain trapped in an emotional and behavioral hell.

Again, if you adopt some of the more positive, or high side behaviors or traits in your stress point, they could actually fill out gaps in your personality and help you to progress in times of stress!

Think of regression as a coping mechanism that prevents you from lapsing into the seriously dysfunctional aspects of your personality. Adopting new behaviors, even if they come in the form of *acting out* your anger or frustration, often helps you vent feelings or suppress them until you can cope in your usual way. If you have extended periods of extreme stress, you may linger in regression to the point at which you misidentify with the other type. However, once rebalanced, you will most likely revert to your true type.

Stages of Psychological Health Within Enneatypes

Traditional analytical psychology typically identifies a basic psychological type (narcissistic, masochistic, bipolar, borderline, depressive) and then delineates classifications occurring within each individual personality (its id, ego, and superego) as well as the behaviors that are indicative of the person's current level of functioning. Most Enneagram theorists use terms like "healthy," "average," and "unhealthy" to delineate various stages of psychological health. However, as mentioned previously, this book prefers to label three major behavioral classifications using Jung's terminology: self-actualized, ego-driven, and pathological.

The essential theory is that self-actualizing, highly functioning personalities function very well and employ balanced, consistent, reliable, and admirable behaviors. Pathological personalities become intractable to the point of obsessive-compulsive behaviors, eventually lapsing into neurosis or psychosis. And ego-driven personalities fall somewhere in the middle.

No one leaps from pathological to self-actualized; you move in the direction of extremely healthy self-actualization or extremely unhealthy pathology in stages. In other words, you don't leap from being healthy to being psychotic, or vice versa. Achieving these behavioral states results from either a progressive movement toward health or a steady, regressive deterioration.

While it's true that part of your type is genetically predetermined, without question your early childhood experiences vastly affect your development. The quality and style of parenting, in conjunction with environmental givens—health, income, education, location, and wealth or dearth of physical, emotional, or spiritual resources—have everything to do with your ability to function at the higher, the middle, or the lower spectrum of your enneatype. You began life whole, but whatever happened in your early life led to the development of a set of adaptive behaviors that suppressed your essence and created a self driven by its own self-constructed ego. An additional drop into pathology brings a set of maladaptive behaviors that really throw you off track.

These traits are sustained by habit and the failure to examine your beliefs. If your childhood was particularly dysfunctional, your coping mechanisms will likely be more rigid and more neurotic than those people who had "normal" or idyllic upbringings. Fear grows in proportion to the dysfunction—the greater your early childhood family's dysfunction the greater your underlying fear, anger, or need for relationship.

Some traditions cultivate and engage negative emotions in an effort to breach the point in your psyche where emotions become uncontrollable. Their theory is that fully experiencing your primary, negative compulsions will help you release them. Gurdjieff, for example, believed in pushing people to their breaking point by deliberately placing them in situations that created maximum stress or went against their adaptive persona. This offered them the chance to consciously live through, and then detach from, their negative compulsions.

To increase your understanding of yourself—and others—it's important to determine where you are and the direction in which you are progressing or regressing. This will help you understand why you swing from one behavior to another and what behaviors serve as warning signs. Understanding the various fluctuations within each of your personality components—your enneatype, wing, security point, and stress point—affords you a truer picture of the full spectrum of traits that define what is really happening within the parameters of your personality and those around you.

Self-Actualized, Highly Functioning Personalities

Within each type, self-actualized personalities have conquered some—or most—of their fears and are breaking free of ego chains. They are free to express the full range of their personality. The most highly evolved or self-actualized personalities have confronted and conquered what happened in early childhood that caused them to subvert, or obstruct, their essence. They have spiritually progressed to the desirable state of self-actualization and live life according to their essence.

On the way to self-actualization, highly functioning personalities evolve from having an ego that is rigid and repetitive in its interaction with others to one that is able to respond to the present situation with full access to its inner adult resources.

Ego-Driven, Reasonably Functioning Personalities

Normal or ego-driven personalities range from a relatively high-functioning person to someone whose self-image is inflated and contradictory. On one end, those progressing toward self-actualization are on the brink of expansion; on the other end, those regressing toward pathology are hanging on by their fingernails. The vast majority of people languish somewhere in the middle—functioning but not self-actualized—limited by their self-image and the adaptive behaviors that drive them; that is, their ego is in the driver's seat.

Ego-driven personalities are more stable than pathological ones, but they are somewhat rigid in the way they cope with reality. Even though they function well within the parameters of their personality, they often aren't aware of why they do what they do and remain overly identified with what they know about themselves or what they want you to know about them.

People who feel compelled to control their behavior and their environment to project a desirable image are essentially prisoners of an inflated ego and will use manipulation, aggression, withdrawal, and a repertoire of other coping mechanisms to sustain their basic needs. Their defense mechanisms, rigid view of themselves, controlling behavior, ongoing internal strife, and consistent disappointments create anxiety that tends to lock them down rather than open them up.

When everything that used to work no longer works, ego-driven personalities slide down the slippery slope toward pathology. They typically feel an increasing sense of failure—their inflated ego begins to deflate—and they often resort to using negative behaviors to get their way. The increased conflict within and without leads to self-absorption and objectionable behavior, which leaves them filled with shame, rage, and/or fear.

While most people occasionally act out as a means of coping with extreme duress, people experiencing posttraumatic stress disorder (PTSD) or those with borderline personalities (functioning neurotics or barely functioning borderline psychotics) tend to flip in and out of their disintegration repeatedly, rapidly, and without clear indications. Their personalities are not sufficiently grounded, and they act impulsively and uncontrollably.

Pathological, Highly Dysfunctional Personalities

Most people who develop pathological personalities suffered painful or abusive childhoods that led to dysfunctional coping mechanisms, which eventually limited their ability to make free choices. Essentially they became prisoners of their compulsions or obsessions. They felt compelled to fortify and defend their inflated or delusional ideas about themselves as evidenced by self-protective defenses, such as lashing out at others, and self-destructive behavior, such as succumbing to addictions. Their compulsive and reactive behavior not only hurts them, it usually cripples or destroys important relationships. A pathological personality is a personality seriously out of balance and rapidly regressing or disintegrating.

As their situation worsens and their personality unravels, pathological personalities primarily cope by denying their real situation. Their ego boundaries have all been trampled, and their internal conflicts are raging out of control, which creates a desperate need to reorder their universe. People with completely disintegrated egos descend from pathological behavior to psychotic behavior. They have lost all sense of reality and will destroy anyone or anything they perceive as threatening, including their real image of themselves. Their psychic pain has become intolerable; they use drugs or alcohol to numb the pain and often resort to threats, intimidation, and violence to control others or make the pain go away. Anyone in total meltdown is dangerous to themselves and everyone else.

Where to Begin

Chapters 7 through 15 each describe one of the nine enneatypes in depth, covering the emotional origins or how each enneatype was wounded in childhood, the three stages that define each personality, the process of individuation and self-actualization, and the balancing of opposites that determines the trajectory of your adult personality development.

Since most people linger in the ego-driven stages, these chapters primarily focus on describing how an ego-driven personality manifests in each type; and then provide descriptions of the pathological stage and the self-actualized personality—your ultimate goal.

Keep in mind that while the gradients reflect the degree of ego consciousness and behavioral imprisonment, a fully integrated, self-actualized personality type is the ultimate fulfillment. People at this ultimate stage have unveiled their essence and opened themselves to spirit; they have broken free of ego limitations and reconnected to the source of life. They know themselves, and they know others. They have faith in themselves, the divine, and others—they are in touch with themselves and the universe.

Chapter 6

The Three Primary Instincts

Humans are born with three primary instincts for survival—physical, emotional, and intellectual. As people develop, they tend to favor one instinct over another—choosing their heads, or hearts, or guts—to observe, interpret, react to, and interact with their inner selves and the outer world. The instinct that suits you most has a major affect on the formation of your personality or Enneagram type. Understanding how your primary instinct affects your type will help you understand your underlying motives and ways of perceiving and operating in the world.

The Three Instincts

The three primary instincts humans employ for survival—physical, emotional, and intellectual—emanate from the head, the heart, and the gut. These three instincts form an important triad within the Enneagram, grouping together personality types according to their preference for one instinct over another. Understanding the instinctual triad increases your ability to understand the primary motivations and behavior of each personality type and its supporting wing.

All human beings develop a preference for using one of the three primary instincts, also know as centers of intelligence. These centers are also known as your emotional self, your intellectual self, and your physical self. Not only do you learn to use one preferred center, you learn to use the benefits or limitations of this intelligence to winnow down, rather than expand into, your true self.

As Enneagram proponents and scholars interpreted the handed-down theories of the system, they incorporated modern psychological concepts to explain the instinctual triad. Most scholars believe that the instinctual triad groups three personality types according to their primary mode of interpreting their inner and outer worlds. It is commonly believed that children choose one method of perceiving, interpreting, reacting, acting, and interacting based upon their proclivity for relying on the head, the heart, or the body. This selection process could be formed by a lack of nurturing or mirroring that reflects all three instincts, or, even more likely, it is environment, parents, and culture in combination with a genetic disposition that favors one instinct or form of intelligence over another. In recent years, books have been written about emotional intelligence and how it can play a more significant role in some people's lives than the more traditional concept of human intelligence centered in the brain. It only stands to reason that some people also rely on a physical, or perhaps intuitive, intelligence centered in their gut.

Theorists are in agreement that your personality is formed in your early childhood, often the result of an inevitable wounding process. Even with ideal parents, all children experience some sort of wounding. If they are lucky, the wounding is superficial; if they are not so lucky, and the wounding is severe emotional or physical damage, it may result in a lifelong quest to overcome neurosis or even psychosis.

QUESTION?

Do people only use one center of intelligence or instinct?
No. According to most theorists, people usually incorporate one of the other two centers as a sort of backup but almost always repress or discard the third, creating an imbalance that stymies growth. Instead of being expansive and dynamic, they become too dependent upon two ways of relating to the world, creating an increasingly fixed personality.

Enneatypes and Instincts

In response to your early childhood experience you learn to process information through your sensitivity to feelings and emotions, your physical or gut instincts that tell you whether you're in a good or bad situation, or through what you see and think using your intellect or brain. Intuition seems to play a role in all three triads in the sense that all the enneatypes have access to their intuition, but they may receive it through their feelings, physical reactions, or thoughts. Enneagram scholars believe that placement on the Enneagram circle reflects which primary instinct you use to navigate through life. The following types are placed into corresponding instinctual modes:

1. **Heart or emotional instinct:** types Two, Three, and Four
2. **Head or intellectual instinct:** types Five, Six, and Seven
3. **Gut or physical instinct:** types Eight, Nine, and One

What this means is that Twos, Threes, and Fours are in tune with their emotions and are keenly sensitive to other people's moods or emotions. They tend to focus on personal relationships and intimacy and will listen to their hearts when it comes to sizing up other people or making decisions about their lives.

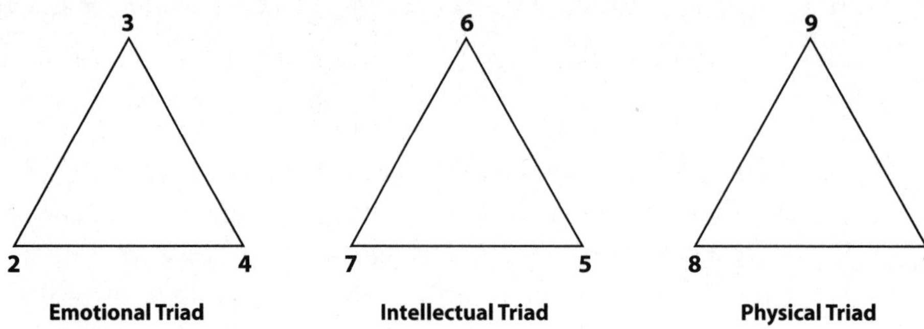

FIGURE 6-1 Triad 1 = emotional instinct, triad 2 = intellectual instinct, triad 3 = physical instinct

Source: Your Secret Self

Fives, Sixes, and Sevens are more in tune with their mental or intellectual processes, which means they rely on rationality and reason to interpret their worlds and interact with others. More than the other six types, they like to process information through their mental intellect.

Eights, Nines, and Ones are more in tune with their physical self or gut instinct when it comes to sizing up people or making decisions about their lives. Since they are acutely aware of their physical bodies, they are more focused on physical survival than the types who rely on other primary instincts.

FACT

Gurdijieff theorized that all humans have a "higher emotional" and a "higher intellectual" center, but most people cannot access their higher selves because their lower selves (personality or ego constructs as determined by how you have learned to use or misuse your thinking, feeling, or physical centers) distract them with their constant chatter, habitual behavior, and functionary defenses. According to Gurdijieff, in order to evolve, you have to unscramble your ego and quiet your mind.

It's also generally agreed that you use a second, subordinate instinct and repress the third. Thus, you may be a heart-centered One who also relies on your head-centered or intellectual instinct. As such, you may be a very sensitive person who also gathers a lot of information before casting judgments or making decisions. Or you may be a gut-based Eight who also relies on a heart-centered or feeling instinct. As such, you may be an aggressive go-getter who is also sensitive to how it makes your partner feel when you are never home. In other words, your two preferable forms of intelligence or instinctual centers work in concert to help you master your world. The third instinct, unfortunately, is often buried in your unconscious and is seldom called upon. A fully actualized personality would ideally use all three instinctual centers in appropriate circumstances—feeling when there is an emotional decision to be made, thinking when a rational decision is required, or following your gut instinct when there is a physical safety issue.

How Instinctual Centers Work

Enneagram scholars are in agreement that triads exists—and concur on how it simultaneously energizes and restricts our personality and suppresses our true self—but they often name them differently.

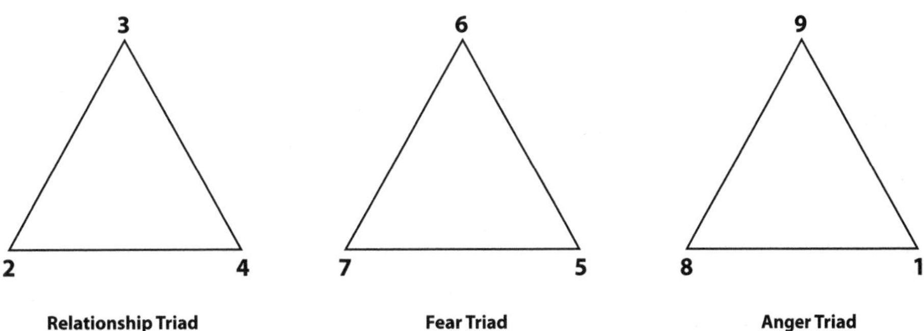

FIGURE 6-2 Triad 1 = relationship instinct, triad 2 = fear instinct, triad 3 = anger instinct

Source: Your Secret Self

In *Your Secret Self*, authors Fensin and Ryan refer to triads within their Enneagram model as "emotional centers" (see Figure 6-2), which they label and define as follows:

1. **Relationship:** This is equated with the "heart" group. People in this category frequently appear to be more focused on human emotions and interrelationships than the other types. It is important to note that the appearance of a heart or emotional orientation is not always integrated. Relationship types do tend to feel and display their emotions more readily than others. They are also more interested in how others perceive them and will dress to impress. Enneagram types Two, Three, and Four fall into this category.
2. **Fear:** This is equated with the "head" group. People in this category tend to live inside their own heads, trying to make logical sense out of life. While they may appear coolly rational, logical, and objective, ironically, they spend most of their time thinking about the success or failure of their relationships. Enneagram types Five, Six, and Seven fall into this category.
3. **Anger:** This is equated with the "gut" group. People in this category frequently respond to their initial gut reaction to people or events. They usually have highly developed intuitive skills and react instinctively, even impulsively, to situations. Their expression or repression of anger is usually an issue in interrelationships. Enneagram types Eight, Nine, and One fall into this category.

In *What's My Type?,* authors Hurley and Dobson refer to this same triad as "the three centers of intelligence, each with its own true purpose and its own everyday functions." They see the "true purpose" as achieving our ultimate wholeness and spiritual awareness and the "functions" as the adaptable ways we use our intelligence to navigate the world. They label these three intellectual centers as affective, theoretical, and effective and define their true purposes as follows:

- **Affective center:** To achieve healthy, perfect union with others, the universe, and with spirit; to understand the stages of human development that create maturity and wholeness. Twos, Threes, and Fours are focused on their affective center.
- **Theoretical center:** To develop creative vision and open you up to the real meaning of life; to be fully conscious of the true nature of self

and others. Fives, Sixes, and Sevens are focused on their theoretical center.

- **Effective center:** To motivate and energize you to actively live your life as it was intended—according to your true purpose and vision; to actively create and complete the work you are meant to do. Eights, Nines, and Ones are focused on their effective center.

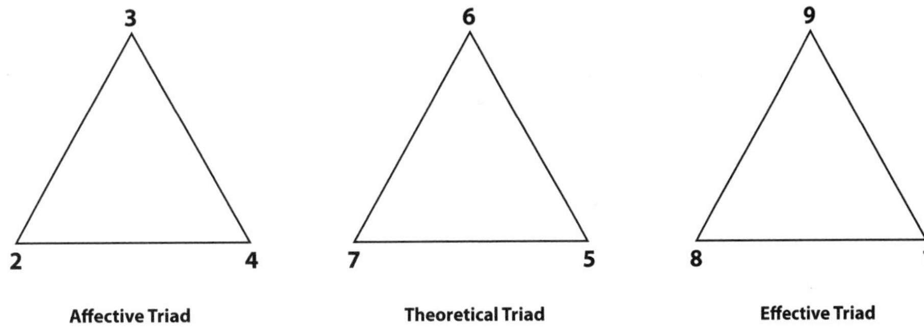

FIGURE 6-3 Triad 1 = affective, triad 2 = theoretical, triad 3 = effective

Source: What's My Type?

Unfortunately, according to Hurley and Dobson, the vast majority of people don't awaken to their true purpose. They limp along married to the illusion that they are just fine and that most problems generate from others. This leaves them with the misappropriate or dysfunctional use of their centers of intelligence, as follows:

- **Affective:** To manipulate your—and others'—way of feeling, including emotions within relationships.
- **Theoretical:** To think, plot, and make intellectual decisions limited to your narrowly defined universe.
- **Effective:** To protect and preserve your physical body and achieve your basic needs, no matter the cost to others.

Hurley and Dobson believe that each instinctual center has a divine purpose: affective or feeling-based types are symbolized by the ear because they can "hear deep movements of the soul"; theoretical or thinking-based types are symbolized the eye because they "see the nature of reality"; and effective or belly-based types are symbolized by the mouth because they are "the center of expression."

Now that your head is probably spinning, it's time to go back to the basics and explain the specifics of the three instinctive triads and how they can help you understand yourself and others, as well as the underlying motivations and the resultant behaviors unique to each type within the triad.

Heart or Feeling Instinct

Types Two, Three, and Four rely on their feelings, or heart, to guide them. They love emotions, deep feelings, and relationships. They are most comfortable in the realm of feelings and are highly motivated to form relationships. They use their heart or heightened ability to feel and observe others and how they appear to them. All three types within this instinctual group develop an image of themselves that becomes crucial to their personal identity. Unfortunately, they can become so focused on what others think or feel about them that they, ironically, often lose touch with their own deepest feelings. They are obsessed with the desired image they create and often depend on others to form favorable opinions about them or to validate their own opinions of themselves. They use their emotions to determine how well they are doing in terms of projecting a desirable image as follows:

- **Twos** want you to like them and will usurp their own needs or anticipate your every real or imagined need in order to gain favor. They need you to need them, and they monitor your feelings, moods, and behaviors toward them to know if they are succeeding.
- **Threes** want you to admire their accomplishments and success. They will stifle sad or undesirable emotions to keep their brilliant,

dynamic, and sterling image intact. They want you to gush over them and compliment their every good deed or victory.

- **Fours** have a vested interest in appearing unique, special, or talented. They can fall in love with their negative emotions and will often heighten or dramatize their emotions so they can then transcend them through art or other creative endeavors. They want you to see just how truly special they are.

Ginger Lapid-Bogda, author of *Bringing Out the Best in Yourself at Work*, which is based on Enneagram principles, describes Twos, Threes, and Fours as so focused on creating positive images to navigate the world that they are always accessing and assessing their feelings to figure out if they are doing well. Twos, she theorized, want to appear warm, optimistic, and enthusiastic, but they succumb to basing their own opinion of themselves on what others think about them. Threes want to project an image of success and are most concerned that others find them worthy of admiration for their accomplishments. They are, in fact, cheerier than Twos, perhaps because they concoct the image they want others to believe and act as if it's really who they are. Fours need to feel like they are both a true individualist and special. They embrace their most painful feelings and wield their hypersensitivity as a shield against withering remarks.

Head or Thinking Instinct

Types Five, Six, and Seven rely on their ability to think to guide them. They value and use rationality, logic, analytical skills, and research to figure out how life works and what they need to do, or not do, to feel safe. They learned at an early age to quell their fears by thinking through or mentally confronting them. When they feel fearful, they try to make sense of whatever is making them feel insecure or unsafe. They like figuring out things and forming complex concepts that explain the world, or your strange behavior, to them. They use their intellect to retreat from scary feelings as follows:

- When **Fives** feel fearful, they will withdraw from the world in order to mull over a problem or strategize a solution. When they can use their intellect to gain control over a situation, they feel safer. They also use their mental abilities to detach from any emotions that threaten their own sense of inner equanimity.

- **Sixes** shrink from their fear by planning ahead and anticipating the worst that can happen. Since they are overly conscious of being fearful, they look for intellectual or philosophical systems that explain the world and offer them a parameter of acceptable behaviors. Sixes cling to belief systems and seek strong leaders who help them limit their mind chatter and who make them think they are safe.
- **Sevens** deal with their fear by thinking about something else. They become highly adept at shoving fearful thoughts out of their minds and thinking happy thoughts. They often look cool, calm, and collected, but underneath they are anxiety ridden. They keep themselves so busy they don't have time to acknowledge their underlying fears.

According to Lapid-Bogda, Fives, Sixes, and Sevens use elaborate analyses of situations to quell their fear: Fives detach emotionally by withdrawing into their imagination; Sixes proactively imagine negative scenarios and create plans to counteract them when they occur; Sevens may look like cool cucumbers when it comes to fear, but their cheeriness is actually a last-ditch effort to circumvent their fear by running madly in the opposite direction, pretending as if hurtful things are not occurring.

Gut or Physical Instinct

Types Eight, Nine, and One rely on their intensified ability to sniff out or sense what is going on with others. They are focused on fulfilling their own physical and emotional needs and will often use their gut instinct to discern how they can manipulate things in their favor. They value action, living life at full volume and maximum velocity, and doing whatever they need to do to best take care of their physical selves. Their central feeling is anger, which they confront in different ways as follows:

- **Eights** love to get angry and will gladly overpower anyone and everyone. When dysfunctional and feeling as if they have been backed into a corner, they resort to threats, intimidation, and verbal assaults to control anyone whom they believe is responsible for making them feel threatened. They also frequently express anger at perceived, if inconsequential, slights.
- **Nines** find their own anger so threatening that they bury it somewhere deep inside and adopt a completely pleasing or passive exterior personality. They eventually lose touch with their pent-up anger and will deny feeling angry or negative about anything or anyone. If pushed or ignored, Nines may show some anger, but they quickly and eagerly return to their easygoing persona.
- **Ones** feel anger but do everything they can to hide it. They have a burning desire to be perfect, and in their minds perfect people don't get angry. When angered, they are more likely to spit and sputter on the surface as they try to suppress an emotional reaction. They will also berate themselves for feeling angry and may turn unspoken anger into depression.

According to Palmer, Eights are acutely aware of the presence and power of other people and will enlarge themselves to gain control, or a sense of control. Eights observe others so they can use the knowledge gained to manipulate people or situations in their favor. Nines, on the other hand, absorb or mirror other people, happily surrendering their own sense of self, their needs, or most certainly their right to either own or express anger. Ones, according to Palmer, use their gut-based sensitivity to ferret out human imperfection and decide what everyone needs to do to make the world more perfect.

Chapter 7

Enneagram Type Two: People Pleaser

Twos believe love is the be all and end all of life. Self-actualized Twos love everyone unconditionally and are genuinely generous, compassionate, and altruistic. Ego-driven and pathological Twos also love deeply, but they attach strings to their love—often cajoling others into loving them so that they can feel fulfilled in life and, above all, needed. Twos want to feel indispensable and work so hard to uphold their loving persona they conceal their aggressive tendencies under a blanket of love. Unless they achieve self-actualization, despite appearances, Twos ultimately stay focused almost entirely on themselves.

Emotional Origins

Twos in childhood usually experienced a disruption or disturbance in their relationship with their father or father figure. Their fathers might have been punitive, demanding, or controlling; or they may have been present but nonresponsive or disengaged, or even totally absent. As a result, Two children felt as if they had to meet rigid expectations in terms of how they appeared or behaved, or they simply felt unworthy of their father's love. Many then harbored deeply ambivalent feelings about their fathers, or father figures, which resulted in feeling as if they had to present a pleasing personality so that their father would finally love them, notice them, or invest any significant energy toward fulfilling their needs.

In other words, Two children probably had a parental authority who overtly or covertly wanted their children to be good in terms of being devoid of any emotional needs, requiring attention, or disturbing them. Many Two children identified more strongly with the nurturing parent to help them feel more secure with the family structure, and they dealt with the father issues by developing an internalized conscientious overseer (superego) that commanded them to act as if they were well intentioned all the time, even when they were willing to be self-centered, manipulative, and controlling in attempts to coerce someone into loving them.

Two children feel ashamed when their needs appear excessive or when they feel unworthy of having even their basic needs fulfilled. Conversely, they develop insatiable needs and covertly try to fulfill them by giving so they can be seen as good people. They act as if they are giving freely, but they secretly keep track of every gift, sacrifice, or act of kindness and who fails to return the favor. Often their unmet secret needs lead to food or drug addictions or shame-based overindulgent behavior.

Two children did whatever song and dance was needed to make their parents pay attention to them and, preferably, to fuss over how "good" they were. They also learned to smother negative emotions to avoid appearing displeasing or difficult. Eventually, Two children willingly and consistently suppressed their own feelings or desires to focus all their energy and attention on whomever they wanted to love them. This eventually led to the surrender of their genuine identity and the creation of a malleable persona that adjusted to present circumstances—functioning like an emotional weathervane, changing shape and form to become whatever the object of their need required.

Two children developed a need for others to validate their own worthiness, which then translated into needing to feel as if they were good all the time. Their need to feel and look good became so ingrained that they would have to feel good about themselves even when they were being obnoxious, demanding, or manipulative. While self-actualized Two children were genuinely caring, ego-driven and pathological Twos translated what they believed was love into a burning desire to dominate or control the person they needed most to love them.

FACT

Twos watch others like hawks and use gleaned information to make the other person love and need them. They are altruistic, but it's often based on narcissistic neediness—they need you to need them. They will suppress, deny, and sacrifice their own feelings or needs to become indispensable and noble. They are at the extroverted point on the feeling triad, which means they are more focused on others than themselves. They are very connected to feelings—somebody else's.

Ego-Driven Twos

Ego-driven Twos love loving others, but they often do so because they need reassurance that they themselves are lovable. Because they need to see themselves as "good people," they often spend more time talking about all the good they do than actually doing good. Rather than focusing their love outward (like self-actualized Twos), ego-driven Twos develop inflated egos—shining the light on themselves, extolling their own virtues, and ignoring their own faults. They are still capable of actually loving people, but they also now occasionally dislike them. Because they cannot admit negative feelings, they bury their conflicting feelings in servitude designed to make you need them and admire them. As a result, when they do help others there is a sneaking suspicion that ulterior motives are at work.

The yin and yang of being a Two: When they are good, they are very, very good—loving, flexible, intuitive, generous, empathetic, and altruistic. When they are bad, they are very, very bad—manipulative, controlling, possessive, suffocating, and needy. A superb Two could be someone as gentle, loving, and devoted as Mother Teresa, while a crazy Two could be a stalker.

Ego-driven Twos see themselves as exemplary mothers, fathers, or bosses because they "love you so much" and "only want what is best for you" (particularly when it is decidedly not what is best for you, such as remaining dependent upon them, or failing to develop self-mastery or confidence in your own abilities). Unfortunately, their ego needs create caricatures of stereotypical codependent mothers or fathers who hover constantly (foisting food, affection, money, or attention upon you), act as if you are the center of their universe, complain that you don't appreciate them, and all the while do not see how they manipulate and use you to get the attention they insatiably crave. They need you to need them, and they will defend their idea that they are giving out of the goodness of their hearts, for your own good, in the face of evidence to the contrary, repeatedly deluding themselves about their own behavior and how hurtful it can be to others. They need you to need them so that they can feel important, secure, and good about themselves; and they need you to pretend that they are the center of your universe.

Ego-driven Twos blindly consider themselves virtuous and admirable, but their loved ones often feel cajoled and manipulated, particularly when asked to consistently flatter the ego-driven Two. Because they are highly sensitive to other people's feelings, they monitor your moods, reactions, and feelings and willfully trample your emotional boundaries—interfering without being asked, dispensing unwanted advice, and imposing themselves to the point of becoming sacrificial martyrs who invent needs to fulfill so they can feel needed.

Coincidentally, the loss of boundaries cuts both ways. Twos will allow themselves to be seduced or taken advantage of, and when they feel invaded and unappreciated, they turn around and invade the boundaries of others. Eventually, their excessive ego needs become pedantic and tiring.

Ego-driven Twos also develop lax emotional boundaries that result in their weeping and wailing on other people's shoulders, often when completely uninvited to do so. When meeting you for the first time, as soon as they decide they want you to like them, they act like they already love you—often to the point of inappropriately touching, hugging, and kissing you.

Signs that you're dealing with an ego-driven Two: She'll put everyone else's needs above her own and pout when she feels ignored. She'll butter up anyone that can raise her social status and jump at the chance to be your best friend, bowling you over with flattery and attention. She'll want to hear all the juicy details about your life, and rarely talks about her own. She loves rescue projects—people, pets, or causes.

Because they need to feel like they are very loving people whose real value comes from self-sacrifice, they need you to praise them constantly, and often brag about how truly incredible they are and how much everyone just adores them. Even though their psychic pain is obvious to others, these self-defended Twos simply don't see it or feel it, which means their unacknowledged neediness prevents honest exchanges about real feelings. Unfortunately, they can become so needy that they will grovel at the feet of anyone who falsely flatters them, leading them into abusive relationships as well as sexual, overeating, shopping, gambling, drug, or drinking addictions. They can also become addicted to serving others and will often spend so much time seeking fulfillment that, ironically, their family ends up feeling neglected or even emotionally and physically abandoned.

Pathological Twos

As Twos dip into pathology—usually as a result of a really traumatizing event (or series of events involving abuse) in their past or present—they become increasingly self-deceptive and manipulative. They have lost the ability to hide their pent-up feelings and become even more emotional when they finally butt up against their own image of themselves as good people. As their relationships crumble, desperate to win back your affection, pathological Twos resort to lies and trickery in blatant attempts to convince you they are lovable. Unfortunately, the more desperate they become, the more they attempt to control their loved ones, resorting to emotional and verbal manipulation designed to undermine their loves ones' confidence in themselves—and their ability to function without the increasingly desperate Two.

According to *The Wisdom of the Enneagram*, pathological Twos on a downward slide may visibly lie to themselves and yet act as if they are entitled to have whatever they want. They become increasingly manipulative, controlling, and jealous. They anger easily and explode over simple misunderstandings. They may drink too much, overeat or stop eating, complain about being wronged, and resort to coercion or seduction to have sex.

Despite increasing evidence that they are hurting rather than helping the people they love, pathological Twos still believe that they are blameless and almost willfully project their own faults onto others. They will belittle or berate loved ones, punish those they love by withdrawing their love, and eviscerate someone they love just to keep them frozen in place. Because they are still motivated by a need to be good and have to repress what is now visible, seething anger, some Pathological Twos now feel compelled to overcompensate by doing for others. Some convert their anxiety into physical ills, consciously or unconsciously resorting to hypochondria to elicit sympathy and loyalty. Still convinced they are unrelentingly loving, they furiously resist therapy or any suggestions that they are flawed—anyone who questions their behavior becomes their enemy.

Despite the demeaning, hurtful, and manipulative way they treat you, pathological Twos feel entitled to your love and now demand that all attention be focused on their increasingly neurotic or psychotic needs. They compulsively hook up with people who embody the primal protective parent or father figure who neglected or failed them—often choosing someone who neglects, abuses, or debases them. They may act out prior sexual abuse and become either sexually promiscuous or abusive toward their partners.

If you attempt to leave a severely Pathological Two, he will issue threats and dogmatically attempt to cajole you into changing your mind. But underneath it is very clear that the "love" they once had for you now has transformed into hate. As a last-ditch effort, they often develop mysterious illnesses and may even become an invalid to force you to take care of them.

Self-Actualized Twos

Self-actualized Twos will listen endlessly to others gripe about their lives, and when most people would have stopped listening and written the person off as a whiner, Twos not only listen but still manage to feel compassion for their plight. As such, they are comforting in the face of disaster and often consistently generous, both spiritually and monetarily. They see the good in others and rarely criticize—even when some criticism would be appropriate. They love the person, not the behavior. They know how to focus on someone with clear eyes and make the beloved feel seen and appreciated without creating or fostering dependency. They imbue self-esteem and create positive, nurturing expectations that help others become the best they can be. They also maintain strong boundaries and take care of their own needs. They are loving, well intentioned, and kind, and they like that about themselves; they are confident without being, feeling, or expressing any sense of superiority.

FACT

Self-actualized Twos are true philanthropists in tune with the physical, emotional, or spiritual needs of others. They are often practical caregivers who uplift and inspire others. Self-actualized Twos whose love for others more than themselves comforted, watched over, and inspired the masses include Mother Teresa, Eleanor Roosevelt, famed therapist Virginia Satir, and children's TV icon Mr. Rogers.

When they reach the pinnacle of self-actualization, Twos are the penultimate altruists—more genuinely considerate and loving than any of the other personality types. They genuinely care about others and perform valuable functions in society. Their love is freely felt and freely given—no strings attached. Unlike ego-driven or pathological Twos, highly functioning, self-actualized Twos don't need others to make them feel loved and are thus capable of loving others enough to encourage them to grow, even when it means that the beloved will separate and live elsewhere. Self-actualized Twos feel honored when others allow them to be part of their lives and have no desire to control them. They have a lot of love to give and have no need, or expectation, of gratitude or recognition for their good deeds.

They are widely admired for their generosity and sincerity; yet they remain humble, grateful, and joyful. They are abundantly happy and often appear radiant. In fact, they have achieved the ultimate ego liberation—their hearts, minds, and souls have room for their true self (essence) and yours. They empower their children, their partners, and their community.

When Twos make a positive connection to Eight, they develop stronger personal boundaries, which helps them acknowledge and fulfill their own needs. With Eight on their side, Twos are also able to bring powerful energy to their altruistic efforts.

The Process of Individuation or Self-Actualization

According to Jung, individuation occurs when you successfully separate your personality from that of your parents and become an integrated personality—becoming what or who you were born to be, what you were before you formed an ego or persona, or suppressed negative behaviors in your shadow. The individuation process is a lifelong, ongoing process or quest. Through therapy or active self-development using introspection and conscious choice, you can work toward the unveiling of your shadow, the unraveling your persona, and the integration of your psyche.

Basically, when merging aspects of Jungian theory with Enneagram theory, one could presuppose that when things in your life are going really well, you are ripe for expansion and are more likely to progress toward individuation and self-actualization by adopting behaviors that support forward movement. On the other hand, when you feel insecure or are under severe stress, you are more likely to regress from the goal of individuation and self-actualization by adopting behaviors that allow you to cope but that do not necessarily help you progress toward health. Again, in some instances, you may uncover traits inherent in your stress point that help you grow during times of extreme stress, e.g., you might both cope and progress toward health by discovering determination, integrity, or industry in your stress point.

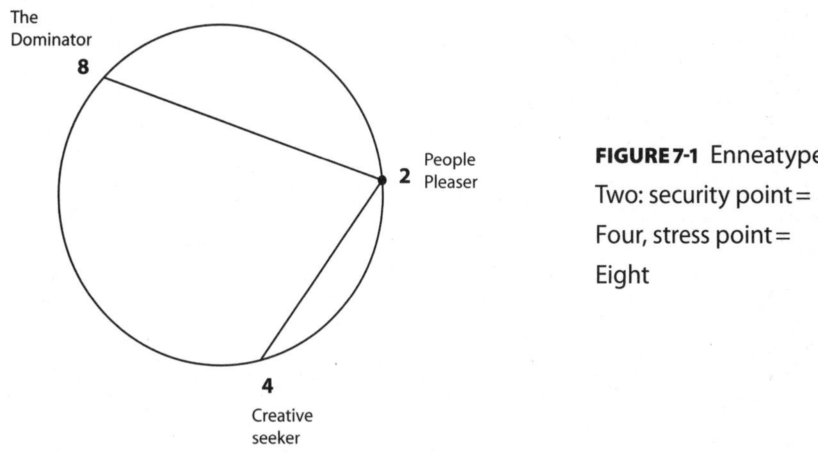

FIGURE 7-1 Enneatype Two: security point = Four, stress point = Eight

How Twos Progress

Twos progress toward individuation by adapting behaviors common to self-searching Fours who love to probe their own feelings in an effort to gain self-awareness and understanding. These self-actualizing Twos learn to accept the light and the dark side of their emotions, and this willingness to achieve emotional integrity offers them new opportunities to experience all of their emotions. They learn to love themselves—and others—unconditionally, allowing them to love others in a healthier way, which then inspires others to love them—just as they are. Self-actualizing Twos also gain an ability to channel their feelings into creative projects and expand their intuitive understanding of themselves and others.

When Twos adopt positive or progressive behaviors from Eight, they gain Eight's gumption and assertiveness, which helps them learn to identify their needs and pursue them proactively. With Eight energy on their side, Twos no longer have to resort to covert manipulation to get their needs met.

How Twos Regress

Twos regress toward pathological, confrontational, combative Eights. They abandon the charming behavior designed to make them look good for rude, far more abrupt behavior. When stressed, particularly about money, they obsessively work, want full credit for whatever they do, brag about their accomplishments, and boss people around. When stressed, they may lose control and denigrate others in a last-chance, desperate attempt to control them. Like Eights, they often lose their temper quickly and lash out verbally or physically. When they want something, they will go after it aggressively. If they feel rejected or spurned, pathological Twos are apt to apply physical and emotional intimidation more common to a pathological eight to try to force someone to love them. The sacrificial lambs who so desperately wanted to be seen as admirable martyrs are now very capable of becoming ruthlessly assertive and dominating.

When Twos disintegrate to Four, they become full of a sense of entitlement, for themselves or others, similar to the way a demanding stage mother fully expects her child to be the star—whether or not she's the most talented. Some authors refer to a "me first" syndrome for Twos who take on the low side of Four.

Balancing the Opposites

According to Jung's personality theory, the psyche is constantly flowing between two extremes, and your primary task is to successfully balance the two polarities. To achieve individuation, each personality has to acknowledge and work through the limitations of its idealized self and shadow, its strengths and weaknesses, and its motivations and fixations (what keeps it stuck). These primary polarities that a Two has to navigate are explored in the following sections.

Shadow and Idealized Self

Every personality forms an inner world that reflects how it feels about itself and an outer world that projects what it wants others to know about it. Jung would also refer to these worlds as the *shadow*, the hidden traits that your psyche squelches and does not want the outer world to see, and the *idealized self*, what your psyche creates and wants the outer world to see.

Twos' shadow hides excessive neediness and the willingness to manipulate others to get their hidden or unexpressed needs met. They don't want anyone to know that, when angry, ignored, or insulted, they swing from feeling martyred to feeling hostile. Twos mask their martyrdom. If they feel outshined, they will undermine the other person's image. They can become possessive, dominating, overprotective, and controlling.

A Two's idealized self contains extreme sensitivity, genuine compassion, and true generosity. A truly healthy Two offers real nurturing based on real love and often inspires others to give selflessly. They are highly perceptive, empathetic, nonjudgmental, and supportive.

It's all about love for Twos, who love feeling needed and will go out of their way to support and nurture others. When self-actualized, they love to use their intuitive skills, sensitivity to others, and ability to communicate to become diplomats, counselors, or therapists.

Turn-Ons and Turnoffs

According to Jung, libido is not connected to your sex drive alone, but instead refers to your overall psychic energy or what gives your personality juice. The opposite of what turns you on would be what turns you off. To individuate, Twos need to seek balance between these two polarities.

Twos thrive on appreciation and gratitude. They love feeling indispensable, helping others through a crisis, and feeling unimpeachable when it comes to relationships. They love behaving in a charitable fashion or being perceived as someone who loves deeply. What they really love, however, is someone who shows real concern for their needs.

They are turned off to the point of being miserable when their love is not returned in equal proportions or when their loved ones aren't sensitive to or fulfilling their needs. Even though they use manipulation to win love, they really don't like it when someone tries to control them.

Fear and Security

These basic and very essential characteristics determine how Twos approach, live in, and eventually conquer their worlds. Fears stop people short and often cause them to regress, and people rarely progress unless they feel a certain sense of security about themselves or their circumstances.

Twos are terrified that no one will love them and that they cannot survive alone. Since they compensate by becoming indispensable, Twos are always afraid that they will let people down. They are afraid of not being needed. When their need for being perceived as essential, unselfish, and saintly isn't met, they feel as if they don't exist.

Twos create a sense of security by using their heightened sensitivity or internal radar to determine the moods and preferences of those around them and then using that knowledge to make loved ones need them. They like feeling unselfish and feel most secure when they are earning praise or gratitude from others.

Motivations and Fixations

Being motivated or being stuck relates to how Twos use or ignore their psychic energy. Knowing their primary motivations and what Twos cling to within their own personality that either helps them progress toward individuation or keeps them stuck in fixations helps you understand how their personality functions.

Twos need to feel important, loved, appreciated, and needed; they need others to validate their feelings and make them feel special. Their egocentric desire to be loved makes them willing to do whatever it takes to prove that others need and love them. They eagerly sacrifice themselves to take care of others in anticipation that the recipient of their love will grow to love them for it. Twos let their needy hearts rule over their heads.

Because Twos are afraid that no one will love them for who they are, they feel as if they have to make others love them by constantly sacrificing themselves. They fear and deny their own aggressive tendencies, which leads to repression and resentment. Terrified that anyone who sees their real, unattractive underbelly won't love them, they are also afraid to show their real feelings. Instead of admitting, owning, and fulfilling their own needs, they project their neediness onto others.

Coping and Failing

This coping-failing dichotomy has to do with the behaviors Twos adopt to cope with their lives, or maintain the status quo, and how those same behaviors can lead to a failure to grow into their full potential.

Twos rely on their intuition, their feelings, and their heart far more than their analytical or mental abilities. Twos cope by taking pride in being more loving and generous than anyone else. As long as they focus on others, they don't notice that they aren't getting their own needs met.

Convinced it will win love, Twos become changelings who alter their personality, appearance, behavior, or mannerisms to be what someone else wants them to be. They use flattery and intense protestations of their undying love to lure someone into their web. They curry favor and will give and give and give—if only you will like them and need them and want them around. Twos are highly sensitive to the moods and preferences of those around them as if they have internal radars to detect what they need to do to win your favor. Twos have a strong desire for relationship. They develop a strong need for affection and approval—they need to feel loved, protected, and valued.

Twos fail when their sense of identity is tied to their unfailing generosity when it comes to time or energy spent serving others, causing them to overextend themselves to the point of exhaustion. They get so used to deflecting attention by obsessing about everyone else's problems that they forget how to focus on themselves. In fact, their need to feel superior—based on their willingness to focus on everyone else's needs—leads them to seriously neglect their own physical, intellectual, or emotional needs. Eventually they lose sight of who they are and what they really need.

Falling Apart and Transcending

Each enneatype has a unique way of falling apart. The types each have specific needs they need fulfilled, or mental concepts they can embrace, before they can successfully transcend their ego limitations and become fully integrated and whole. Twos become angry, accusatory, and abusive toward anyone they feel is ignoring their needs or who isn't returning their affections. This is especially apparent when their excessive giving becomes compulsive and openly goal oriented or manipulative and wakes others up to their games or causes them to reject them. When all of their coping mechanisms fail, their emotions may become volatile and escalate disproportionate to the conflict or situation. When they feel thwarted or threatened, they verbally or emotionally berate their partners, fly into rages, or lapse into crying jags.

To become self-actualized, Twos need to recognize their neediness and learn to fill it in healthier ways. They also need to uncover their hidden motives and forgive themselves for being underhanded when it comes to love. They need to truly recognize that everyone is responsible for their own needs, that people will love them simply for being themselves, that boundaries need to be honored, that their needs are as important as anyone else's needs, and that filling their needs from the inside out is healthier than meeting them from the outside in. As they integrate, Twos save themselves by becoming increasingly attracted to spiritual enlightenment.

Chapter 8

Enneagram Type Three: King of the Hill

Threes are the kingpins and the stars of their universe. When they bond with healthy mothers, they become the most authentic souls on the planet. When they bond with narcissistic mothers, they become sham artists, hawking false personas to hide undeveloped souls. They are hard-driving achievers who claw their way to the top and crow when they get there. Unfortunately, they desperately want congratulations and adoration from the people they just worked so hard to beat. When self-actualized, Threes attract others with their magnetic personalities; when pathological, their narcissism drives others away.

Emotional Origins

Right out of the gate, Three children were extremely sensitive to how other people were feeling, particularly when they were feeling pleased with the child. Three children identified with the parent or parental figure who fulfilled their physical and emotional needs. Consequently, Three children developed a strong desire to win their parents' love. Whether it was the father, mother, grandmother, or a doting aunt, as infants, Three children picked up subconscious or intuitive signals from their primary caretakers and willingly adjusted their personalities to embody the values that person or the family as a whole cherished. They not only wanted attention, they wanted to impress their family. They learned to earn validation and love through accomplishing what the family most valued.

If the caretaker was self-actualized, he or she mirrored the baby's personality and contributed to the formation of a healthy personality. However, if a doting parent showered a Three child with over-the-top adoration, the child most likely grew up expecting everyone to adore him and to immediately cater to his every need. This type of nurturing created narcissistic Three children who required constant attention and admiration and who grew so dependent on outside validation that without someone around to admire them they felt lost and empty.

Most Three children escaped blatant narcissism but nevertheless ended up so anxious to please their parents that they became very adept at doing things because their parents would admire them for it, even if they had no interest in it or if it went against their grain.

In school, they focused on popular or powerful people and then did whatever they thought those people would find impressive, whatever it took to be noticed and admired by the ones that counted. Because their actions were done to make themselves look like kings of the hill, Threes became easily frustrated and unhappy if their chosen person ignored them. They based their image on what they could achieve, and when they fell short, their egos bruised easily. They hid what they considered unattractive sides of their personalities and felt as if they had been exposed as frauds if someone saw beneath the veil.

On the flip side, if his parents were narcissistic, no matter how hard he tried, the Three child couldn't win the admiring gaze he coveted, which left him feeling unworthy. Eventually a Three child in a pathological home surrendered his own needs, disconnected on some level from his feelings, and lost touch with his essence—all in the vainglorious attempt to be a star.

Ego-Driven Threes

Ego-driven Threes are so invested in being the best that they become the straight-A students and overachievers. They become so competitive that they put their noses to the grindstone, constantly compare themselves to others, and strive to beat them. Like Twos and Fours, Threes get their energy and validation from matters of the heart—they need a response from those around them in order to feel loved. They feel energized when someone else validates their value.

Because Threes confuse applause with love, they learn to excel at whatever will win them accolades, whether in the form of grades or the ability to make a lot of money. Because they possess unusual charisma and have an exceptional ability to create and sustain false personas, which include what appears to be very attractive trappings, Threes overidentify with the roles they create. Often the role becomes larger than life yet more real to the Three.

Threes believe that they have to perform or produce something spectacular in order to deserve your love. As such, they set high achievement standards for themselves and care way too much about how others perceive them, particularly in relation to their accomplishments or the trappings of financial success. They push themselves to create a successful image at all costs. Unfortunately, this frequently leads to ego inflation and turns Threes into boastful showoffs who replace confidence and benevolence with arrogance and contempt.

Threes need you to be highly impressed with their charisma, their intelligence, their possessions, their knowledge, or whatever is attached to the image they want you to admire. Because of this, they are particularly susceptible to advertising gimmicks, particularly those that equate money and possessions with status. Threes will choose being shallow and deceptive over being deep or honest. They become so attached to their image that anything that indicates failure could send them into an identity tailspin.

Between believing that their success will earn them your undying love and their inflated ego requiring that they maintain their fictive image, they develop a clamorous drive to garner attention and win rewards, especially money and fame. They are the workaholic overachievers of the world who will do whatever it takes to make a whole lot of money, warrant a grand entrance, and be honored as the best at their chosen game. At this point, they are the inflated image they have created—out of touch with any real feelings or desires to the point they appear robotic and unfeeling. Terrified that a romantic partner will see their vast emptiness, they rarely let down their guard and always try to "sell themselves" based on their carefully crafted persona.

According to *The Wisdom of the Enneagram*, a Three on a downward slide compulsively drives himself to the brink of physical, mental, or emotional exhaustion. He lies to preserve a false self in a manner that goes way beyond pretending everything is great when it is clearly not even remotely okay. He is vastly insensitive to loved ones and will fly into jealous rages, threaten, and intimidate loved ones in a last-ditch, desperate attempt to control them.

If their life isn't working, ego-driven Threes are so afraid you will realize they are fakes, they spend most of their energy seeking ways to sustain, or fortify, the charade. In social settings they dominate the conversation, using them as opportunities to brag. It's glaringly all about them—their accomplishments, their possessions, and their superiority. Their increasing narcissism starts to reveal their underlying sense of inferiority, and they respond by being hypersensitive to criticism and hostile if they feel threatened.

Pathological Threes

Pathological Threes desperately try to prop up a rapidly disintegrating personality by doing whatever they feel they have to do to maintain the façade—lying on job applications, buying things they cannot afford, exaggerating their accomplishments, denying that their spouse left them, and posturing on a multitude of superficial levels. They have become so adroit at deception and so invested in their successful persona even they believe their own lies. They also still feel so threatened and jealous of their competitors' success that they will sink to the dark pits of hell to sabotage or beat them. No longer aware of what they might actually feel or really need, they use people as pacifiers, someone to gratify their insatiable need for adulation. If a person meets their needs, they want to keep that person around; if not, they throw him away like a used paper towel. They have become so adept at deluding themselves and hiding their reality from others that Threes under extreme pressure may inadvertently create a crisis situation that leaves them feeling naked and vulnerable. When their worst nightmares come to pass and they are exposed, rejected, or abandoned, some Threes are able to snap their rather substantial defense mechanisms back into place while others come completely unglued and disintegrate into a deep depression.

Eventually, pathological Threes view the truth as whatever they need it to be. The lie has become all, and everyone and everything becomes expendable. A Three lies when they pretend that you are not important to them or that they've got everything under control. Their deepest deceit, however, is not in the multitude of lies they tell; it is an existential deceit—they are not whom they seem to be. With pathological Threes, what you see is not what you get. What you see is the role they play to impress, conquer, and control.

As the pathological Threes' lives deteriorate, their desperation makes them vindictive and dangerous—willing to destroy anyone who gets in their way or who could conceivably expose them as fakes. They become increasingly hostile, jealous, and malicious—desperate to squash anyone who has something they want but can never have, and desperate to hold onto the very people they profess to love yet abuse. When they've hit rock bottom on the pathological scale, Threes feel threatened by anyone or anything that reminds them of their failures. And when they feel angry or threatened, they often lash out at the person rejecting them, becoming cruel, jealous, possessive, vindictive, abusive, and ultimately, at the end of the pathological spectrum, capable of murder. Male psychopathic Threes tend to attack women who look or act like the mother whose love they could never win or who make them feel rejected.

Self-Actualized Threes

Self-actualized Threes have everything they need—confidence, brains, personality, balance, energy, and charm. Instead of seeming to have it all, they definitely have it all, and they are so secure they have no need to flaunt it. At the top of their game, self-actualized Threes inspire others to emulate their energetic and competent pursuit of life, work, and love. Wafting through the universe with their assets looks like a breeze, and they draw admirers like bees to honey. On top of all this, self-actualized Threes are modest, innocent, and benevolent—giving of themselves and their assets freely.

Threes at their best know who they are, what they want, and how to get it. Instead of focusing on an exterior locus, they are inner directed, self-generating, and integrated—they possess, speak, and live with integrity. Unlike pathological Threes, with healthy Threes what you see *is* what you get. Self-actualized Threes are realistic about and accepting of themselves and others as human beings doing the best they can, which allows them to love themselves and others freely.

FACT

According to the *Enneagram Movie and Video Guide*, because they are so adept at creating a successful image, selling themselves in all situations, and excelling at work in order to bolster their carefully crafted image, Threes may trend toward careers as corporate or self-development gurus, such as Anthony Robbins, or become superstars in their field who also have a head for business and self promotion, such as Oprah Winfrey, Dick Clark, Michael Jordan, and Tiger Woods.

Self-actualized Threes give credence to the opinions of those they admire, but they have firm personal boundaries allowing them to feel confident, realistic, and grounded—no matter what anyone else thinks. They are often extremely charismatic, accomplished, self-assured, and charming, yet rarely are they arrogant or harbor any secret feelings of superiority.

Self-actualized Threes have their share of approval needs and compensate for them by setting their goals high and striving to meet them, which they often do. They employ dogged determinism to focus on the tasks at hand and complete projects—they earn respect through hard work rather than posturing. Truly healthy, fully integrated, self-actualized Threes are the superstars, the people who catch your eye and make your heart pound faster because they are the real deal.

The Process of Individuation or Self-Actualization

According to Jung, individuation occurs when you successfully separate your personality from that of your parents and become an integrated personality—becoming what or who you were born to be, what you were before you formed an ego or persona, or suppressed negative behaviors in your shadow. The individuation process is a lifelong, ongoing process or quest. Through therapy or active self-development using introspection and conscious choice, you can work toward the unveiling of your shadow, the unraveling your persona, and the integration of your psyche.

Basically, when merging aspects of Jungian theory with Enneagram theory, one could presuppose that when things in your life are going really well, you are ripe for expansion and are more likely to progress toward individuation and self-actualization by adopting behaviors that support forward movement. On the other hand, when you feel insecure or are under severe stress, you are more likely to regress from the goal of individuation and self-actualization by adopting behaviors that allow you to cope but that do not necessarily help you progress toward health. Again, in some instances, you may uncover traits inherent in your stress point that help you grow during times of extreme stress, e.g., you might both cope and progress toward health by discovering determination, integrity, or industry in your stress point.

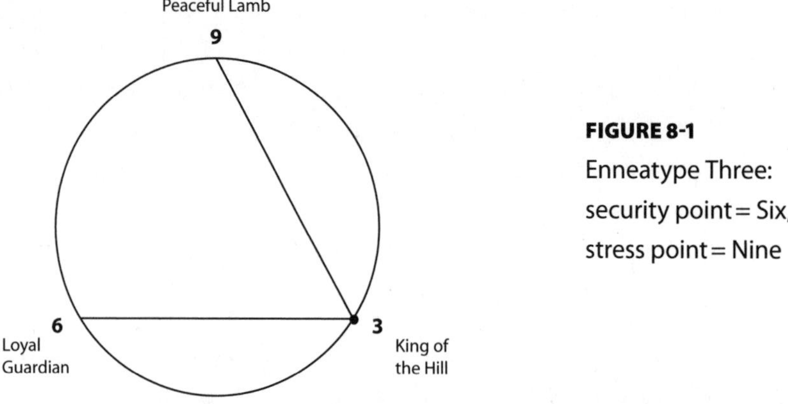

FIGURE 8-1
Enneatype Three:
security point = Six,
stress point = Nine

How Threes Progress

When self-actualized Threes further integrate by adopting Six behaviors, they expand their level of commitment to something or someone other than themselves. They develop a better understanding of team and community. As a result, they become more rooted in their values. They also have a better chance of opening themselves to intimacy, which helps them appreciate their inner self and grow. If they continue to integrate, they lose interest in status, or the quest for personal best, and become cooperative and supportive. Their sense of fulfillment comes from understanding the value of intimacy over the surface value of needing to look good or climb to the top of the heap. As their competitive nature and narcissism subsides, their real self, or essence, bubbles to the surface. In other words, they blossom.

When uptight, ambitious, eye-on-the-prize Threes assimilate the positive energy of style Nine, they mellow considerably. Many learn to relax and slow down, and even acquaint themselves with the contemplative side of life.

How Threes Regress

When under duress, Threes gravitate toward pathological Nine behaviors—hiding in the background and slowing their workaholic pace. Feeling burned out, they disengage and disassociate their feelings. If their career is not going well, they may become increasingly disillusioned and depressed and remain stalled—lost without their ego-driven get-up-and-go—for a long period of time. Severe stress can lead to a meltdown in which they may take the first honest look at themselves. Unfortunately, Threes are so entrenched in the fictional version of their life that breaking through their ego defenses rarely happens. As they plummet to the breaking point, Threes create bigger lies about their imaginary accomplishments, lose all sight of their true self, and fly into controlling or jealous rages. Because they are so invested in an image of success, Threes often experience quite difficult midlife crises. Their successes suddenly seem shallow and worthless, which leaves them feeling as if they don't know who they are.

When Threes adopt the negative energies of Six, they see their competitive success as creating hostility among those they competed against. In extreme cases, they can become paranoid and worry about not being able to take the actions they know they should. They may attempt to cover their insecurity by taking individual credit for team and community efforts.

Balancing the Opposites

According to Jung's personality theory, the psyche is constantly flowing between two extremes, and your primary task is to successfully balance the two polarities. To achieve individuation, each personality has to acknowledge and work through the limitations of its idealized self and shadow, its strengths and weaknesses, and its motivations and fixations (what keeps it stuck). These primary polarities that a Three has to navigate are explored in the following sections.

Shadow and Idealized Self

Every personality forms an inner world that reflects how it feels about itself and an outer world that projects what it wants others to know about it. Jung would also refer to these worlds as the *shadow*, or hidden traits that your psyche squelches and does not want the outer world to see, and the *idealized self*, what your psyche creates and wants the outer world to see.

A Three shadow hides insecurity, insincerity, and dishonesty. Although they do everything to hide or deny it, they assess other people's feelings and vulnerabilities for the primary purpose of exploiting them. Since they mask extreme insecurity with posturing, they view even minimal objective criticism as insulting and often retaliate with verbal, emotional, or physical abuse. When dysfunctional, they become classic narcissists.

FACT

Threes love the fact that they are multitalented, organized, creative, and decisive, and that they know how to tackle problems and get the job done. They love being exceedingly focused and efficient, as well as very creative with strong marketing skills. They make loquacious and effective salespeople and love being leaders.

As far as their idealized self, on the positive side a Three can be very persuasive and inspire others to believe in their dreams. Fully self-actualized Threes are self-sufficient, loving, generous, thoughtful, and optimistic. If they are happy, they radiate confidence and exercise wisdom.

They embrace the truly finer things in life—beauty, art, culture, spirituality, and romance. They use their vast creativity, energy, and dedication to support social causes that benefit humanity.

Turn-Ons and Turnoffs

According to Jung, your libido is not connected to your sex drive alone, but instead refers to your overall psychic energy or what gives your personality juice. The opposite of what turns you on would be what turns you off. To individuate, Threes need to seek balance between these two polarities.

Threes are gluttons for recognition and monetary success. They love being so successful that everyone looks up to them. They become obsessed with earning money, fame, and recognition, and totally love being the most successful person in the room. They get turned on by anything that helps them project the desired image of success—impressive real estate, expensive furniture jewelry, art, fancy cars—and makes others envious.

Because it makes them feel vulnerable, Threes get very turned off when anyone tries to pierce their armor by delving into their real feelings. They get really crazy, defensive, and intimidating if anyone tries to expose their weaknesses. They hate it when someone wants something from them that they can't give. They don't like themselves—or their family—looking less than perfect.

Fear and Security

These basic and very essential characteristics determine how Threes approach, live in, and eventually conquer their worlds. Fears stop people short and often cause people to regress, and they rarely progress unless they feel a certain sense of security about themselves or their circumstances.

Threes are terrified that no one will love them and that they cannot survive alone.

Threes are terrified of feeling—or having anyone guess—that they are empty inside. Their desperate need to create a successful image leaves them afraid that someone will discover their real limitations or view them as a failure. Threes are afraid that any display of real vulnerability will unmask them. Down deep they don't feel lovable and live their lives terrified that the people they love and need so desperately to love them will leave them.

Threes don't like being so overly concerned about image that they feel compelled to create and wear a social mask to fit every occasion. They aren't proud of their tendency to blame others for their problems. Threes don't mind being narcissistic, but they don't want it to be obvious to others that their insecurity is at the root of it. They hate appearing less than adequate in any way.

Threes feel most secure when they can bury their emotions by working night and day. They are most comfortable in the world of accomplishment and feel good about themselves when they are the best at whatever they do. Achieving monetary success or having everyone think they are very successful helps them sleep at night. If they feel like they have everything under control and can manipulate people successfully, they gain confidence in their ability to fool everyone.

Motivations and Fixations

The feeling of being motivated or stuck relates to how Threes use or ignore their psychic energy. Knowing their primary motivations and what Threes cling to within their own personality that either helps them progress toward individuation or keeps them stuck in fixations helps you understand how their personality functions.

Because Threes either received unsubstantiated praise or no praise, they have a burning desire to be admired by their family, friends, coworkers, and community. They want to be accepted and loved for who they are, but they also want to be the best they can be and, more particularly, better than anyone else. They need others to fuss over them and to act as if they are the center of the universe. Threes need validation from others to feel worthwhile. Threes want to have every means of visible success—attractiveness, intelligence, competence, charm, personality, a physically attractive family, tons of money, fame, and recognition. Threes want others to pale in comparison; they want to be the king of the hill at all times.

Threes are weighed down by an inner nagging voice that tells them that they have no real value and that everyone else is better than them. Once they have created an inflated persona designed to trick others into believing they are superior, Threes live in fear that someone will unveil them and expose them for the sham they are. Because they have lost touch with their feelings and true identity, they are afraid to develop true intimacy lest their beloved discover that they are far less than what they project and are in reality empty inside. They are like the wizard Dorothy discovered hiding behind a curtain in Oz. Since their inflated image has been carefully crafted, they are terrified of failing and being exposed as a failure, which is just one of the many fears that keep them stuck.

Coping and Failing

This coping-failing dichotomy has to do with the behaviors Threes adopt to cope with their lives, or maintain the status quo, and how those same behaviors can lead to a failure to grow into their full potential.

Threes cope by focusing on work and achievement, particularly by setting lofty goals and then doing whatever it takes to achieve them. They concoct a successful persona and become facile at deceit—doing or saying anything to hide their underlying insecurity. They buy fancy cars, mansions, bling, and lavish wardrobes—all designed to project extraordinary financial success. They keep themselves too busy to think about feelings, eventually becoming workaholics whose success feeds into their inflated ego. They are supported by the culture of the United States. Psychological classifications for pathology have equivalents for every other Enneagram style, but being a workaholic is not considered an aberration or mental illness.

Threes fail when they create a totally false persona to disguise their insecurity and actually believe the inflated myths they created. They set their goals too high, keep a lot of balls in the air, and overextend themselves for all the wrong reasons. When they feel insecure, they often project their negative qualities onto their loves ones and criticize or berate them in hopes of making them feel so insecure they won't leave them. Their narcissism ends up alienating the very people they wanted so desperately to impress. Meanwhile, they spent so much energy chasing their own tail and are so obsessed with work and money that they neglect their families.

Falling Apart and Transcending

Each enneatype has a unique way of falling apart. The types each have specific needs they need fulfilled, or mental concepts they can embrace, before they can successfully transcend their ego limitations and become fully integrated and whole.

Threes fall apart when something cataclysmic happens in their lives, particularly when it ends up exposing their soft underbelly. If they feel in danger of losing a job, a large amount of money, their spouse, or anything they think is crucial to their existence or their inflated image, they resort to threats and intimidations in hopes of controlling the situation. If they suffer severe blows to their image, they may become deeply depressed or suicidal.

Threes transcend their own ego when they finally realize that people will love them for who they and not for what they can accomplish. If they surrender the need to be the center of attention, they can learn to focus on others and develop reciprocal intimacy—realizing that their real feelings are valuable and sharing them also improves intimacy. They need to learn that it's okay to feel vulnerable and that others aren't judging them as harshly as they judge themselves.

Chapter 9

Enneagram Type Four: Creative Seeker

Fours possess a multitude of qualities: introspective, intuitive, sensitive, compassionate, artistic, self-motivated, ambitious, true to self, and emotionally vulnerable. They often have a steel core—when they sink into despair, they bounce back to reinvent themselves. Fours have an emotional, romantic nature. They love beautiful, sensual surroundings to feel their feelings, and they use their vivid imagination to create fantasies, stir passions, or simply exaggerate emotions. Often called overly sensitive or dramatic, they harbor and nurture deeply felt emotions, particularly a bittersweet melancholy that they seen to cherish despite their complaints.

Emotional Origins

Fours are often born into a family where alcoholism (or other addictions), divorce, or perhaps illness left one or both parents unable to care for their infant, or at least the Four child perceived it that way. Sometimes their caregivers were mentally or emotionally unstable, swinging unexpectedly from nurturing to abusive behavior toward the child. Whether it sprang from an unbalanced parent, the absence of parents, or some outside cataclysmic event, Fours felt as if they were literally abandoned in early childhood. Since the perpetrator is usually physically or emotionally unavailable, the Four child turned whatever anger or grief she felt toward the caregiver inward, blaming herself for being inadequate. Thus, at an early age, Four children spent too much time wallowing in hurt feelings, which led many to develop a lifelong pattern of succumbing to recurring bouts of melancholy or enduring chronic, low-grade depression.

As is the case with all of the other types, not all Fours were literally abandoned or rejected. Some simply didn't mesh with otherwise healthy parents and grew up feeling out of sync or different from their parents. Even if their parents attempted to dote on them, Fours simply didn't see themselves reflected in their parents' eyes. Lacking external validation, Four children learned to cultivate a rich imagination and relied upon themselves to interpret their own feelings and create a unique, sensitive identity. Throughout their childhood and well into adulthood, they often felt like outsiders and so different from everyone else they felt as if they were a character in a story.

Ego-driven or pathological Fours suffer from an abandonment complex. Their wound resulted from feeling as if the parents who should have loved them failed to do so, which leaves them forever in search of someone who could truly love them. This quest, however, is often conducted when they are feeling desperately lonely and consequently leads to poor choices and a succession of potential lovers that do what Fours fear most—abandon them—recreating the original emotions that resulted from not feeling loved or accepted.

Four children typically felt as if they couldn't rely on anyone and interpreted the lack of emotional bonding as rejection. Rather than blaming the parents for being deficient in some way, they buried whatever hostility arose and elected to blame themselves for not being the kind of child their parent could love. They struggled to define themselves by their own terms, which created a lifelong quest to find their real (hidden) identity.

This quest for knowledge about who they really are provides their primary source of self-esteem. They like being in search of themselves and mining their emotions. While they long to feel normal, in reality they come to relish being different, as in "special" or brilliantly unique. Unfortunately, Four children often turn introspection into inhibition, becoming increasingly self-conscious and shy. They may rightfully feel quite angry toward their parents, but rarely do they feel secure enough to express it. Instead, they turn it inside against themselves where it manifests as a self-flagellating depression.

Because they don't bond with their mother or their father, Four children often feel compelled to look for a suitable substitute, someone who will truly see them for whom they really are and applaud their efforts at further self-discovery. This search for an idealistic parent often transforms into a search for an ideal romantic partner who will whisk them away and give them the life they truly deserve.

Ego-Driven Fours

Fours don't learn who they are by emulating their parents. And instead of using their likes and true characteristics to define themselves, the majority become ego-driven Fours whose deflated ego requires them to identify who they are by the qualities or habits they don't have. This only solidifies an image of being deprived. On one hand it's good that they forge an individualistic personality that makes them feel outside of society and yet marvelously unique. On the other hand, it can turn into a bad thing if they identify so strongly with being different that they fear becoming just another normal person living a normal life. Many Fours spend their lives doing whatever it takes to avoid being "normal," even when fitting in and having a normal life is something they secretly desire.

As a result of feeling abandoned, rejected, or unlovable, Fours begin life with an inferiority complex, which leads many to identify with their perceived failings. If they are relatively typical, they then transform this obsession with being different into proof that they are extremely sensitive and special and become the sort of deeply feeling, creative artist who willingly suffers for her art.

Fours have fixations. They imagine that others possess what they are missing and secretly envy them. They feel attracted to and focus on what they cannot have while virtually ignoring what's right in front of them. They require external validation that they are lovable. They enjoy a bittersweet melancholy, and they use emotional intensity to feel alive. And they feel that their real life will only begin when someone truly loves them.

Even if they aren't talented, ego-driven Fours are vastly attracted to the idea that they feel everything more deeply than anyone else. If they can express their feelings through art, it offers them an opportunity to show the world that they are indeed unique and special. If they are posing behind their art, they often become withdrawn, secretive, and elusive in hopes that others won't discover that they are not whom they appear to be.

Unfortunately, ego-driven Fours also harbor an extremely critical, internal judge who is constantly second-guessing their every move, a connection to the ego-driven side of One. This often results in self-censorship and striving to achieve an idealized image that is always just out of reach. Their underlying feeling that they are not lovable creates overcompensation in the form of seeking to impress others with their exceptional intelligence or discriminating taste when it comes to all things cultural. Fours will dress for success and uphold a graceful image that they design to match their desired image and impress others.

Because ego-driven Fours fall in love with their feelings and will do anything to prolong them, they often create a vast fantasy to substantiate a dramatic approach to life and love. They are the ones who seem to willingly spend their lives waiting for a romantic ideal rather than falling for the real person right in front of them. They often embody the quintessential Cinderella or Snow White—waiting for their princely rescuer to arrive and whisk them away from banal reality.

Wounded Fours are also in danger of turning their feelings in upon themselves to the point of becoming self-absorbed and disconnected. When this happens, they become shy, moody, and hypersensitive. Because they start to pity themselves, they often overindulge by spending too much, eating too much, drinking to excess, or adopting other addictive behaviors—all meant to soothe hurt feelings. If they are under undue stress, or come from a particularly dysfunctional family, they eventually squeeze out anyone who doesn't appreciate their heightened sensitivity or who isn't willing to listen to their long list of woes, becoming increasingly self-conscious and withdrawn and retreating further and further within themselves.

Pathological Fours

As small children, pathological Fours learned to withdraw into an increasingly solitary world, sinking into a depression that felt as if they were in their darkest hour and that there was no way out of the black pit of despair. Because they felt powerless to make any positive changes, any offers of outside help fell on deaf ears. Pathological Fours replicate those feeling by falling in love with melancholia because it feels intense and awakens their unconscious through imagery and metaphor, creating what Palmer called a "unique temperamental sensitivity."

According to *The Wisdom of the Enneagram*, a desperate Four on a downward slide exhibits moodiness that leads to reactive anger and emotional outbursts. He withdraws from social interactions and is increasingly melancholy and morose. He constantly sabotages himself and then suffers self-created, unbearable guilt over his perceived unworthiness. He paints himself into an emotional corner, eventually spiraling into a deep depression that could lead to self-mutilation or suicidal thoughts.

When a Four personality hits the skids, what was once sensitivity becomes an obsessive need to be the center of attention. A pathological Four whines, complains, acts out, and falls apart—all in the name of expressing her hypersensitivity and fulfilling her self-absorbed needs. What was once sensitivity focused on themselves first and others second transforms into a reedy, high-strung, overly dramatic compulsion to be viewed as tragic and, therefore entitled to everyone's undivided attention. Their emotional and psychological needs soon become tiresome, repetitive, and incapable of being successfully addressed. They have virtually fallen in love with disappointment, tragedy, and suffering.

Eventually, pathological Fours turn all their imagined or real humiliations inward, becoming deeply reclusive and depressed. The more they withdraw, the more they feel and act immobilized. They often plead for time to sort out their feelings and could spend months—or even years—rehashing past events to no avail. They never forget or forgive, and clearly, if pathologically, get satisfaction from recounting—over and over and over—their litany of complaints about what everyone else has done to them. When they direct their contempt inward, however, their self-reproach turns into self-hatred, which can result in late-stage addiction or a steep fall into suicidal depression.

Self-Actualized Fours

Self-actualized Fours have a highly developed sense of artistry and artistic meaning. They are frequently multitalented and make significant contributions to the arts. Their penchant for sensitivity makes them empathetic, compassionate, and poetic—in tune with the human existence in all its pain and glory. They may have highly developed tastes for sophisticated elegance in art, music, literature, furniture, architecture, and decorating. If so, they bring charm, grace, and style to every setting, and often transmit knowledge of and appreciation for the arts to future generations.

Since they are capable of seeing the divine in the ordinary, integrated Fours who have risen above their ego needs often become spiritual guides who are adept at understanding, guiding, and supporting others in their quest for spiritual growth. They love sharing poems, fairy tales, and myths that they feel are very meaningful, and they are extremely good at verbalizing the delicate symbolism of their rich inner lives, particularly when it serves as inspiration to others.

Self-actualized Fours, according to *The Secret Self,* surrender to self-pity, perk up, express their blossoming creativity, buckle down to get work done, complete projects, think less and act more, positively assert themselves, unconditionally love themselves, surrender fantasy, embrace reality, and appreciate their blessings. They feel unique yet also very connected to others and to life. They accept things as they are and enjoy life!

Their love for symbols along with their feeling-oriented sensibility leads many Fours to become creative artists—writers, photographers, artists, musicians, dancers, actors, directors—or if not a true artist, they typically spend their lives searching for a way to express their individuality through creativity. Healthy Fours can be exceedingly charming people who inspire others to become more in tune with their inner lives and to find their own means of creative expression.

Integrated Fours are also excellent at ferreting out complicated, intertwined information and are able to present it in a way that helps others understand difficult subjects. As such, they make excellent communicators and often become teachers, mentors, and leaders. Self-actualized Fours are also original thinkers who have a thirst for adventure, particularly the quest for self-discovery, and often inspire others to seek their own unique life journey. According to Jung, individuation occurs when you successfully separate your personality from that of your parents and become an integrated personality—becoming what or who you were born to be, what you were before you formed an ego or persona, or suppressed negative behaviors in your shadow. The individuation process is a lifelong, ongoing process or quest. Through therapy or active self-development using introspection and conscious choice, you can work toward the unveiling of your shadow, the unraveling of your persona, and the integration of your psyche.

FACT

Talk about star power! Accroding to the *Enneagram Movie and Video Guide*, lists of classic Fours are rife with actors, writers, dancers, poets, and musicians. Among them: Johnny Depp, John Malkovich, Marlon Brando, Ingmar Bergman, Bob Dylan, Kurt Cobain, Eric Clapton, Rudolf Nureyev, Martha Graham, Judy Garland, Edgar Allan Poe, Charles Baudelaire, Marcel Proust, Virginia Woolf, J. D. Salinger, Sylvia Plath, Anne Rice, and Tennessee Williams.

Basically, when merging aspects of Jungian theory with Enneagram theory, one could presuppose that when things in your life are going really well, you are ripe for expansion and are more likely to progress toward individuation and self-actualization by adopting behaviors that support forward movement. On the other hand, when you feel insecure or are under severe stress, you are more likely to regress from the goal of individuation and self-actualization by adopting behaviors that allow you to cope but that do not necessarily help you progress toward health. Again, in some instances, you may uncover traits inherent in your stress point that help you grow during times of extreme stress, e.g., you might both cope and progress toward health by discovering determination, integrity, or industry in your stress point.

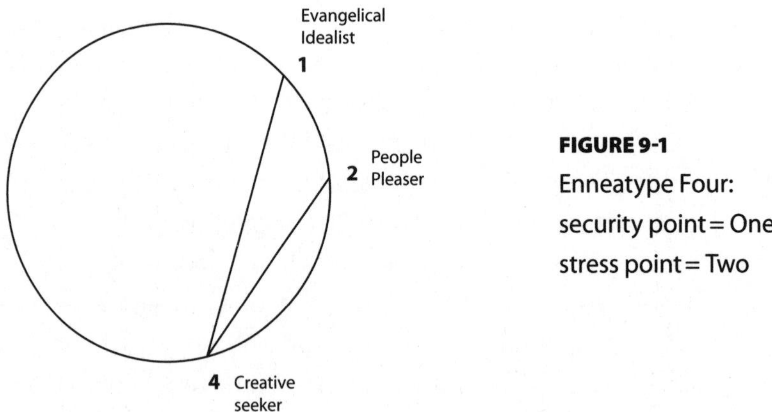

FIGURE 9-1
Enneatype Four:
security point = One,
stress point = Two

How Fours Progress

Self-actualizing Fours progress toward One behaviors, which helps them become more grounded in their own being. They often synthesize their proclivity to create with a strong sense of moral justice and high-minded principles, which helps alleviate self-absorption. When Fours feel more secure about themselves, they surrender their quest for a fantastical life and their preoccupation with what could have been and become more rooted in, and appreciative of, what is happening in the immediate present—right here, right now.

When Fours assimilate the positive side of Two, they become more focused on others and less focused upon themselves—they opt to use their unique sensitivity to serve others. Developing authentic concern for how others think and feel helps Fours overcome their self-absorption. Also, as they become a bit more extroverted and open to interaction, their social skills improve.

How Fours Regress

When pathological Fours gravitate toward negative Two behaviors, their desperate need for love often resorts in the use of manipulation to win the object of their affection. Typically, they are so desperate for a balm for their loneliness, and so convinced that it must come from outside of themselves, they will latch onto someone—anyone—who can temporarily quell that horrifying sense of feeling empty and undesirable. Fours who adopt negative Two behaviors are in danger of becoming emotionally dependent on others to fulfill their emotional needs. As such, they are willing to repress their own needs in order to win the affection of their partner.

When Fours assimilate the negative energy of One, they often assume their private and highly individual tastes are objectively a norm, and then insist that their tastes or their creativity become the norm for others. A Four, in the throes of ego-driven One energy, can act like the ultimate snob.

Balancing the Opposites

According to Jung's personality theory, your psyche is constantly flowing between two extremes, and your primary task is to successfully balance the polarities. To achieve individuation, each personality has to acknowledge and work through the limitations of its idealized self and shadow, its strengths and weaknesses, and its motivations and fixations (what keeps it) stuck. These primary polarities that a Four has to navigate are explained in the following sections.

Shadow and Idealized Self

Every personality forms an inner world that reflects how it feels about itself and an outer world that projects what it wants others to know about it. Jung would also refer to these worlds as the *shadow*, or hidden traits that your psyche squelches and does not want the outer world to see, and the *idealized self*, what your psyche creates and wants the outer world to see.

A Four shadow hides a person who feels both deprived and fatally flawed. Because Fours usually deal with this inferiority complex by becoming self-absorbed, they also hide jealousy, envy, and a transverse elitism. When they succumb to their weaknesses, they become moody, withdrawn, hypersensitive, melodramatic drama queens. In their darkest corners of their personalities they are hypercritical to themselves and others, intractable, moralizing, shame ridden, rejecting, and self-punishing.

A Four's idealized self contains the highly desirable qualities of being extroverted, warm, empathetic, and supportive to self and others. Self-actualized Fours have poetic souls that are passionate, sophisticated, and intelligent, with a gift for creativity and an exceptional ability to verbally express their thoughts and feelings. Optimal Fours are introspective and intuitive, and many are uniquely talented, original artists.

Turn-Ons and Turnoffs

According to Jung, your libido is not connected to your sex drive alone, but instead refers to your overall psychic energy or what gives your personality juice. The opposite of what turns you on would be what turns you off. To individuate, Fours need to seek balance between these two polarities.

Fours are enchanted by romance and spend their lives hoping against hope to be truly seen, understood, and loved. They covet deeply meaningful experiences, crave reciprocal passion, and long for undying commitment. Feeling safe energizes Fours and leads them to a full expression of their artistic abilities. Fours find beauty, art, serenity, romantic stories, evocative symbolism, and poetic meaning inspirational. They love writing in journals, soul searching, feeling deeply, and being unique.

Fours fall into funks when they feel insecure, disappointed, or misunderstood. They fall apart emotionally if they feel emotionally or physically abandoned. They lose their normal drive toward creativity when they feel forced to deal with shallow people or a long string of ordinary days.

Fear and Security

These basic and very essential characteristics determine how Fours approach, live in, and eventually conquer their worlds. Fears stop you short and often cause you to regress, and people rarely progress unless they feel a certain sense of security about themselves or their circumstances.

Fours have a primal fear of rejection and abandonment. Fours are also terrified that they will never discover their essence, or truest self. They are afraid that no one—not even themselves—will know who they really are and what contribution they are supposed to make to society. They also fear having an "ordinary" life and will create carefully spun fantasies to amuse themselves and others. Fours live in constant fear that they will never find their soul mate, someone who ultimately clearly sees, understands, appreciates, and celebrates who the Four really is underneath her stockpile of feelings.

Fours feel most secure when they have a substantial inner life they can withdraw into and indulge their fantasy life. They love symbols and rituals—the symbol becomes its content and rituals become reality. They also fare well when they have a well-defined sense of self that includes everything tragic that has ever happened to them (so they can weave it into art). They love having intimate friends who are willing to listen to their stories and empathize without buying into or supporting their drama.

Motivations and Fixations

The feeling of being motivated or being stuck relates to how Fours use or ignore their psychic energy. Knowing their primary motivations and what Fours cling to within their own personality that either helps them progress toward individuation or keeps them stuck in fixations helps you understand how their personality functions.

Fours have a burning desire to create meaningful works of art that fully expresses their deepest emotions, or at the very least to create a beautiful environment in which they feel comfortable exploring their deepest emotions. They dream of finding their soul mate and creating a fantasy life together. Fours want to safeguard their inner selves and yet expose them through works of art that reflect their essence, or real being. They are caught in the dichotomy of wanting to retreat from the world and wanting the world—and most of all themselves—to finally discover who they really are. Fours are seekers in search of themselves, and when they find out whom they really are inside, they fervently hope that they will be someone special, someone who makes a meaningful, artistic contribution to the world.

Fours get stuck in ruts because they don't want to surrender past hurts and the swell of emotions they created. Fours romanticize their shadow and believe that becoming "normal" will destroy their talent. Despite their occasional longing to be like everyone else, they love being the wounded artist and actually learn to enjoy prolonging their sadness for the sake of their art. They sink so deeply into their self-absorption that they lose social desirability. Because they've often been pegged as "too intense," Fours may mask their real feelings, particularly the painful ones, by talking about inconsequential feelings while hiding their real feelings, and this can lead to them actually losing touch with their real feelings.

Coping and Failing

This coping-failing dichotomy has to do with the behaviors Fours adopt to cope with their lives, or maintain the status quo, and how those same behaviors can lead to a failure to grow into their personality's full potential.

Fours cope by focusing on fantasy and spend their time searching for a romantic ideal. They use their aloofness and moodiness to keep others at bay. They channel their dramatic excesses into creative projects. They envision themselves as nobly different from ordinary people and cling to a feeling that they will one day find the perfect someone who will finally recognize their essence through their many veils and finally, truly love them exactly as they are—someone special.

Fours fail themselves when they believe their own fantasy and settle for unrequited longing. Because they believe that something is always missing from their life, they form and fall in love with a bittersweet melancholy. They nurse past hurts and all the juicy emotions connected to them; in fact, they embrace angst and often succumb to self-created depression. They get stuck because they feel that their flaws make them special and thus cannot be surrendered.

Falling Apart and Transcending

Each enneatype has a unique way of falling apart. The types each have specific needs they need fulfilled, or mental concepts they can embrace, before they can successfully transcend or become fully integrated and whole.

Depression

When Fours fall apart, their emotional seams come unglued, leading to excessive tears or blistering anger. They bury their anger and turn it into depression. They become overly dramatic, defensive, sarcastic, and irascible, deliberately pushing others away. No matter how you attempt to comfort or reassure them, they remain inconsolable and typically fall into a serious funk.

Fours transcend their ego when they connect to the universe, the divine, and every other living person. Whenever and wherever they find the beauty that exists in everyday life, it elevates them out of their gloomy feelings and helps reduce the pressure to create an exceptional life based on fantasy. Once they realize that they are lovable and sufficient, grieve their losses, and move on, they will find many opportunities that prove that they are neither alone nor abandoned.

Healthy Fours lose their fascination with being different and use their creativity to see special qualities in other people, whom they animate or empower by discovering and revealing that person's potential. This helps Fours surrender their self-absorption. Self-actualized Fours compress the broad spectrum of their emotions and really start feeling. Once they stop being in love with their own sensitivity and become willing to fall so deeply into a feeling that they experience it through all its various stages, they transform themselves from an aspiring artist to artists capable of fully expressing all of their multifaceted capabilities.

Chapter 10

Enneagram Type Five: Masterful Hermit

Fives are the cool, calm, collected thinkers of the world. They are the ones who endlessly use their considerable intellect to mull things over, albeit from a safe distance. Fives are quiet, reserved, self-contained, and famously contemplative. They stand in the corners at parties survey the crowd, and silently amass information they can use later to form opinions about whom they can and cannot trust. Even though they long to belong to a circle of friends, they don't take the initiative in forming relationships but wait for others to come to them.

Emotional Origins

Many Five children grew up in a family where personal boundaries barely existed or where one or both caregivers consistently overstepped the child's physical, emotional, or psychic boundaries. Their mother, or primary caregiver, may have been possessive, controlling, or smothering. As quiet, private souls, Five children experienced this behavior as an intrusion and guarded themselves against it by retreating into the safe, private world of their imagination.

Other Five children felt abandoned by both parental figures, or failed to bond with their mother and learned to cope with their despair by detaching from or compartmentalizing their feelings. Sandra Maitri, author of *The Spiritual Dimension of the Enneagram*, described a Five's memory of the early relationships as "tinged with the sense of not being fully related to, deeply loved, wanted, or fully nourished. . .a sense of having futilely sucked at a dry tit."

Five children adapted to feeling rejected or to feeling smothered by skirting intimacy, by hiding themselves from the sight of others and observing others from safe distances. Five children became calm, cool observers who retreated from life and felt safer dealing with mental concepts than messy feelings. If they experienced their mother—or mother figure—as devouring, they probably developed a belief that intimacy was draining and that they were better off conserving their energy than feeding into someone else's emotions. Suffering from early disappointment, Five children lose their faith in hope, preferring predictability to surprise.

Five children learned to retreat to their own rooms or to a compartmentalized psychic space that permitted them time to mull over their emotional reaction. They learned to like their time alone and often resorted to hiding even when in public. Eventually, they became observers of life more than fully engaged participants and often would not know what they felt about an interaction until they had time to think about it later.

Five children needed order and strongly preferred to know ahead of time what was on their agenda. They developed an affinity for mental preoccupations and would rather fade into the background than be singled out or put on the spot. They would often feel drained when around others and resisted authority at every turn. They spent a lot of time alone and liked working on projects on their own. They often say they felt like aliens in their family, as if plopped down from the sky into a family that was nothing like them.

Ego-Driven Fives

Fives represent Jung's quintessential thinking introvert; they retreat from the world and process everything through the sharpened sieve that is their mind. Although they are great at analyzing, categorizing, and postulating, they also idealize their privacy, their emotional detachment, and their mind. Fives desperately want to believe that if they merely think things through and plan well, they can control what happens to them. They love knowledge, particularly knowing more than anyone else, and feel most safe when they fully understand what is happening in their world and what is likely to happen tomorrow.

FACT

Singer, songwriter, and poet, Bob Dylan (a Four with a heavy Five wing) portrays the Five personality's reclusive nature. Dylan often felt estranged from life and was reticent about being in the limelight. In interviews, he evaded questions, openly challenged the reporters, replied flippantly, and averted eye contact. Dylan's reclusive and protective nature provided ample time alone to channel his emotions into his potent lyrics.

Because they rely on their first-rate thinking process to decipher what they consider an illogical world, ego-driven Fives can appear very cool, calm, and collected. Given the choice, they circumvent feelings by quietly observing what is going on around them and then retreat to the safety of their private room to mull everything over and order it in their mind. Fives do best when they have ample time alone to sort through their memories and dreams.

Since their basic personality formed around a sense of violation, abandonment, or never having their needs met, Fives are often (functional) collectors or (dysfunctional) hoarders who clutch money, possessions, and energy tightly to their chest. Oddly enough, however, they don't consider their own feelings, needs, or desires important and rarely see any value in sharing their innermost thoughts, which makes it difficult for those who love them to know how to respond to them. In fact, Fives aren't aware of what their feelings really are until they think them over in private—their thoughts and feelings suffer from a time lag.

In order to survive the disappointment of not being fully seen—or cherished—by their primary caregivers and to avoid feeling the pain of neglect, they adapt by isolating themselves and hiding their essential self. Emotional and physical withdrawal thence becomes a Five's primary coping mechanism, which leads to a faltering sense of who he actually is, which eventually requires virtually hiding from life. When a Five chooses to interact, he likes having ultimate control over the quantity and the quality of what he perceives as draining experiences.

FACT

According to *The Enneagram* by Helen Palmer, Howard Hughes careened from an ego-driven Five to a psychotic Five. Feeling drained by having to deal with others, Hughes retreated so far he became a hermit. Choosing to live frugally despite his massive wealth, Hughes ran his empire from the safety of a few small rooms. It's said that he found the daily chores of living so exhausting that—even when hungry—he would sit at the table for hours without lifting a spoon to his mouth.

Their fundamental fixation or delusion is that they are truly separate from other human beings, which also ultimately seals their fate: a life devoid of connection, unity, or love. Fives' emotional withdrawal both protects and defeats them. Their inner lives—and their souls—are always in danger of drying up and disintegrating. Feeling the impact of losing their inner juiciness, Fives often become increasingly frugal with their energy, time, emotions, and money—parceling out limited quantities and believing that others are, or should be, doing the same.

Even wealthy Fives feel as if they are empty inside and fear that no amount of money or possessions can fill that void. In fact, wealthy Fives often eschew material possessions and live far below their means and rather enjoy feeling superior to others in not craving things or needing outward signs of wealth to feel important.

Pathological Fives

As their personalities disintegrate, Fives suffer from excessive mind chatter and a debilitating lack of self-esteem. They no longer trust their own judgment or their ability to navigate life. In addition, because their exceptional mental abilities allow them to see all sides of a problem, they overthink and confuse themselves to such an extent that they end up not doing anything to solve their problems. Instead of clear thinking, they get distorted, jumbled thinking that amplifies their inability to make decisions or take action. They often dramatically switch from being intellectual and theoretical to being defensive and aggressive.

Secretly they fantasize about having a real life, but they have grown too complacent to wish for, or to expect, anything to occur. Eventually, pathological Fives resign themselves to living a limited life that is devoid of passion, lust, or desire for anything or anyone. As they become increasingly passive and isolated, they feel dried up, wasted, and of no use to anyone, not even themselves. Pathological Fives frequently lose their vitality, including whatever fragments of their sex drive remained.

According to *The Wisdom of the Enneagram*, Fives on a downward slide live an increasingly hermetic life, rebuffing all social opportunities. They compartmentalize their life and become apathetic, exhausted, and neglectful of their own daily physical needs. They appear trapped in their overactive mind and become both bitter and spiteful. They appear schizophrenic or obsessive-compulsive, and eventually approach a catatonic state.

Some pathological Fives become dictatorial, impatient, petty, hypercritical, and blame others for things that go wrong. Sadly, they themselves become victims of their own crushing superego, which punishes them regularly and harshly for failing to meet its high standards. Unlike a One, who integrates or identifies with her superego, a Five's superego berates, belittles, and nags him constantly, making him feel even worse about himself. In a desperate attempt to control his environment, a longing for order turns into obsessive-compulsive behavior in which both his thinking and his actions become rigid.

Disintegrating Fives often feel empty inside and do whatever they can to avoid actually feeling the emotions connected to their own sense of deprivation and poverty of spirit. They become increasingly antisocial and withdraw from work, social, or family events. When asked personal questions, they clam up and refuse to share their feelings. They appear frozen or paralyzed with fear and often act as if nothing matters and nothing can change, as if they have lost all hope that their lives will be happy or fulfilled.

Self-Actualized Fives

While ego-driven Fives use detachment to cope, self-actualized Fives achieve healthy detachment—they feel the full range of emotions appropriate to each situation yet allow the feelings to flow through them and dissipate. They have developed an inner observer that helps them order their world without attempting to control their world.

Self-actualized Fives have defeated their fears, calmed their overactive mind, and learned to love themselves and others unconditionally. They have ample evidence that all of their needs will be met and that others love them for who and what they are without reservations. This helps quiet their overactive minds and steady their emotions. As they integrate into whole, healthy beings, they unleash their natural talents for finding order in the midst of chaos and become extremely intelligent, prophetic seers equivalent to Jung's Wise Old Man.

In fact, self-actualized Fives have the uncanny ability to open all their channels—mental, emotional, and intuitive—when it comes to observing and synthesizing information. Their clarity, and confidence in their clarity, allows them to see beyond what most people see and to envision new choices. Their acute mental clarity and laserlike intuition results in visionary ideas in terms of anticipating problems and solving them before they materialize. They go beyond the creation of theories to reordering the universe and often appear as if they have been divinely inspired.

When Fives actualize their connections to types Seven and Eight, they find the energy to deal effectively with external reality. Bill Gates, for example, is a Five with a powerful connection to Eight traits that helped him create vast wealth. When Fives assimilate healthy Seven traits, they often develop a fine sense of humor, like Johnny Carson, a Five who was able to incorporate Seven's wit and charm.

According to authors Hurley and Dobson, self-actualized Fives are extremely curious and interested in absorbing new information. They embrace change and inspire others to open up to their infinite possibilities. They love adventure and have the courage to strike out on their own. They accept diversity and rarely judge anyone. They love to lend a helping hand to anyone trying to expand their horizons and enjoy watching others develop and trust their own inner voice. They can be quite charming, witty, and engaging, which makes them attractive to the opposite sex.

The Process of Individuation or Self-Actualization

According to Jung, individuation occurs when you successfully separate your personality from that of your parents and become an integrated personality—becoming what or who you were born to be, what you were before you formed an ego or persona, or suppressed negative behaviors in your shadow. The individuation process is a lifelong, ongoing process or quest. Through therapy or active self-development using introspection and conscious choice, you can work toward the unveiling of your shadow, the unraveling of your persona, and the integration of your psyche.

FACT

Fives, especially with a Four wing, are often philosophers, theologians, or psychologists who turn their intellectually oriented, rational observation of human behavior into coherent theories. Often, they not only make astute observations, they discard antiquated theories and create a new order or system of their own. The Buddha is an example of a fully self-actualized Five, and Sigmund Freud is an example of an ego-driven Five.

Basically, when merging aspects of Jungian theory with Enneagram theory, one could presuppose that when things in your life are going really well, you are ripe for expansion and are more likely to progress toward individuation and self-actualization by adopting behaviors that support forward movement. On the other hand, when you feel insecure or are under severe stress, you are more likely to regress from the goal of individuation and self-actualization by adopting behaviors that allow you to cope but that do not necessarily help you progress toward health. Again, in some instances, you may uncover traits inherent in your stress point that help you grow during times of extreme stress, e.g., you might both cope and progress toward health by discovering determination, integrity, or industry in your stress point.

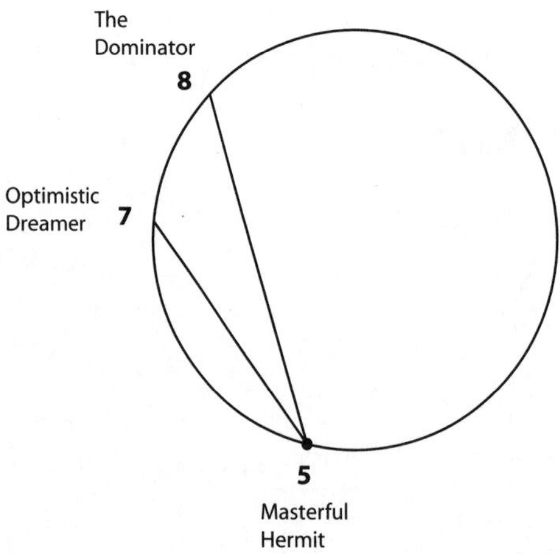

FIGURE 10-1: Enneatype Five: security point = Eight, stress point = Seven

How Fives Progress

Fives progress toward Eight, and when it's working well, Eight energy lights a fire, motivating fearful Fives to actually do something to improve their lives. Often, when feeling the Eight's confidence and physicality, they actually inhabit their bodies and not only surrender to an urge to congregate with others but will risk intimacy. Instead of withdrawing, they socialize, and as they do they grow more comfortable being visible.

They also get more in touch with all of their feelings, including the dreaded fear. Once they learn that fear is part of being human and that they can express it without damaging anyone or looking foolish, they will often acknowledge rather than repress it. Unleashing the energy behind repressed fear helps Fives feel confident and assertive, even to the point of being willing to take on leadership roles.

When Fives adopt positive behaviors from Seven, they come out of their reclusive shells and venture into the outer world. Seven energy helps them loosen their more typical inhibitions and express an atypical playful side, which translates into pleasurable socializing and connecting with others on a more intimate level than a guarded Five would usually achieve.

How Fives Regress

Fives regress toward Seven, which manages to confuse them further, meaning Fives lose their grip on order. They become restless, insatiable, and lose their ability to focus. They become so distracted that they find it difficult to finish what they start. They also lose their patience more quickly and lose control of their feelings in general. They find justifications for being self-absorbed and feeling as if they are superior to other lesser beings. They dominate conversations and may be both flippant and disrespectful. They find even more reasons to distract themselves by overthinking or by fantasizing about how it could be instead of how it is.

If reclusive Fives adopt behaviors from the low side of Eight, they may develop a cold ruthlessness and may use their love for isolation, coupled with a desire for revenge, as a way to plot revenge from a distance—similar to the infamous Unabomber, Ted Kaczynski, who went after his victims in an orderly manner and who wrote volumes about his thoughts on the state of the world.

Balancing the Opposites

According to Jung's personality theory, psyches are constantly flowing between two extremes, and your primary task is to successfully balance the two polarities. To achieve individuation, each personality has to acknowledge and work through the limitations of its idealized self and shadow, its strengths and weaknesses, and its motivations and fixations (what keeps it stuck). These primary polarities that a Five has to navigate are explored in the following sections.

Shadow and Idealized Self

Every personality forms an inner world that reflects how it feels about itself and an outer world that projects what it wants others to know about it. Jung would also refer to these worlds as the *shadow*, the hidden traits that your psyche squelches and does not want the outer world to see, and the *idealized self*, what your psyche creates and wants the outer world to see. (For more on shadows, see Chapter 4.)

The healthiest, most integrated Fives are in touch with their feelings and use their perceptive abilities to look for ways to enrich other people's lives. They trust their own instincts and trust that good things are going to happen in their lives. They open themselves to new experiences and inspire others to do the same.

A Five shadow hides the type's tendencies to be greedy, miserly, and stingy. Caring more about facts than feelings translates into an unattractive, cold rationality. Even though they remain socially awkward loners, when they are anxious, they tend to show off and can be arrogant, glib, and mean. In personal relationships they can be stubborn, think they are always right, remain closed to alternate points of view, blame others for mistakes, and be condescending to the point of appearing contemptuous.

Self-actualized Fives have the fabulous qualities of being mentally acute, resourceful, inventive, and competent. They are excellent communicators, efficient project coordinators, and are headstrong yet effective leaders who embrace progress. These highly integrated Fives are both independent and adventuresome. They are often extremely perceptive, sensitive, objective, introspective, reflective, and loving to their inner circle. Self-actualized Fives possess inner wisdom and form a healthy philosophy for living life. They are incredibly loyal to principles and to the people they admire and consider worthy.

Turn-Ons and Turnoffs

According to Jung, libido is not connected to your sex drive alone, but instead refers to your overall psychic energy or what gives your personality juice. The opposite of what turns you on would be what turns you off. To individuate, Fives need to seek balance between these two polarities.

Fives love an orderly pattern and crave nothing more than sufficient solitude to think anything and everything through and order their private universe. They have a high appreciation for lucidity and adore a mental challenge. Since Fives love acquiring extensive knowledge, they, more than any other sign, covet and generally acquire a library full of fabulous books. While they love time to reflect, they also like spending their time wisely and do their best when they've got puzzles to solve and obstacles to overcome.

Fives cringe when anyone asks them how they feel or wants to discuss their mutual feelings for each other. Crowds, parties, weddings, funerals, or any social event—where they might be required to chat about mundane matters or have to deal with unpleasant emotions, like anger, resentment, or grief—strike fear in their hearts. They hate unruly feelings, passionate family arguments, or anything that makes them feel confused or disoriented.

They also hate repetitive conversation, when people are vague or attempt to stonewall them, and being asked to talk about anything before they feel ready.

Fear and Security

These basic and very essential characteristics determine how Fives approach, live in, and eventually conquer their worlds. Fears stop them short and often cause them to regress, and they rarely progress unless they feel a certain sense of security about themselves or their circumstances.

Fives are afraid that they are empty, that the universe is falling apart, and that you will reject them or drain them of their energy. Fives are afraid of actually feeling their emotions, especially the ones that tell them they are desperately lonely. Since they spend far more time fantasizing in their heads about, rather than participating in, a relationship, when confronted with a real relationship that they cannot contain they feel overwhelmed by the velocity of their emotions. They are afraid of appearing foolish and avoid it by arming themselves with knowledge.

Fives feel most secure when they have accumulated a lot of knowledge on whatever is intriguing or puzzling them. If they can create sense out of chaos, they feel in control. They like having plenty of time to plan ahead so they can be extremely efficient in executing projects. Fives require safe and trustworthy relationships, understandable and reasonable expectations, and social propriety. They need plenty of private time and space and are happiest when they can progress in relationships at their own pace.

Motivations and Fixations

Being motivated or stuck relates to how Fives use or ignore their psychic energy. Knowing their primary motivations and what Fives cling to within their own personality that either helps them progress toward individuation or keeps them stuck in fixations helps you understand how their personality functions.

Fives love tackling a project that requires a mental challenge, especially acquiring extensive knowledge on an obscure or fascinating subject. They like to make order out of chaos and exhibit their impressive intellect, from a safe distance of course. They love creating a home that becomes their

sanctuary and having plenty of time to pursue their private hobbies, read books, reminisce about their past, or fantasize about their future. They prefer to make progress rather than cling to the past.

Fives feel pressured, rather than liberated, by love. Not wanting to admit their growing emotional dependence, Fives will seek solitude within the relationship and avoid confrontation at any cost. They also prefer to consider all the angles before making decisions, which means they bog down when making even simple decisions. Their preference for solitude creates limited interpersonal skills. They feel the way they think or work is superior, which leads them to rely more and more only on themselves and to eventually ignore other people's opinions. They give precedence to facts over feelings when making decisions.

Coping and Failing

This coping-failing dichotomy has to do with the behaviors Fives adopt to cope with their lives, or maintain the status quo, and how those same behaviors can lead to a failure to grow into their full potential.

Fives cope with what they consider an intrusive life by creating an ordered personal universe that includes firm boundaries designed to protect them from awkward situations or unwelcome demands on their energy. They protect themselves by observing life rather than actively participating in it. They methodically organize and categorize information so they can make logical conclusions when pressed. They will avoid emotional entanglements that distract them from their work and tend to circumvent criticism by blaming others when things go wrong. Fives keep their sanity by retreating into their sanctuaries.

Fives are infatuated with their intelligence and take great pride in knowing more than others. They love nothing more than to withdraw into their extensive libraries to pour over books. The more planning they do or knowledge they collect, the happier they are before undertaking any new venture. Nothing gets them more excited or makes them feel safer than feeling like they have a firm and precise handle on how their life is going.

Fives fail themselves by retreating from active life to live in a world of ideas. Remaining aloof or distant means they spend way too much time alone, overanalyzing what could happen and how they might cope with it, instead of getting in the trenches and living their lives. Eventually, they go from avoiding others and not reaching out to anyone to not being emotionally available to loved ones. Over time, the more hermetic Fives become, the more they disconnect from their true inner strengths.

Falling Apart and Transcending

Each enneatype has a unique way of falling apart. The types each have specific needs they need fulfilled, or mental concepts they can embrace, before they can successfully transcend their ego limitations and become fully integrated and whole.

Unlike Twos, who deal with their fear of feeling strong emotions by repressing them, Fives deal with their fears by detaching from them and retreating from social interaction. When Fives are angry, they typically retaliate passive-aggressively by withholding conversation or emotion or by using subterfuge and quiet rebellion to express their unhappiness or disapproval. An out-of-control Five unleashes pent-up anger by flying into a rage. If they feel like they are losing control, they often become increasingly obsessive-compulsive.

Fives transcend their ego limitations when they turn their focus from observing others to observing their own behavior and seeking to change it. Once they fully realize that other people can be supportive and nurturing, and that there is enough energy for everyone to get all of their needs met, they can loosen their strictures and enter into a reciprocal relationship. Once they realize that everyone needs other people, they can find and embrace opportunities to build relationships. They transcend their ego by connecting all of their feelings to what is occurring in present time and by giving themselves permission to be who they are, to feel truly seen and accepted for who they are, and to communicate what they feel, need, and want.

Chapter 11

Enneagram Type Six: Loyal Guardian

Sixes tend to expect the worst while not exactly hoping for the best. Like Fives, Sixes also rely on their minds, which are often reeling with possibilities—negative, fearful possibilities. Their personalities are filled with paradox. They display characteristics of being equally weak and strong, shy and outgoing, and they flip-flop from one ego state to another. They spend their lives rebelling against authority or surrendering to it. Sixes need someone or something to believe in, and once they find that person, philosophy, cause, government, or theology, they devote themselves to it.

Emotional Origins

Some Six children become neurotically attached to the memory of being solely dependent on two caregivers and never successfully separate from their parents. If the father or father figure was strong, clear, authoritative, and healthy, the child may have fared better but probably began a lifelong quest to find another perfect father. If the father, or father figure, was weak or absent, Six children often felt insecure and frightened, and they rarely received the mirroring they needed to develop confidence in themselves.

Other Six children grew up in a family where their parental figures were overbearing, unpredictable, unreliable, dishonest, and physically or emotionally threatening. If the parents or authorial parent had substance abuse problems, the Six child most likely endured erratic behavior that left him or her feeling unsettled, off balance, and fearful. If the parent was an alcoholic, for example, a Six child learned to deal with her anxiety about what might happen by becoming a vigilant observer—watching her parent closely to determine whether he came home drunk or sober and when he was most likely to go off the deep end and behave badly.

Six children coped with stressful situations—or situations they expected to prove stressful—by constantly being on guard. They sought to avoid disaster by anticipating it and generally fearing the worst. Unfortunately, most Six children also felt like they created the problem. As a result, they grew up mistrusting themselves and the very people they were dependent upon, leading to a generalized fear of intimacy. Despite a longing for connection, they learned to push away potential friends or romantic partners. Six children grew up with an exaggerated need for reassurance and guidance, as well as financial, physical, and emotional security.

Ego-Driven Sixes

Ego-driven sixes are the most ambivalent type in the Enneagram. No matter what is going on, how big or small the decision is, or what is on the line, they waffle. Torn between the rules and regulations they have chosen to create a sense of stability and safety in their lives, and a growing sense that these same rules have failed them, their minds become a battleground of indecision.

Their behavior becomes reactive instead of active and is often erratic, as when they first trust and then abruptly revolt against authority. Similar to Nines, but without as much conviction, Sixes can occasionally exemplify passive-aggressive behavior—passive when they want to express their negative emotions but continue to fly under the radar within a family, an organization, a government, or a religion; aggressive when they want to break away and find a new belief system or partner.

Sixes prefer governing by consensus. In fact, our American culture is a Six. Our Founding Fathers were willing to fight to the death for the principles of democracy and dedicated their lives to protecting and preserving the fledging country. When belief in principles reach critical mass—when they make perfect sense in their minds and warrant loyalty—Six governments become dogmatic fundamentalists whose passion inspires enough followers to launch a nation.

Sixes are also chronic worriers—insecure, nervous, fearful—and as such will go overboard to make themselves useful in hopes that their loved ones or employers will want them around and take good care of them. They need constant reassurance, and since they don't trust themselves to navigate life solo, will often go from one dependent situation to another.

Because they constantly question their own judgment, they also tend to jump from one set of beliefs to another, primarily by second-guessing themselves and even at times opposing themselves. They may create a situation in which they could fall prey to a cultlike mentality, but luckily their tendency to war within themselves often saves them. They will carefully scrutinize and investigate new ideas—like the good devil's advocates they are—but once they understand all the intellectual constructs and firmly believe in something or someone, they commit body, mind, and soul. In fact, many Sixes become dogmatic political, religious, or social fundamentalists. They love rules and regulations and are thus attracted to mathematical, legal, scientific, engineering, military, or accounting professions.

Sixes generally have problems identifying and expressing their thoughts or feelings. They also overdeliberate even simple decisions, weighing every possible outcome in their mind relentlessly. They can't help imagining the worst and create unnecessary anxiety. They are doubters or naysayers who shoot down ideas. Since they expect disaster, they cringe at anything perceived the least bit problematic. They love to complain about how others are making their lives difficult, but they rarely take personal responsibility or do anything to change their stressful situations.

However, when healthy and functioning at their peak, Sixes are among the best problem solvers in the world. They pay close attention to what's going on, have x-ray vision when it comes to anticipating everything that can go wrong, and will protect themselves by fixing problems if they can. They make excellent middle managers, and you can thank Sixes for helping bureaucratic agencies function.

Pathological Sixes

Pathological Sixes manifest their chronic anxiety by becoming phobic—convinced everyone is against them and either accusing or avoiding perceived troublemakers. Or they manifest their anxiety by becoming counterphobic—proving they are not afraid by being confrontational and aggressive toward the object of their fear. They believe everyone has suspect motives and are convinced that someone is out to get them. The more they isolate themselves, the more paranoid they become.

According to *The Wisdom of the Enneagram*, a desperate Six on a downward slide suffers from panic or anxiety attacks and may flip from being extremely needy and dependent to being openly rebellious and defiant. She may suddenly hook up with a bad crowd or tolerate abusive situations in which she is clearly being hurt. She becomes increasingly fearful and paranoid and, if pushed to her limit, may strike back aggressively at perceived enemies.

Unfortunately, Sixes project their weaknesses onto other people. While this gives them some respite, it also gives their power away—allowing them to skirt responsibility or to realize that they have the power to make changes. They become too dependent on someone else, surrendering their confidence, their energy, and their motivation to take control of their own lives. This makes them susceptible to abusers, and they often stay in relationships in which they swing from being professional victims to abusers. When they blame others for their problems and direct their anger outward—usually inappropriately and disproportionately to the situation—their outbursts are startling and make people around them uncomfortable.

In a desperate attempt to order their lives and feel safe, pathological Sixes often latch onto a religion or cult and project all of their power onto the chosen leader or theology. They often project godlike omniscient powers onto the person leading the group. This can leave them feeling like they don't have the power within themselves to change their situation or even to make intelligent decisions about their life.

When Sixes become fundamentalists they ascribe to one set of structures. Like all dogmatic fundamentalists, they live within the narrow scope of beliefs that exclude anyone who doesn't feel the same way they do. Fundamentalists no longer question authority, re-examine their beliefs, or show compassion and understanding toward those who don't share the same beliefs. They think suppressing others will make them safe, so when they feel threatened or when they cannot accept their own dark side, they project their fears or weaknesses onto others and label them as evil to justify violence against them.

Self-Actualized Sixes

The basic difference between ego-driven Sixes and self-actualized Sixes is that integrated Sixes don't suffer from the same anxiety producing dichotomies in their personality. Self-actualized Sixes are comfortable in their own skin and confident that they not only have sound judgment, but the ability to excel at whatever they choose to do. They have progressed beyond the need to have an external locus—they trust their own instincts. They also trust others, but they still ask a lot of questions, albeit to qualify or quantify their own perceptions and to protect society from ill-intentioned organizations.

FACT

According to *The Enneagram Movie and Video Guide,* famous real-life Sixes who possess Six phobic personalities include Woody Allen, Warren Beatty, Albert Brooks, Richard Lewis, Penny Marshall, Carly Simon, and Brian Wilson. Famous real-life Sixes who possess Six counterphobic personalities include Jerry Brown, George Carlin, Carrie Fisher, Mel Gibson, J. Edgar Hoover, Michael Moore, Paul Newman, Robert Redford, and Ted Turner. Disintegrated Sixes range from J. Edgar Hoover to Charles Manson to the epitome of a destructive Six, Adolf Hitler.

Self-actualized Sixes find the courage to accept all the nuances enfolded within their personality. The less they project their weaknesses, their strengths, and their fears onto other people and claim the whole shebang as their own, the more courageous and confident they become. They maintain their high standards in terms of seeking valiant people, causes, governments, or religions to trumpet, but they now understand that nothing and no one is perfect. Once they determine a cause or person is good enough, they offer their allegiance and their service from a place of strength instead of weakness. In other words, they are loyal participants who no longer have a neurotic need to stand guard but who can now more competently step into the ring.

The Process of Individuation or Self-Actualization

According to Jung, individuation occurs when you successfully separate your personality from that of your parents and become an integrated personality—becoming what or who you were born to be, what you were before you formed an ego or persona, or suppressed negative behaviors in your shadow. The individuation process is a lifelong, ongoing process or quest. Through therapy or active self-development using introspection and conscious choice, you can work toward the unveiling of your shadow, the unraveling of your persona, and the integration of your psyche.

According to Judith Searle in *The Literary Enneagram*, Shakespeare's character Hamlet accurately portrays a Six in the throes of ambivalence. Some of the telltale signs of Sixes include their mental agility, excessive anxiety, fixation on worst-case scenarios, and their disarming ambivalence. In the height of his torment, Hamlet vacillated between emotions, and ultimately sealed his tragic fate when his distorted thinking forestalled productive action.

Basically, when merging aspects of Jungian theory with Enneagram theory, one could presuppose that when things in your life are going really well, you are ripe for expansion and are more likely to progress toward individuation and self-actualization by adopting behaviors that support forward movement. On the other hand, when you feel insecure or are under severe stress, you are more likely to regress from the goal of individuation and self-actualization by adopting behaviors that allow you to cope but that do not necessarily help you progress toward health. Again, in some instances, you may uncover traits inherent in your stress point that help you grow during times of extreme stress, e.g., discovering determination, integrity, or industry.

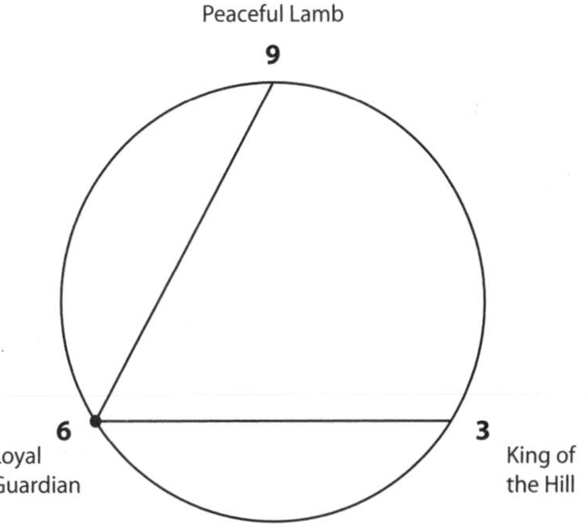

FIGURE 11-1: Enneatype Six: security point = Nine, stress point = Three

How Sixes Progress

Sixes progress by adopting behaviors common to a Nine. When they use their inner resources from style Nine, they are able to live in their own bodies and learn to experience emotions—particularly those pesky polar opposites such as love and hate, or fear and trust. It also helps them discern subtle differences between experiencing true intuition instead of anxiety-induced paranoia. Once their anxiety dissipates, Sixes take on positive qualities of Nines by becoming emotionally stable and confident. They open their hearts and risk interactive rather than reactive relationships. As Sixes leaning toward Nines learn to see nuances and further trust their own judgment, they can give themselves and others the benefit of the doubt.

When Sixes access the positive resources of Three, they use their problem-solving skills to achieve excellence and confidently claim their native abilities. Instead of languishing in the grey zone, or seeking outside sources, Sixes are finally able to recognize and claim their inner authority.

How Sixes Regress

Sixes regress to Three behavior in which they seek to allay their inferior feelings and to calm their fears about being alone in the world by becoming overachievers. They can become so intent upon building an impressive and lucrative career that they will consistently work to the point of physical exhaustion. Like Threes, Sixes on the ropes focus on image rather than true qualities, which all too often results in competitive actions and sabotage so that they can come out on top. Their inferiority is masked by an inflated ego that attempts to convince everyone that they have it all together, often by bullying or belittling perceived competitors.

Sixes in full regression often project their fears and negative behaviors onto an enemy and then secretly desire to be as bad as the person whose behavior they've just been trashing. Like Threes, Sixes in decline may hide a disintegrating ego through lies and manipulation. If they crash, Sixes locked into Three behaviors may turn the contempt they feel toward themselves outward onto someone or something and feel justified—even if they have no justification for doing so—in attacking or destroying.

If Sixes adopt some of the negative attributes of a Nine, they fall into the Nine trap of becoming even more passive. Soon they feel overwhelmed and lose their ability to focus. This can be catastrophic, leading from a broadening inertia to depression and immobility.

Balancing the Opposites

According to Jung's personality theory, psyches are constantly flowing between two extremes, and your primary task is to successfully balance the two polarities. To achieve individuation, each personality has to acknowledge and work through the limitations of its idealized self and shadow; its strengths and weaknesses, and its motivations and fixations (what keeps it stuck).

Shadow and Idealized Self

Every personality forms an inner world that reflects how it feels about itself and an outer world that projects what it wants others to know about it. Jung would also refer to these worlds as the *shadow*, or hidden, traits that your psyche squelches and does not want the outer world to see, and the *idealized self*, what your psyche creates and wants the outer world to see.

A Six's shadow hides his rigidity, the same rigidity that leads to a dogmatic approach to life. Sixes would rather that no one knows how truly insecure they feel. Unfortunately, they are indecisive, second-guess themselves and others, and worry about inconsequential things. They are often overly analytical, overprotective, shallow, and narrow-minded. Sixes like to hide their paranoia and their secret attachment to revenge. When provoked, Sixes can become extremely belligerent and aggressive, two qualities they would rather you didn't see.

FACT

Sixes have an authority complex. More than any other type, they over-identified with and idealized, or feared and reacted against, their patriarchal figure and then transposed that dependence upon, or fear of, onto real world authority figures. Sixes react to authority by either latching onto it as a way of quieting their anxiety or rebelling against it when they project their fears onto it. Like Ones, Sixes occasionally battle with their own strict, interior superego, but generally they're more concerned with outer world moral codes.

A Six's idealized self is someone very capable of committing to worthy endeavors. Their values are in line and integrated, which provides them with courage to make decisions, act responsibly, and sustain positive loyalty. Optimum Sixes are mentally acute, conscientious, persevering, and extraordinarily reliable. Confident Sixes make strong leaders who will support, sustain, and inspire everyone in the organization from the bottom up. Sixes at their best are comfortable in their own skin, which makes them very charming and sociable.

Turn-Ons and Turnoffs

According to Jung, libido is not connected to our sex drive alone, but instead refers to your overall psychic energy or what gives your personality juice. The opposite of what turns you on would be what turns you off. To individuate, Sixes need to seek balance between these two polarities. More than any other enneatype, Sixes struggle between whether they should adhere to an inner or an outer authority. To cope with their phobic fear, Sixes commonly surrender their power to an external authority. But when tension develops, they flip into counterphobic behavior and attack the very authority figure they had been relying upon for direction.

Sixes are happiest when they feel that they can truly trust other people, as well as themselves, to behave properly and do the right thing. They like people who behave responsibly toward each other and the world, and they love discovering a philosophy or religious belief system that fully sustains and supports their view of the world. They love opportunities to use their sharpened intellect and pride themselves on always knowing the right answer.

Sixes hate it when anyone betrays their confidences or sabotages them. Also, they feel pressured if people clamor for an immediate answer without giving them time to investigate or review all the pertinent factors that weigh into a decision. They also get hot under the collar when people ignore their needs, or when they can't trust others to do the right thing.

Fear and Security

These basic and very essential characteristics determine how Sixes approach, live in, and eventually conquer their worlds. Fears stop you short and often cause you to regress, and you rarely progress unless you feel a certain sense of security about yourself or your circumstances.

Because they lack sufficient self-confidence or faith in their own abilities, one of a Six's deepest fears is that they cannot survive on their own. They don't trust their own instincts and live in fear of making mistakes or failing at important tasks. They always feel that they aren't good enough and crave the approval of others; they often seek help making even simple decisions. Sixes are afraid that they aren't safe anywhere, that they can't trust anyone, that they will be left alone with their own devices and be caught short, and that they will fall into a dark hole and not be able to find their way out without a guide, counselor, protector, or true friend.

Sixes feel secure when they know that they can rely on their exceptional intelligence and ability to see everything that is going on to analyze every situation. If they can anticipate what's going to happen and manipulate people and events so that they feel safer, they'll feel like they can make it in this dangerous, unpredictable world. They feel more secure when they belong to, trust in, and dogmatically follow a religious, political, or social philosophy.

Motivations and Fixations

Being motivated or stuck relates to how Sixes use or ignore their psychic energy. Knowing their primary motivations and what Sixes cling to within their own personality that either helps them progress toward individuation or keeps them stuck in fixations helps you understand how their personality functions.

Sixes have a burning desire to achieve some sense of lasting security and thus constantly search for someone or something that they believe virtually guarantees them a safe journey through life. If they find someone or something to believe in, they throw all of their weight behind it and become the most devoted and loyal supporters. They also want to achieve a clearly delineated place in the hierarchy of whatever organization they work for or participate in. Their desire to be in control of their feelings leads them to gain as much knowledge as possible.

When Sixes blindly obey rules and laws, they surrender both their opinions and their free choice for the sake of social congruity. This prevents them from developing trust in their own instincts, perceptions, or abilities and often leaves them feeling groundless in the face of indecision. Sixes get stuck whenever they allow their fear of calamity to smother any sense of security or self-reliance. Whenever they weigh too many conceivable consequences before undertaking even small risks, or always want to know what everyone else is thinking before they express an opinion, Sixes are dragging an oar in the water.

Coping and Failing

This coping-failing dichotomy has to do with the behaviors Sixes adopt to cope with their lives, or maintain the status quo, and how those same behaviors can lead to a failure to grow into their full potential.

Sixes learn to quell their fears by thoroughly investigating and questioning conventional wisdom before making up their own minds. They protect themselves by devoting themselves to what they are certain are good people and good causes, and then proving to them that they are reliable, trustworthy, and decent. Following traditions, keeping their schedules packed to avoid overthinking or worrying, supporting leaders they have learned to trust, and feeling a part of a community all help Sixes deal with anxiety.

The worst thing Sixes do to themselves is blame themselves for what happened to them in their childhood and any other transgressions or overstepping of boundaries that others perpetuated. Sixes fail themselves when they get trapped in their own mind—always considering a multitude of options, imagining the worst, and expecting disaster. They rely almost solely on their mind instead of reaching out to others and building strong relationships based on common human fallibility. They have difficulty figuring out how they really feel (as opposed to think). They resist new ideas and question the need to do anything different.

Sixes look outside for an organization, a religion, or a philosophical orientation to quell their anxiety. They don't trust their own intellect to make crucial decisions. However, once they find an authoritative system, they swing back and forth from complete acceptance to outright rebellion. Sixes suffer from an internal anxiety that creates an ongoing battle to figure out what will make them feel most comfortable at the time. Sixes react rather than act, and they feel an excruciating ambivalence within their own souls.

Falling Apart and Transcending

Each enneatype has a unique way of falling apart. The types each have specific needs they need fulfilled, or mental concepts they can embrace, before they can successfully transcend their ego limitations and become fully integrated and whole.

When Sixes come unglued, they walk around in a state of constant anxiety that can manifest in being completely phobic and paranoid or being completely rebellious and belligerent. They may rebel against the very authority they have long followed and question everything and everyone that they used to believe in. They could shrink from normal activities and cower from even slight challenges. They actively push people away by becoming overly critical, acerbic, and confrontational. When angered, disintegrating Sixes will use their sharp wit to intentionally wound someone else's ego. Sixes with their backs to the wall may become so afraid that they have trouble leaving the house, or they may project their problems onto a scapegoat and then behave sadistically toward them.

Sixes transcend their ego limitations when they realize that they were not responsible for how their parents behaved and that whatever happened was outside their control. If they also realize that the world is filled with decent, honest, trustworthy people whom they can both truly rely upon and trust, they can let down their guard and allow their best qualities to blossom. When they do, they can discover that other people like, value, and trust them for who they are and not who they think they have to be. If Sixes inhabit their own bodies and stop their mind from interfering with feeling their feelings, they can integrate body, mind, and soul to become a whole, centered human being.

Chapter 12

Enneagram Type Seven: Optimistic Dreamer

Sevens believe in the pleasure principle and live life with gusto. They love life, people, parties, and everything wonderful that life can bring. There's no looking back and no reliving unhappy experiences. Sevens just want to be happy, and they'll have a fascinating life—even if it only happens in their daydreams. They are bright, energetic, enthusiastic optimists. Sevens are the dreamers and schemers who are so compelled to keep themselves busy that they are constantly creating new goals and trying new activities.

Emotional Origins

A Seven child began life as the apple of his mother's eye, but then something or someone distracted the mother and left the Seven child feeling either rejected or dejected. Even if the mother returned and once again bestowed her affections, the Seven child experienced heartbreaking despair from which he never fully recovered. He experienced what it felt like to be emotionally abandoned and developed an aversion to ever feeling it again.

Other Seven children feel as if they have to save their mother, or that their reason for existing was to fulfill their mother's need to feel like a valuable person in the world. In other words, some Seven children may have felt a mixture of attraction and repulsion for their mother. Even if they had warm and fuzzy memories of their mother, underneath they may have felt pressured when around her—pressured to be more than they were, to be perfect, or simply to be constantly happy.

FACT

Sevens embody Jung's *Puer Aeternus* archetype, or eternal youth. Like Peter Pan, most Sevens glorify their childhood and prefer immature, playful emotions to grownup, painful ones. Like Peter Pan, on some level Sevens believe in and constantly search for their particular fantastical Neverland, a place where they can abolish pain and adult responsibility in favor of fun and games.

Seven children may have had a supremely happy childhood and be pain averse simply because they don't know what it is to feel depressed, sad, unhappy, stressed, or angry. Or they had a superprotective mother who made sure they didn't see, hear, or feel anything painful. While the mother did this out of love, she inadvertently created a child who developed a fear of pain because he don't know how to handle it. Other Seven children my have had a mother who needed a cheerful child and rewarded that child when he hid all those nasty little feelings and remained sweet and charming. Or they may have had a mother who never left her child alone with his own thoughts and feelings, or a mother who thought whatever wasn't talked about didn't really exist—like getting angry or feeling sad.

Ego-Driven Sevens

Like their counterparts in the thinking triad (Fives and Sixes), Sevens appease anxiety through thinking; however, there is a basic difference between the way Fives use thinking and Sevens use thinking. Introverted Fives use their mental acuity to defend against what they view as a perilous outer world; extroverted Sevens use their mental acuity to defend against what they view as a perilous inner world. Fives retreat inward and spin facts and knowledge around in their heads to avoid having to socialize or form relationships in the scary outer world. Sevens reach outward and create a whirlwind of physical or social activity to avoid experiencing scary emotions inside. Sevens will jump at many opportunities to experience life, but don't ask them to look backward or talk about any negative feelings or experiences. They like keeping their eyes on future possibilities.

Sevens escape painful emotions by keeping themselves extremely busy. A person in motion is not a contemplative, inward looking person. When life becomes unpleasant, Sevens distract themselves by thinking positive thoughts, finding something new to think (and dream) about, and taking on new challenges. Because they are gifted thinkers, Sevens need stimulation and have no patience for boring situations or people. Unfortunately, they often become addicted to excitement and will sabotage themselves many times over for the sake of a momentary adrenaline rush.

According to *The Enneagram Movie and Video Guide*, Sevens make great characters. In movies they are often portrayed as adventurers, pirates, scoundrels, rogues, gourmands, lovers, dreamers, drifters, con men, gluttons, visionaries, and hedonists. Most Sevens are depicted as debonair, charming, vivacious, and endearing; rarely are they either villains or tragic characters.

Sevens are closely tied to Jung's extroverted sensate in that they are focused on external objects and experiences. They believe more in the external world than the internal world—that everything valuable is found in the outer life you live, replete with possessions and experiences. They value the world of things, ideas, and real world experiences more than they value the internal life of emotions, spirit, or soul. As such, Sevens require a life filled with adventure.

Sevens are also quick thinkers with minds that are always searching for fresh stimulation. They come up with fabulous ideas but are more likely to discard them and move on to the next than do anything to make them happen. After a while, they crave newness and can flit from one idea to another whether or not those ideas have any merit. Eventually, they may end up with a long string of ideas but nothing to keep them warm at night. In other words, they can be all show and no product.

Sevens like to keep their options open and always have a roster of backup plans. According to Helen Palmer, any time a Seven makes a commitment, it is always buffered by backup plans. "Agreement is which one feels right at the time," Palmer explained. This defensive planning is designed to avoid negativity, failure, or boredom. Alternative plans also allow a Seven to employ their favorite defense mechanism—rationalization. If one plan bores them, they can rationalize a decision to move on and try something new. On the surface this works, but it also contributes to the characteristic flitting that prevents Sevens from reaching their own depths. They make choices based on what makes them feel happy in the moment, which keeps their life experiences on the surface and delays discovery of their deeper, truer self, or essence.

Pathological Sevens

Pathological Sevens don't take themselves seriously, which means they bury possibilities along with potential problems. Their once busy life becomes a frenetic life that further loosens their grip on reality. They can delude themselves into thinking that the dreamy life they created in their own mind is what is really occurring. They can become so desperate to believe their fantasies that when a close friend or family member attempts to interject a slice of reality they will refuse to listen.

Pathological Sevens hunger for excitement. Hyperactivity provides them with a seductive adrenaline rush that leaves them feeling compelled to chase it. The more they get caught up in the chase, the more they become impulsive, indulgent, irresponsible, and unreliable.

According *The Wisdom of the Enneagram*, a desperate Seven on a downward slide refuses to acknowledge painful feelings, which leads to frenzied activity and desperate attempts to sublimate or supplant sadness, anger, or depression. Bombarded by all the memories and feelings he suppressed, his behavior becomes increasingly erratic, often swinging from mania to depression. His addiction escalates into dangerous territory, and he may abuse other substances. As his personality disintegrates, he may suffer panic attacks or fall into a deep depression. A Seven at the end of his rope is often suicidal.

Pathological Sevens focus solely on what benefits them. Their narcissism becomes pathological when they start feeling that they are not only superior but deserve everything they want, and they are willing to trample anyone who gets in their way. They walk around feeling and acting superior but cower in constant fear that someone will discover that they are not who they pretend to be.

Self-Actualized Sevens

Self-actualized Sevens have learned to accept all of their experiences and the complicated feelings they generate—the good, the bad, and the ugly. They have integrated their past, forgiven their transgressors, and can now live comfortably very much in the present. They have a more realistic view of themselves and others and are able to both listen and be truly empathetic. As a result, they form healthy, fulfilling relationships. As they grow and mature emotionally, Sevens also learn to embrace solitude and the sort of nourishing meditative silence that allows their souls to blossom. This helps them appreciate life as the gift it is and to feel truly joyful.

FACT

What Sevens desperately need is sobriety—a soulful sobriety that goes beyond refraining from excessive ingestion of alcohol or drugs. According to Sandra Maitri in *The Spiritual Dimension of the Enneagram*, "Sobriety for Sevens means temperance, moderation, self-restraint, seriousness, staidness, and soundness of reason and judgment. It means being unhurried and calm, with no trace of impatience or haste, facing reality and not being fanciful, as well as not being showy."

Integrated, self-actualized Sevens see, honor, and reinforce the positive qualities of people and situations. They maintain a youthful, happy attitude, but they no longer cower from reality to do so; instead, they see the sadness in others and themselves and face it squarely instead of running from it. They genuinely believe in possibility, resurrection, and rebirth for everything and everyone.

These highly integrated and whole Sevens become the ultimate visionaries, capable of imagining a bright future for the whole planet. Their lively minds and superior imagination help them see beyond limitations and to hold dreams that embody love, generosity, peace, and prosperity for all. A mature, self-actualized Seven also has the ability to go beyond mere dreaming and will put ideas into action.

The Process of Individuation or Self-Actualization

According to Jung, individuation occurs when you successfully separate your personality from that of your parents and become an integrated personality—becoming what or who you were born to be, what you were before you formed an ego or persona, or suppressed negative behaviors in your shadow. The individuation process is a lifelong, ongoing process or quest. Through therapy or active self-development using introspection and conscious choice, you can work toward the unveiling of your shadow, the unraveling of your persona, and the integration of your psyche.

Basically, when merging aspects of Jungian theory with Enneagram theory, one could presuppose that when things in your life are going really well, you are ripe for expansion and are more likely to progress toward individuation and self-actualization by adopting behaviors that support forward movement. On the other hand, when you feel insecure or are under severe stress, you are more likely to regress from the goal of individuation and self-actualization by adopting behaviors that allow you to cope but that do not necessarily help you progress toward health. Again, in some instances, you may uncover traits inherent in your stress point that help you grow during times of extreme stress, e.g., you might both cope and progress toward health by discovering determination, integrity, or industry in your stress point.

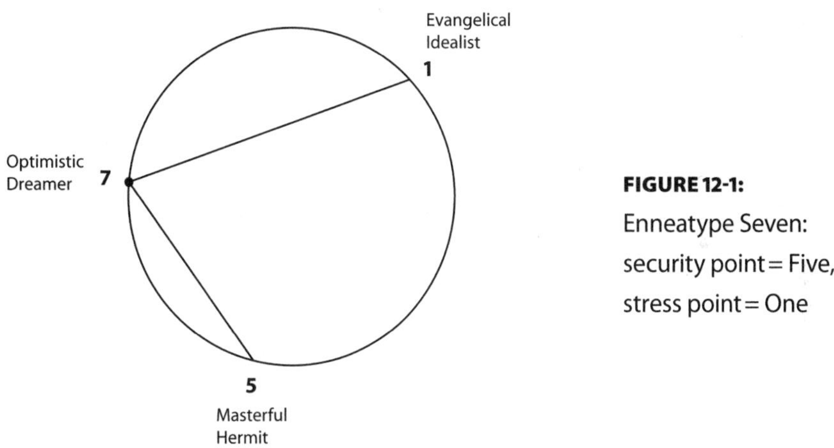

FIGURE 12-1: Enneatype Seven: security point = Five, stress point = One

How Sevens Progress

When Sevens progress, they move toward Five behavior. They find a still point, slow down the frenetic activity, and create time and space for further investigation, actual planning, and following through. They go from daydreaming about to manifesting their ideas. With Five on their side, Sevens are finally able to put their clever minds to work on concrete tasks and stick with projects until they are actually completed. As their comfort level increases for alone time, Sevens explore their internal life, including those pesky negative feelings and memories. Doing so helps them integrate and become more truly whole.

When Sevens can connect to positive One energy, they become more responsible than usual, follow the rules and norms of society, and can sustain their focus long enough to pay attention to detail. Best of all, they often harness the critical ability of One and that helps them learn to substitute quality for quantity.

How Sevens Regress

When Sevens regress, they move toward One behavior, which brings out a nasty streak of unfamiliar pessimism. They fall under the sway of One energy by setting very high standards for themselves and others and then issuing harsh judgments when anyone, including themselves, falls short. Sevens may adopt One's black-and-white thinking, think they have all the answers, and turn their frustration outward, blaming others for any bad fortune. As their optimism fades, Sevens in retrograde experience black moods, often sinking into depression or swinging back and forth between manic-depressive episodes.

If Sevens adopt negative Five energy, they can become parsimonious, shrinking their lives to a subsistence level and stifling their natural expansiveness. They may use their intellect to become highly speculative, but they don't muster the energy to take action. Instead, their natural tendency to rationalize becomes heightened, and they become liars instead of creative storytellers.

Balancing the Opposites

According to Jung's personality theory, psyches are constantly flowing between two extremes, and your primary task is to successfully balance the two polarities. To achieve individuation, each personality has to acknowledge and work through the limitations of its idealized self and shadow, its strengths and weaknesses, and its motivations and fixations (what keeps it stuck).

Shadow and Idealized Self

Every personality forms an inner world that reflects how it feels about itself and an outer world that projects what it wants others to know about it. Jung would also refer to these worlds as the *shadow*, or hidden traits that your psyche squelches and does not want the outer world to see, and the *idealized self*, what your psyche creates and wants the outer world to see.

Sevens' shadow hides a smoldering anger that is unleashed if anyone tries to manipulate or even control them or asks them to do their bidding. Their penchant for constant and instant gratification leads them to hop from one idea, job, or romance to another without sinking their teeth into anything, producing anything, or committing to anyone. They are great at envisioning but weak at follow-through. They are impulsive and escapist, which often creates havoc in their lives. If life throws them a curve, they completely lose their optimism and become resentful, spiteful, bitter, rude, and often aggressive. They have an addictive personality and a gluttonous hunger that cannot be satisfied.

A Seven's idealized self is extremely intelligent and extremely likable and charming. They have charisma in spades and are easily capable of spellbinding people. Sevens are highly imaginative and visionary thinkers. They like viewing life in a very positive way and often possess a certain joie de vivre that helps them go through life partying. They use their discriminating taste for all things good to delight and entertain their family, friends, and coworkers. Their idealized self is always upbeat, positive, and blazingly optimistic—they'll be the person championing your dreams.

Turn-Ons and Turnoffs

According to Jung, libido is not connected to your sex drive alone, but instead refers to your overall psychic energy or what gives your personality juice. The opposite of what turns you on would be what turns you off. To individuate, Sevens need to seek a balance between these two polarities.

Sevens are turned off when anyone tries to bring them down to earth or asks them to face reality squarely. They don't like feeling or discussing negative emotions or painful memories and consider anyone who does a wallowing, pessimistic stick-in-the-mud. Their sharp minds grind to a stop whenever anyone or anything bores them, which leaves them feeling pressured to find something more interesting lest they feel depressed, sad, or lazy. They are afraid of slowing down or being alone with their thoughts. If any sad, angry, or aggressive feelings seep into consciousness, Sevens are afraid it will lead to an avalanche of feelings and long-buried pain that they won't be able to control.

Sevens love telling stories, particularly when they have a happy ending. They also love talking about future plans, creating a long to-do list, and setting new goals. They love discussing ideas, philosophies, and psychology, but only on an intellectual level. They don't go near true feelings, particularly if they are painful. Offer them a good time, and they are on board. Sevens are social butterflies who love having a full dance card—anything to keep them on the go and fully distracted from pesky negativity.

Fear and Security

These two basic and very essential characteristics determine how Sevens approach, live in, and eventually conquer their worlds. Fears stop you short and often cause you to regress, and you rarely progress unless you feel a certain sense of security about yourself or your circumstances.

Sevens are afraid to face anything that reminds them that life is difficult and that painful things happen. They are terrified that slowing down will let the darkness in. They feel insulted when anyone bosses them around and hemmed in when anyone tries to tie them down. They are so afraid that something better might come along they are afraid to commit themselves.

Making a long list of fantastical dreams or ambitious goals helps Sevens move their energy forward. If Sevens can form a juicy image of their personal utopia and hold it in their minds, they feel rooted and on course. They feel most secure when they have their options open and don't feel imprisoned or restricted. Since they don't like unpleasantness, Sevens covet happy times and living life full tilt. If they are having fun, they feel that all is right with the world.

Motivations and Fixations

This relates to how Sevens use or ignore their psychic energy. Knowing their primary motivations and what Sevens cling to within their own personality that either helps them progress toward individuation or keeps them stuck in fixations helps you understand how their personality functions.

Sevens are motivated to keep painful feelings or memories at bay. They are motivated to keep the flow of fresh ideas coming and to keep their eyes on the future—their future. They are motivated to develop the next scheme, diversion, or job, or romance. Their burning desire to live life to its fullest motivates them to catapult toward experiences and adventures like moths to flame. Nothing excites a Seven more than the possibility of discovering something or someone new that they can believe—if only for a short while—will totally change their lives and bring them the riches they deserve.

Sevens get stuck when they deny themselves the experience of owning all of their feelings, which prevents them from growing or developing any real character. The need for constant activity prevents them from ever experiencing absolute stillness or meditating about their life constructively. Instead, they keep themselves one-dimensional and on the run. They create an idealized self—based on fantasy—that amuses them but keeps them from developing a real self based on grit, substance, and genuine depth. Their flitting tendency also prevents them from sticking with a craft long enough to achieve mastery, which weakens their opportunities to use the full force of their intelligence and capabilities.

Coping and Failing

This coping-failing dichotomy has to do with the behaviors Sevens adopt to cope with their lives, or maintain the status quo, and how those same behaviors can lead to a failure to grow into their full potential.

Sevens escape their fear by distracting themselves and making life a party. As long as they are surrounded by happy people doing fascinating things and have plenty of opportunities open, Sevens believe their lives are going fine. They focus all their energy on things in the external world to avoid feeling anything painful in their internal world. They use their exceptional mental skills and gift for brainstorming to generate new ideas in hopes of covering the fact that they aren't very good at completing anything. They keep themselves busy and make sure they always have options to forestall the dreaded boredom they inevitably feel if they allow the pace to slow down.

Sevens fail by choosing a superficial life over a fully integrated one. They cut off one part of their personality and thus fail to know the riches that can be hidden in their shadow and in their childhood pain. Denying their pain keeps them from learning from it and making other choices. They fail by not giving themselves the gift of solitude where real dreams can materialize. And they prevent themselves from discovering what they could really accomplish if they stopped chasing their tails. They also don't allow themselves to learn that they can handle difficult emotions, which means they don't develop the self-confidence that helps them go forward.

Falling Apart and Transcending

Each enneatype has a unique way of falling apart. The types each have specific needs they need fulfilled, or mental concepts they can embrace, before they can successfully transcend their ego limitations and become fully integrated and whole.

Sevens fall apart when reality crashes down—when they get rejected, someone betrays them, or they don't get that big job they wanted and deserved. Setbacks turn into traumas, and traumas lead to a major slippage in their subconscious where all those nasty feelings have been stashed, which causes a meltdown in their psyche. Their fragile hold on patience is gone, leading to open hostility, temper tantrums, and excessive drinking, eating, shopping, or other addictive behaviors. They lose their charm entirely and become belligerent, aggressive, bullying, and insulting. A Seven off the deep end is in danger of becoming hysterical, panicked, and claustrophobic. They feel like all their options have dissipated and a deep despair leading to suicide feels inevitable.

Sevens transcend their personality by realizing that being conscious in the moment is the only way to really live the life you were meant to have. They also transcend by remembering their entire past, processing the emotions they shoved under the rug, and then living from that point on fully conscious and fully present. When they integrate all the parts of their personalities into a cohesive whole, they learn to own and share all of their emotions—opening them up to opportunities for genuine intimacy. They transcend their ego limitations when they surrender the need to feel superior and embrace the totality of their personality—when their ego inflation transforms into true self-esteem.

Chapter 13

Enneagram Type Eight: The Dominator

13

Eights are powerhouses—in the boardroom and in the bedroom—who have a large appetite and the lust to fulfill it. Primarily motivated by sensory instincts, they like anything that makes their body sing—monetary success, power rushes, hot romances, and the robust assertion of power. Eights are authoritative, direct, assertive, and amazingly resourceful. In personal and professional relationships they are often argumentative, dominating, controlling, and intense. Eights love to face reality head on and rebel against injustice. Oddly enough, they make the ultimate revolutionaries or missionaries.

Emotional Origins

Children who develop an Eight personality often witnessed exploitation within their home or within their closely knit neighborhood. In many cases, Eight children had a controlling father figure who dominated a weaker mother figure, from which the Eight child learned the necessity for appearing strong, particularly when caught in a confrontational exchange. In such cases, the Eight child decided the world was a dangerous place and ramped up his own energy to claim a stake in it. Eight children braced themselves for combat and puffed out their literal and metaphorical chests to frighten off perceived opponents.

If Eight children developed their personalities in abusive or poverty-stricken families, they most likely became outright aggressors who willfully defended themselves and anyone they cared about. For example, they identified with the hotshots, bullies, or delinquents that reigned over the neighborhood. If Eight children grew up in wealthy or psychologically and sociologically healthy families, they most likely identified with movers and shakers in the corporate world or moral leaders in government or religious arenas.

Eights often develop an anger fixation. Once they discover the psychic energy that provokes—and results from the expression of—anger, Eights become addicted to the thrill of battle and anger excites them. Verbal confrontation becomes second nature, something that defines their own sense of themselves as a competent defender and protector. While most people cringe in the face of explosive outbursts, Eights climb giddily into the ring.

Because they frequently grew up in abusive situations, Eight children learned to be on their toes at all times. They constantly sized up the competition, particularly if they felt threatened, so they could be ready to defend themselves verbally or physically. They developed a strong sense of self that allowed them to feel in charge and to take control when they felt threatened in any way. They subsequently buried any visages of their softer side and surrendered the privilege of introspection. Eight children learned to view themselves as fierce competitors who were stronger, smarter, tougher, sharper, and almost always right. If they desensitized themselves to their own and others' feelings, Eight children became bossy, demanding, manipulative, and hard edged. Healthy Eight children often became inspiring, venerable class presidents; dysfunctional or wounded Eight children often became vicious, domineering gang leaders.

Ego-Driven Eights

Ego-driven Eights have their eye on the ball and their energy focused on the outer world. They are extroverted in the truest sense of the word—they love being vocal and visible powerhouses among. Eights have a real zest for living life full tilt and thrive on challenge, confrontation, and accomplishment. You can spot Eights the moment they enter a room—they'll be the ones projecting their huge personality through the way they swagger, strut, and preen.

FACT

According to *The Enneagram Movie and Video Guide*, famous Eights include Gloria Allred, Charles Barkley, Humphrey Bogart, Johnny Cash, Fidel Castro, Michael Douglas, Indira Ghandi, Geronimo, John Gotti, Ernest Hemingway, Marilyn Horne, Saddam Hussein, Joan Jett, Evel Knievel, Rush Limbaugh, Norman Mailer, Golda Meir, Dennis Miller, Queen Latifah, Grace Slick, Charlize Theron, Barbara Walters, and Denzel Washington.

In every area of their lives, Eights are proactive, take-charge personalities. They are people on a mission, even if the mission is somewhat self-serving. However, when they are motivated more by a desire to be the hero than a desire to help others, Eights roll up their sleeves and do philanthropic work. Unlike Ones, who do good deeds on behalf of moral principles, Eights do good deeds to feel powerful They definitely win kudos for championing underdogs, but they do it partly because they feel compelled to attack perceived injustice and partly because they simply like being combative.

Eights are often portrayed as abrasive, brutally honest, loud, crass, profane, sexually explicit, and overwhelming, but what many fail to see is that this posturing hides a somewhat tender vulnerability and childlike innocence. The secret behind Eights is that they actively suppress their fears and act as if they are strong. Perhaps more than any other type, they have mastered the ability to look self-assured, assertive, and fulfilled in the way they live life—in the way they walk, talk, eat, work, love, play, plan, and dream—while very much feeling insecure, vulnerable, and needy.

Nevertheless, without question, fully functioning, ego-driven Eights are genuinely dynamic and strong. They have both the courage and the will to make changes, take risks, and lead others. It both helps and hinders that they don't feel a need to justify or defend their opinions. They send out a clear message that anyone willing to take them on had better be prepared for a knockdown-dragout fight. Their abrasiveness or aggression often makes them controversial figures, but conflict suits them—they actually feel emboldened and energized by it. Eights have the gift of vision and everything they need to bring those visions to fruition. If you want something done, call an Eight.

FACT

Donald Trump embodies Eight energy. In business, he triumphed at negotiation and rebounded several times from the brink of bankruptcy, and he constantly blows his own horn. He also transforms undeveloped real estate into showy buildings and blazes his name across them. When the public tired of him, he found another way to flaunt his ego through his television show *The Apprentice*. His drug is power and prestige, but his vulnerable underbelly lies just beneath the surface.

Eights will freely admit to being driven by lust—lust for life, lust for money, lust for culinary excellence, lust for yachts, lust for luxury cars, lust for sexual fulfillment. To Eights, life is an adventure begging to be lived, and restraint is the kiss of death.

Pathological Eights

Pathological Eights are hypercritical, possessive, unforgiving, and crudely insensitive. They bulldoze over anyone that gets in their way, leaving a string of antagonistic relationships behind them. Not only have these Eights long ago lost connection to their softer side, they go through life defensive and combative—exerting their power over others by arguing about everything. To supplicate their underlying vulnerability and—mostly due to their own bad behavior—susceptibility to betrayal, they constantly test others' loyalty by pushing their buttons to see how they react. They will also indiscriminately act arrogant, bullying, and intimidating simply to bolster their own sense of being in control. Eventually they believe everyone is against them and plot vindictive revenge.

According to *The Wisdom of the Enneagram*, Eights on a downward slide are confrontational to the point of vociferously bullying loved ones or coworkers. Their ego has a grandiose quality—almost kinglike. They actively seek revenge for perceived transgressions or threats to their authority. They resort to physical and emotional rages in a last-ditch effort to control. An Eight on the brink of total meltdown can literally go into a murderous rage and feel justified in doing so.

Pathological Eights are victims of their own inflated image. When their image implodes, they disintegrate into dictatorial sociopaths—dysfunctional to the point of breaking every moral and ethical code to get what they want or to maintain control. They become ruthless power mongers who use their negative power to control, dominate, and destroy anyone who makes them feel insecure or who gets in their way. At the farthest reaches of the scale, pathological Eights become megalomaniacal, sadistic dictators—on the level of Saddam Hussein or Idi Amin—who are capable of feeling justified in annihilating masses of innocent people.

Self-Actualized Eights

Self-actualized Eights believe in truth, no matter what, and justice as long as it is both tolerant and fair. They are exceedingly loyal, caring, honest, generous, and courageous. They are straightforward in all their dealings—what they say is what they mean. They are accomplished, confident, persistent, dedicated, and they love empowering others. They have limitless energy for life, love, family, community, and work.

Self-actualized Eights would have made the perfect Arthurian knight. According to *What's My Type?*, not only are they strong competitors and excellent combatants, ideal Eights are also refined, cultured gentlemen who would as easily write love poems as they would triumph in heated battle. Eights love successfully blending their macho strength with a sentimental heart.

Fully integrated Eights have achieved the level of inner security required to be truly magnanimous. They still have a strong, proactive personality, but they now wield their power—or more correctly use their personal magnetism and strength of character—for the right reasons. Lucky for the rest of us, highly functioning Eights are very willing to assume leadership roles, particularly when they serve a common good. They exhibit tremendous courage and commitment in truly defending, supporting, and uplifting the poor and downtrodden.

Eights at the peak of emotional health become not only honorable and inspirational but truly heroic, As passionate defenders of justice, they play an essential role in society by protecting those not yet strong enough to protect themselves. When their energy is focused on spiritual reawakening, they can be powerful spiritual leaders who inspire multitudes to behave responsibly toward self and society.

The Process of Individuation or Self-Actualization

According to Jung, individuation occurs when you successfully separate your personality from that of your parents and become an integrated personality—becoming what or who you were born to be, what you were before you formed an ego or persona, or suppressed negative behaviors in your shadow. The individuation process is a lifelong, ongoing process or quest. Through therapy or active self-development using introspection and conscious choice, you can work toward the unveiling of your shadow, the unraveling your persona, and the integration of your psyche.

Basically, when merging aspects of Jungian theory with Enneagram theory, one could presuppose that when things in your life are going really well, you are ripe for expansion and are more likely to progress toward individuation and self-actualization by adopting behaviors that support forward movement. On the other hand, when you feel insecure or are under severe stress, you are more likely to regress from the goal of individuation and self-actualization by adopting behaviors that allow you to cope but that do not necessarily help you progress toward health. Again, in some instances, you may uncover traits inherent in your stress point that help you grow during times of extreme stress, e.g., you might both cope and progress toward health by discovering determination, integrity, or industry in your stress point.

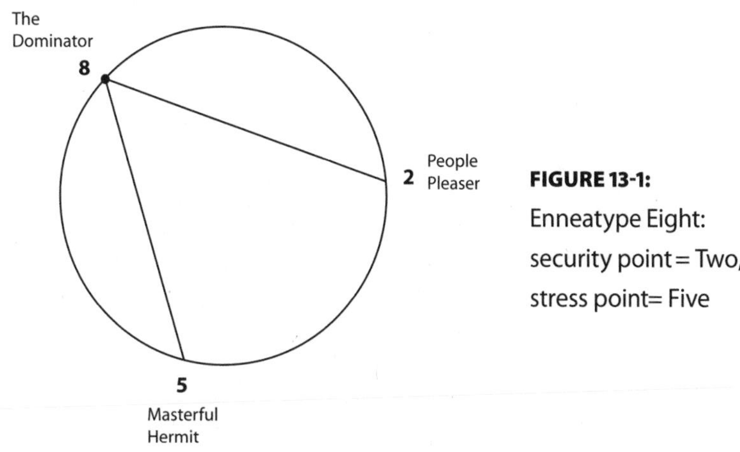

FIGURE 13-1: Enneatype Eight: security point = Two, stress point= Five

How Eights Progress

Eights progress by adopting Two behavior that helps them feel comfortable enough to risk being vulnerable occasionally and to soften their feelings for those around them. Instead of dominating loved ones, they offer them the respect and love they deserve. Like self-actualized Twos, when Eights progress, they identify with others and develop a healthy interdependence that serves both parties. The more they get in touch with their softer side, the more Eights become genuinely altruistic.

When Eights access the positive resources of style Five, they often develop more of their inner life and become less combative. They also learn to see the value of reflection and contemplation, which helps them curb their tendency to barrel through life like a bull in a china shop.

How Eights Regress

Eights regress by shrinking into Five behavior that causes them to withdraw further from the world and to fabricate stories about themselves that support their dysfunction. Instead of brimming with confidence, they feel weakened and ineffective, which often leads to further reflection on how they have been cruel and misguided, which leads to feeling guilty and depressed, emotions Eights normally squelch. If they linger in isolation, Eights falling too far into negative Five behavior can become masochistically self-punishing and suicidal.

When Eights degenerate into the low side of Two, they lose their focus on the wider implications of justice and insist on "me first." Their struggle is no longer for justice but to get what they have coming, regardless of what happens to others.

Balancing the Opposites

According to Jung's personality theory, psyches are constantly flowing between two extremes, and your primary task is to successfully balance the two polarities. To achieve individuation, each personality has to acknowledge and work through the limitations of its idealized self and shadow, its strengths and weaknesses, and its motivations and fixations (what keeps it stuck). These primary polarities that an Eight has to navigate are explored in the following sections.

Shadow and Idealized Self

Every personality forms an inner world that reflects how it feels about itself and an outer world that projects what it wants others to know about it. Jung would also refer to these worlds as the *shadow*, or hidden traits that your psyche squelches and does not want the outer world to see, and the *idealized self*, what your psyche creates and wants the outer world to see.

Eights use aggression to mask their vulnerability. On top of this, Eights view others as caricatures instead of real people, which means an Eight's shadow often contains the following qualities: arrogant, self-serving, hypercritical, liar, unforgiving, cruel, confrontational, demanding, short-tempered, controlling, rigid, combative, domineering, bully, violent, and narcissistic. Since Eights are pretty up front and in your face, many of their more ordinary, if negative, peccadilloes are in plain sight. However, in the darkest corners of an Eight shadow one finds megalomaniacs who are capable of destroying whomever or whatever is in their way.

An Eight's idealized self has flipped negative traits to their positive counterpart. Instead of being dependent, insecure, and domineering to subvert unrecognized vulnerability, they are vulnerable souls who are also self-sufficient, enterprising, independent, and bold. Instead of flubbing interpersonal relationships by pretending to be the king of the jungle, they are honest, trustworthy, empathetic, magnanimous, and supportive. An idealized Eight models healthy assertive behavior tempered with sensitivity, compassion, responsibility, and vision.

FACT

When Josef Stalin was reportedly approached to purchase a machine to detonate the land mines that were planted throughout Russia when the Germans invaded, he rebuked the offer curtly and said simply, without compassion or any sense of impropriety, "We use peasants."

Turn-Ons and Turnoffs

According to Jung, libido is not connected to your sex drive alone, but instead refers to your overall psychic energy or what gives your personality juice. The opposite of what turns you on would be what turns you off. To individuate, Eights need to seek balance between these two polarities.

Eights love showing others how loyal, competent, enterprising, resourceful, and brilliant they are, particularly when under pressure. They get turned on when they can take charge of a situation and solve problems, especially when doing so reflects well on them. They want others to admire them as champions of justice and will happily crusade for worthwhile causes or seek revenge when someone has stepped over the bounds of propriety. They are at their best when they have a firm grip on how things are occurring and how they can achieve the desired effect.

Eights get turned off when people lie to them, attempt to control them, or manipulate them into doing something inherently against their nature. They don't like rules or strictures that fence them in too tightly. They don't like people who won't stand up for the right thing to do. They don't like evidence of weakness, in themselves or anyone else.

Fear and Security

These basic and very essential characteristics determine how Eights approach, live in, and eventually conquer their worlds. Fears stop people short and often cause them to regress, and they rarely progress unless they feel a certain sense of security about themselves or their circumstances.

Since Eights always want to know where they stand, they squirm when anyone shows signs of being ambivalent about or questions their authority. Eights see the world as a battlefield, so they are afraid of being betrayed and thus constantly monitor other people's emotional and commitment temperatures. Since they consciously and unconsciously hate appearing vulnerable, they live in constant fear that others will discover their weaknesses and exploit them. They are afraid that you will think less of them if you know how frightened they really feel. They abhor the idea of ever being physically or emotionally dependent on anyone else.

Eights feel secure when they are locked in a power struggle they know they can win. They love feeling confident that they have the upper hand in all arenas of their life. They feel most comfortable when they are making a lot of money, amassing assets, and building a financially secure future. If they are extremely confident that their families and their inner circle of coworkers and friends are completely on their side and supportive of their goals, they can let down their guard long enough to enjoy life.

Motivations and Fixations

Feeling motivated or stuck relates to how Eights use or ignore their psychic energy. Knowing their primary motivations and what Eights cling to within their own personality that either helps them progress toward individuation or keeps them stuck in fixations helps you understand how their personality functions.

Eights are motivated to fight for justice. If they see weaknesses in a traditional way of doing things, conducting business, or governing that they think needs to change, they will attack it head on, fighting city hall and whomever stands in the way. Also, if they see something they want—a person, a job, a house, or an investment property—it becomes the treasure they have to have no matter the cost. Eights love the thrill of a win and get juiced by the combative game required to get what they want. They also want to live life at a frenzied, adventurous pace and are motivated to keep on the move, seeking new experiences and discovering new empires.

Eights get stuck when they defend their image of themselves so vehemently that they don't listen when friends or family try to give them useful feedback. When they actually feel guilty for hurting someone's feelings, they tend to minimize the other person's feelings and cover the appropriate feeling of guilt with aggression. Eventually, they numb so many of their feelings that they don't have access to them when they really need them. Eights stay stuck by disconnecting their feelings in the present from anything that happened in their past. Unclaimed childhood pain or abuse prevents Eights from integrating their personality and locks them into impulsivity.

Coping and Failing

This coping-failing dichotomy has to do with the behaviors Eights adopt to cope with their lives, or maintain the status quo, and how those same behaviors can lead to a failure to grow into their full potential.

Eights adopt a personality based on contention—the belief that they have to counteract rather than interact. Eights believe in survival of the fittest and cope with what they see as a decidedly unfriendly world by convincing themselves that they are stronger than the average person and fully capable of getting what they want. Consciously or unconsciously, they cover any evidence of internal weakness or vulnerability with an aggressive posture. They cope with disappointment by acquiring status, money, and possessions. They cope with inner loneliness by luring others to them with promises of financial support and establishing a one-up mentality that convinces them the other person will never be strong enough to actually leave them.

Eights fail themselves by overidentifying with power and exerting it over others. This creates antagonism rather than the intimacy they really desire. Their lust for power often distorts their thinking and skews their judgment. When Eights don't listen to spirited discussions from objecting family members, business associates, or friends, they delude themselves into thinking they are 100 percent right and justified—especially when they aren't. When they cut off their sensitivity to others, they also cut off their ability to connect on intimate levels. Eights isolate themselves further by thinking, believing, and acting as if they are superior.

Falling Apart and Transcending

Each enneatype has a unique way of falling apart. The types each have specific needs they need fulfilled, or mental concepts they can embrace, before they can successfully transcend their ego limitations and become fully integrated and whole.

Eights fall apart when they feel like they've lost their grip on those around them. By the time they lose their measured and highly controlled composure, Eights have amassed a long list of real and imagined enemies, leading to raging paranoia and complex, vindictive strategizing. When they think all is lost, Eights become full-blown sociopaths who resort to lying, cheating, stealing, threatening, intimidating, and violent behavior. An Eight in total disarray literally falls apart at the seams and can be both unpredictable and extremely violent.

An Eight transcends by remembering that humanity is all in the same boat—we all have weaknesses and vulnerabilities, and we all need each other to survive. They transcend their own tendency to fake strength by reinforcing their innermost feelings of love and respect for themselves and others. Once they have evidence that the majority of people have good intentions, they can drop their guarded stance and open the emotional floodgates. The more they drop the pretense, the more others will validate and value their true qualities. And the more they learn to listen to what others and both honor and accept suggestions, the more they grow. Eights need to reacquaint themselves with their own inner self and embrace the place of stillness that fosters a fully integrated, whole personality.

Chapter 14

Enneagram Type Nine: Peaceful Lamb

Nines are the sweethearts of the Enneagram. They typically have no hard edges and will go along with ideas, plans, or group consensus purely to get along. Nines often prefer the agendas, values, and ideas of others, so much so that eventually they lose of their own preferences. To them, peace and harmony are graceful, ideal states well worth personal sacrifices. As such, Nines willfully suppress or deny their needs, wants, dreams, desires, ambitions, or genuine emotions for the sake of everyone else. They have big hearts, and they can be genuinely generous and exceedingly reliable.

Emotional Origins

Nine children repressed their own feelings for the sake of peace in a turbulent family. Whether they grew up with embittered and argumentative parents, a dominating parental figure, or simply in a loudmouthed family, Nines quivered in the face of opposition and sold themselves short for the sake of a peaceful existence. If the parents banged heads, the Nine child learned to cope by seeing both sides of the argument and employing blatant or subliminal negotiations as a way to bring them back together and reunite the family. If one or both parents derided or blatantly rode over the Nine child, for the sake of peace the Nine child quietly surrendered. In a family where vociferous parents, relatives, or siblings created a lot of white noise, the Nine child tried to see everyone's viewpoint and may have done whatever she could to quell the debates and quiet the room.

Nine children desperately wanted congruity and a quiet, orderly life, and as such they often sought to appease both parental figures, or all the warring family members, hoping against hope to bring everyone back together again. Nines learned the art of acquiescence—surrendering their needs for the sake of others, empathizing with everyone else's viewpoint, and appeasing all sides in a disagreement.

FACT

According to *The Enneagram Movie and Video Guide*, famous Nines include Jennifer Aniston, Tony Bennett, Sandra Bullock, Julia Child, Connie Chung, Bill Clinton, Kevin Costner, Dwight Eisenhower, Tipper Gore, Patty Hearst, Audrey Hepburn, C. G. Jung, Grace Kelly, Nancy Kerrigan, Abraham Lincoln, Ronald Reagan, Jerry Seinfeld, Ringo Starr, and James Stewart.

If a Nine child had narcissistic or alcoholic parents, she may have interpreted their lack of engagement as emotional abandonment. Or she may have decided that the parents didn't love her sufficiently enough to notice her unique personality or individual needs. A Nine child may also have been the firstborn of many and felt superseded when other children entered the picture. Or she may have been far down in birth order and gotten lost among the shuffle.

Ego-Driven Nines

Ego-driven Nines are the fence sitters of the world. From early childhood on, they coped with life by sitting on the fence as long as possible, withholding decisions about their own lives. They silently hoped someone else would establish goals that they could support or at least go along with until they either grew tired of doing so or were pushed, pulled, or cajoled in another direction. Because they don't feel special enough to matter, Nines assume their voices will not be heard. They can easily lose focus on what they really want because they feel from the outset they will not be able to have it.

Nines surrender self-development for the sake of obtaining and maintaining relationships. In hopes of winning love, they focus their energy on providing a nurturing environment in which their family members' dreams have the chance to evolve. They may look happy, secure, and even noble, but they are, in fact, self-sacrificing to the point of neglecting their needs and denying their sense of self. Nines eventually lull themselves into a deep inner sleep that silences, denies, and hides their needs, drives, and desires.

Eventually their denial of self and constant acquiescence to others takes a toll on those around them. At some point, most previously compliant and passive Nines grow weary of the congenial, lackadaisical, angelic persona they created just to get along and begin to actually want something for themselves. It turns out that all that time Nines were eagerly attending to your every need, on some level they may also have been blaming you for their own failure to pursue their dreams. Even if their unwavering devotion left you feeling mysteriously obligated, Nines generally eventually discover newfound ambition, or at least a renewed drive to discover themselves, that leaves you reeling when they make it your fault that they failed to discover their own unique characteristics long ago.

Being at the center—and most noncommittal—of the anger triad, Nines typically deal with their anger issue by suppressing it so diligently it eventually shows up as what they see as inexplicable fatigue. Anger is simply too volatile and too explosive an emotion for Nines; it blows them off course and out of otherwise stable relationships. Terrified of any major shifts in their lives, Nines covet the status quo. They have a comfort level they don't want breached and thus strongly prefer predictable routines and living life in measurable and manageable proportions. Feeling an intense emotion like anger would upset their apple cart and quite possibly force them to get off the fence and mobilize their forces for a change in direction. This feels so overwhelming to Nines that they will gladly sacrifice those pesky emotions for a hyperactive schedule or a list of chores to be done for their husband or children such as selling Girl Scout cookies or volunteering to serve on the organizational committee for the community center's charity drive.

Nines frequently take on more than they can handle and then undermine the people who gladly handed the projects over to them by diddling around until everything is seriously behind schedule. Sometimes they can't help themselves, but don't fall for their helpless pose. They are generally very capable people who deliberately sunk an oar in the water to slow you down.

While Nines are busy being charitable and generous, they are usually also harboring resentment and amassing a large stash of perceived slights. They won't openly express any of them, but they will drag their feet and inadvertently forget to follow up on essential tasks or drop the ball on a special project. And if anyone dares to push their buttons through direct confrontation or attempt to control them, they may smile sweetly and slow down the pace to a crawl.

Pathological Nines

Pathological Nines barely live in their own skins. They have suppressed so much of their personality and projected it onto others that they no longer have an inner sense of who they are. They have lost the ability to ferret out their needs or desires and survive by keeping themselves so busy fulfilling someone else's needs or meeting someone else's agenda that they don't have time to ruminate on what they have lost or denied themselves.

According to *The Wisdom of the Enneagram*, Nines on a downward slide become openly argumentative, defensive, and bitter, often accusing others of taking advantage of them. They develop a long list of past affronts and wield them to break off long-term relationships. Or they become increasingly needy, dependent, and submissive, remaining in dysfunctional relationships even when being clearly physically or emotionally abused. They may lapse into a deep depression or disassociate from their emotions by creating a false persona.

However, as their personalities disintegrate and their propped up worlds crumble, all that anger Nines pressed down into the darkest corners of their soul comes bubbling to the surface. Suddenly nothing works anymore, and they feel angry often to the point of rage. They may uncharacteristically explode, dumping years of previously unspoken frustration on their loved ones or coworkers. They are, in fact, furious with themselves for sabotaging their own lives, but they still find spoken anger so frightening that they project it onto the people they chose to serve.

Some pathological Nines react to the realization that they subverted their lives by becoming immobilized—locked in place and incapable of or completely resistant to change. Their energy often plummets to the point of serious depression. Some Nines feel so overwhelmed by a rush of intense emotions, they literally disassociate from all of their feelings and either consciously concoct or unconsciously spin off an alternate personality or personalities.

Self-Actualized Nines

Self-actualized Nines are the true mediators of the world. Because they can truly see and understand all the variances of opinions, attitudes, or behavior, Nines are natural politicians—capable of making others feel seen, heard, understood, and valued. Nines have an implicit understanding that polar opposites are only two very divergent attitudes and that a lot of middle ground exists. More than any other enneatype, Nines are comfortable with the juxtaposition of opposing viewpoints. They understand paradox and appreciate diversity. Nines hold a higher vision for the world and foresee compromises that leave everyone intact and fulfilled.

FACT

According to *The Nine Ways of Working*, Psychologist Carl Rogers embodied Nine energy when he created a system of psychotherapy based on "unconditional positive regard." Rogers encouraged psychotherapists to acknowledge their patients' sense of their own worth without evaluating or judging them. He believed complete emotional acceptance freed the patient to uncover his own neurosis and find his own answers to his psychological dilemma.

A fully integrated Nine has recognized, claimed, and taken action to fulfill her own desires and is able to offer her loved ones her true self, not a self encumbered by a needy undertow. These self-actualized Nines do truly love everyone unconditionally, and at last they are able to express that love fully and spontaneously. Nines who have transcended to their highest self take an active stance in every aspect of their lives and have plenty of energy left to facilitate community development.

The Process of Individuation or Self-Actualization

According to Jung, individuation occurs when you successfully separate your personality from that of your parents and become an integrated personality—becoming what or who you were born to be, what you were before you formed an ego or persona, or suppressed negative behaviors in your shadow. The individuation process is a lifelong, ongoing process or quest. Through therapy or active self-development using introspection and conscious choice, you can work toward the unveiling of your shadow, the unraveling of your persona, and the integration of your psyche.

Basically, when merging aspects of Jungian theory with Enneagram theory, one could presuppose that when things in your life are going really well, you are ripe for expansion and are more likely to progress toward individuation and self-actualization by adopting behaviors that support forward movement. On the other hand, when you feel insecure or are under severe stress, you are more likely to regress from the goal of individuation and self-actualization by adopting behaviors that allow you to cope but that do not necessarily help you progress toward health. Again, in some instances, you may uncover traits inherent in your stress point that help you grow during times of extreme stress, e.g., you might both cope and progress toward health by discovering determination, integrity, or industry in your stress point.

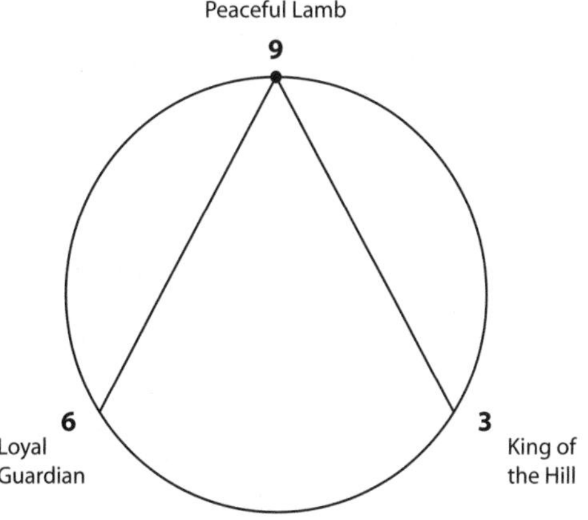

FIGURE 14-1: Enneatype Nine: security point = Three, stress point = Six

How Nines Progress

Nines progress by adopting Three behavior, which helps them engage in life. With Three energy on their side, Nines often develop ambition, create realistic goals, and muster the energy to put it in motion. Feeling reinvigorated by their newfound clarity, Nines can get really focused on what they want for themselves, create a proactive game plan, and go after the success they deserve. Three energy helps them make huge strides when it comes to taking risks and overcoming minor setbacks. Motivated Nines become self-sufficient and action oriented from the inside out and rightfully earn the self-esteem that follows.

Nines also progress by assimilating some of the energy of their other connecting point, style Six. With Six on their side, Nines learn to contribute to the community without harboring unspoken resentment. They may suddenly feel as if they have woken up and realized that they are important to the group. Positive Six energy helps them learn to set and keep firm personal boundaries that guard their self-interest.

How Nines Regress

Nines regress by adopting dysfunctional Six behavior, which unfortunately leads to increased anxiety. Nines under the influence of Six energy become even more self-doubting and more frozen in place. They go from waffling to complete decision avoidance, from minimizing emotional dissonance to exaggerating disagreements, from relying on their own conservative judgment to latching onto an outside authority to provide structure. Suddenly Nines are following all the rules laid out by someone else, but often to the point of blind acceptance and potential disaster.

When Nines swing toward the low side of Three, they get fired up. Remaining passive is no longer an option. Their tendency to mask their real feelings through passive aggression morphs into outright aggression. They also adopt Three energy when they look for ways to do very little and disguise their laziness by creating an image of activity and achievement.

Balancing the Opposites

According to Jung's personality theory, the psyche is constantly flowing between two extremes, and your primary task is to successfully balance the two polarities. To achieve individuation, each personality has to acknowledge and work through the limitations of its idealized self and shadow, its strengths and weaknesses, and its motivations and fixations (what keeps it stuck). These primary polarities that a Nine has to navigate are explored in the following sections.

Shadow and Idealized Self

Every personality forms an inner world that reflects how it feels about itself and an outer world that projects what it wants others to know about it. Jung would also refer to these worlds as the *shadow*, or hidden, traits that your psyche squelches and does not want the outer world to see, and the *idealized self*, what your psyche creates and wants the outer world to see.

A Nine's shadow hides a nasty stubborn streak that manifests in resistance to anyone else's ideas, even when those ideas are both necessary and appropriate. Nines typically hide their intractability—their outright refusal to change—even when maintaining the status quo is harming them. They can be lazy, indecisive, tedious, detached, and unresponsive in a very passive-aggressive, irritating way. Despite their laid-back disposition, Nines are fully capable of displaying an explosive rage that could easily, if unexpectedly, decimate those around them.

A Nine's idealized self is virtually angelic. Blissful peace almost literally streams out of their lavender scented pores, and their unwavering allegiance uplifts anyone lucky enough to be its recipient. Self-actualized Nines have earned the right to be proud of being extremely dedicated, loyal, and steadfast. They are also receptive, patient, accepting, and easygoing in general. Any expectations they have in terms of relationships are well within reach, and they are genuinely grateful for whatever you do for them. Integrated, whole, actualized Nines bring an essential vision of diplomacy, peace, and harmony to their families and to the planet. They, more than any other type, believe idealized coexistence is possible, easily achieved, and virtually inevitable.

Turn-Ons and Turn-Offs

According to Jung, libido is not connected to your sex drive alone, but instead refers to your overall psychic energy or what gives your personality juice. The opposite of what turns you on would be what turns you off. To individuate, Nines need to seek balance between these two polarities.

Nines are turned on by harmony and outward displays of cohesiveness and congruity. Nines want smiles on everyone's faces and peacefulness all around. They love so cleverly fulfilling your needs that you don't even notice their hand in it. They like helping someone else go for the gold so that they don't have to. Nines love having time to putter and seek variable, entertaining, or amusing distractions that will keep them so busy that they simply don't have time to contemplate their own lives and whether they are truly happy or not.

Nines are turned off by pressure to perform. They don't want the limelight and cower when given responsibility to lead. Since they strongly prefer moving at a slower pace and allowing things to unfold naturally, they recoil when anyone attempts to control them. Nines hate dissension, particularly when someone comes forward bracing for a fight. Nines prefer to stay in the background, but if you neglect them or their needs, the anger they seek to hide may surface in an abrupt, sharp, and unexpected way.

Fear and Security

These basic and very essential characteristics determine how Nines approach, live in, and eventually conquer their worlds. Fears (for Nines it's a sense of hopelessness) stop people short and often cause them to regress, and they rarely progress unless they feel a certain sense of security about themselves or their circumstances.

Deep down inside their emotional core, Nines remain convinced that they were neglected or abused because they were somehow unlovable or simply not compelling enough to be important to their parents. This leaves Nines so discouraged about their dreams and aspirations that they decided they would borrow and assimilate those of others. They decided to go for the minimum: seeking comfort and little else. They live their lives afraid that any discord will ultimately lead to emotional or physical abandonment. Thus most Nines withdraw from verbal confrontations. They also refuse to take risks, avoid decisions, and do whatever they can to keep everything in their lives unchanged.

FACT

Perhaps the most potent movie about Nines is the 2004 remake of *The Stepford Wives*. In it, husbands band together to turn their wives into robots programmed purely to appease and please their spouses. Once converted, the wives have no interests of their own and are all smiles when they greet their husbands each night. They are Nines who have been forced to surrender any desires they might once have had into complete and blind devotion to their family.

Nines feel secure when they know everyone's place in a family or business and when everything is proceeding according to known expectations. They prefer having their lives follow an orderly pattern that rarely fluctuates, and they strongly prefer a natural unfolding rather than an unnatural rushing of events. If they are permitted to proceed at their own pace—in relationships or in business—they function efficiently; if they feel pushed, cajoled, manipulated, or controlled in any way, they push back in their passive-aggressive way by dropping an emotional oar deep into their private ocean, by claming up, or by dragging their feet in one of their clever and annoying ways.

Motivations and Fixations

This relates to how Nines use or ignore their psychic energy. Knowing their primary motivations and what Nines cling to within their own personalities that either helps them progress toward individuation or keeps them stuck in fixations helps you understand how their personality functions.

Nines are motivated by the desire to bring everyone together as one. They are all about peaceful coexistence and cooperative compromise. Like Rodney King during the Los Angeles riots, they want everyone to "just get along." Nines like flying under the radar, doing their job well enough to be appreciated without feeling pressured or forced to ramp up the pace. Nines want a peaceful, happy, easygoing life with enough pleasant diversions to keep them unaware of nagging feelings of unhappiness or any lack of fulfillment. Nines want to help the people they love—spouses, children, siblings, coworkers—excel at what they do so they can live vicariously through them.

Nines get stuck when they sell themselves short for the sake of a quiet, orderly existence. They are so afraid to narrow down choices and make controversial, or even singular, decisions that they may spin their wheels in the rut they themselves created. They could spend years doing things that had no real relevance to their life as they might have envisioned it had they given themselves the option to put themselves first occasionally. Nines are so desperate to maintain the status quo that they may fail to make potent, positive changes. Often they will stay in dysfunctional relationships long after any of their needs have been met or even voiced.

Coping and Failing

This coping-failing dichotomy has to do with the behaviors Nines adopt to cope with their lives, or maintain the status quo, and how those same behaviors can lead to a failure to grow into their full potential.

Nines cope by surrendering huge chunks of themselves, and often unconsciously erasing their sense of self, for what they believe is necessary to maintain maximum comfort—at work, at home, at church, or in the community. They project their best qualities onto others, sublimating their ambitions by being supportive and nurturing to people they feel have an actual chance to succeed. Unfortunately, this means that they negate themselves and often lose any sense of their own potential. They may cope by keeping their focus on inconsequential things and by distracting themselves and others from what they see as their personal weaknesses. They use diversionary tactics to prevent family members or coworkers from escalating disagreements into open conflict.

Nines fail themselves by never fully exploring their true interests. If they don't acknowledge their needs or desires, they don't have a fighting chance to realize that they are fully capable of fulfilling them. They deny themselves opportunities to reinforce their own self-esteem or opportunities to grow beyond their own limited expectations. They fail themselves every time they deny the importance of their anger as an emotion that signals an important need not being met. In other words, they don't learn to value themselves enough to give credence to their needs, wants, desires, or emotions, which ultimately means they evade their own very distinct destiny. They also deny their family the true benefits of healthy love.

Falling Apart and Transcending

Each enneatype has a unique way of falling apart. The types each have specific needs they need fulfilled, or mental concepts they can embrace, before they can successfully transcend their ego limitations and become fully integrated and whole.

Nines fall apart in a passive way—by almost literally falling asleep. They often use drugs, sex, or inconsequential activity to purposefully dull their minds. Like couch potatoes, they will sit on the sidelines and passively watch their own lives go by. Their foot-dragging, eventually-I'll-get-around-to-it approach turns into complete and blatant avoidance, leading very quickly into serious disarray in all aspects of their lives. They swing from becoming so needy they beg others for help to becoming openly obstinate and intractable—even to the point of raising their voices or uncharacteristically lashing out at loved ones. Their normal resignation goes from low-level functioning to sleepwalking through life. Some Nines become so depressed they take to their beds and refuse to participate in life.

Nines transcend by waking up and claiming their deepest selves and their long dormant passions. Nines transcend their ego limitations when they love themselves as much as they love everyone else and allow themselves the right and privilege of having their own thoughts, opinions, desires, and destiny. When Nines can keep the focus on their own being long enough to set some defining boundaries, recognize meaningful desires, and establish their own priorities, they have a far better chance of unveiling their soul's purpose and have a real shot at achieving self-actualization. They have to realize that they are as important as everyone else and that it is not beneath them to have real desires or competing ideas. Instead of surrendering self for the sake of peace, they have to be willing to surrender peace for the sake of self.

Chapter 15

Enneagram Type One: Evangelical Idealist

Ones are the crusaders of the world. They formulate principled ideas and will almost virtually fight to the death for them. Purposeful, orderly, self-controlled and die-hard perfectionists, Ones are people on a mission to improve the world. They love to overcome moral adversity and will eagerly sacrifice themselves for the overall good of their community. They are rational idealists who are moved by a higher calling but want to serve in practical ways. Ones often become reformers, teachers, activists, crusaders, moralists, and religious leaders.

Emotional Origins

Ones frequently come from families in which they perceived that the father, or whoever served as the disciplinarian, failed to fulfill his fatherly duties. The One's paternal figure may have been stern, judgmental, and rigid; verbally, emotionally, or physically abusive; alcoholic; emotionally unavailable; punishing; physically absent; or simply inept. Even if a father was physically and emotionally present, a One child basically received a spoken, or unspoken, message that he was not acceptable as he was, and that he must constantly strive to behave more appropriately or appear perfect.

The blow could have come in the form of regular sharp criticism that left One children feeling humiliated, as if there were something critically wrong with them—something they must control or hide if they wanted to avoid rejection or expulsion from the family. Their parents may have heavy-handedly enforced a strict moral code that forbade normal, healthy human appetites and left One children feeling impure, dirty, or simply too impulsive for their own good.

Since most One children felt that they couldn't rely on their fathers, or authority figures, they established their own rules of conduct and internalized a moral compass that they then used to monitor and judge their own and others' behavior. Ones often judged others harshly if they didn't possess the level of commitment, conviction, or activism that Ones believed was necessary. This sense of self-justification formed their identity and affected how they dealt with emotions.

Ones internalized rules so deeply they felt guilty for very forgivable "sins," such as eating two pieces of cake in one sitting or speaking out of turn. Eventually, Ones felt angry toward the father or authority figure in their lives, but they repressed what they perceived as dangerous, dark emotions and punished themselves for failing to meet their own internal codes for acceptable behavior or only feeling acceptable emotions. Any angry or overly emotional outbursts occurred when they had already disappointed themselves to the breaking point and lost control.

Ego-Driven Ones

Because ego-driven Ones find or create a set of principles, rules, or religious or philosophical precepts that they then internalize, they set very high standards for themselves and often feel anxious and guilty when they fail to meet their own ideals. They judge themselves and others, acting as if they are morally superior and therefore know how everyone should behave. When people inevitably fail to live an exemplary life, idealistic Ones often feel as if they alone carry the burden of preserving the world.

Ego-driven Ones develop a kind of watchdog superiority complex. They use rigid rules to hold themselves—and everyone else—to high standards and then constantly strive for perfection in everything they do, berating themselves when they fall short. They need to feel like they've got it all together. They spend a lot of time mentally comparing what they have, what they accomplished, or what they are to what others have, what others accomplished, or what others are. Even in normal conversation, they often sound as if they are preaching or moralizing.

Ego-driven Ones get so entrenched with being perfect that they start to believe they know better than anyone how things should operate. And they don't hesitate to let everyone know. They eagerly climb onto soapboxes for everything from the proper use of car seats to the moral imperatives of stem cell research. Ego-driven Ones develop purposeful agendas, don't believe in wasting time, and are always creating new and loftier goals. Because they like belonging to a structured group with principles they can trumpet, they are particularly drawn toward political or religious activism.

The real trouble starts when Ones become so rigid they can't withstand losing face. They are afraid to fail, or to appear less than perfect, so they tighten their grip on propriety. Their neat, methodical ways increasingly become regimented; they tend to judge themselves—and others—in black and white, right or wrong, and good or bad categories. Since they can't waste time, they feel compelled to order their lives and everything in it, rating activities, people, and events in terms of what is most worthy of their time and effort.

If normal coping mechanisms stop working, they cling even tighter to their rules and become agitated when you question what they are doing. When out of balance, their need for order often becomes compulsive—they insist that everything is neat, organized, and hyperefficient. The more they cling even tighter to rigid moral or religious principles, the more intimacy becomes a high-risk endeavor—sexual urges threaten their own image of themselves as morally superior and pure.

Ego-driven Ones are compulsively neat and organized. They are compulsive about punctuality, appearances, and what one should do. They tend to criticize everyone, but they are hardest on themselves. Convinced they know more than you, Ones love to debate issues. They have something—a religion, a philosophy, a government—they believe in so strongly they are always searching for recruits or converts. They tend toward black-and-white thinking.

Ego-driven Ones under pressure frequently lose touch with what was once their gentle, loving inner guide, superego, or internalized principles. As their need for order heightens, or when they feel pressured or out of control, they often become harsh, demanding taskmasters. They are so focused on order and correctness, they become unglued if things get messy in their environments—at the workplace, in their families, or in their own minds—and may dump a barrage of insults on anyone whom they perceive as the root of the problem, even when it's clearly a projection of their own failings.

Their conscientious habits have morphed into compulsions that turned them into workaholics, perfectionists, and nitpickers who judge others harshly for what they see as fallible behavior—even when it's a minor transgression. Feeling both internal and external pressure, they counteract by becoming impatient, hypercritical, controlling browbeaters. Unable to withstand, let alone admit, a breech in their own high standards, they hide their feelings and attempt to repress their physical desires, succumbing to puritanical, fastidious, and pedantic attitudes and behaviors.

Pathological Ones

Pathological Ones have flipped to the dark side of their orderly, fair-minded ways and can be openly self-righteous, intolerant, cruel, and rigid. Because they are vainly trying to hold onto the rigid rules that once helped them feel safe in a dangerous and corrupt word, they often become obsessed, controlling, and compulsive. They attempt to force themselves—and everyone else—into an extremely narrow box of acceptable behaviors or beliefs. Anyone who resists or steadfastly remains unwilling to live in the Ones' narrow box of propriety often warrants condemnation and punishment.

When they've gone off the deep end into true pathology, Ones can get locked into absolutes and become increasingly intractable—refusing to bend, or mend, their minds or their ways. They can do nothing wrong; everyone else can do nothing right. Because they feel so conflicted inside, they obsess about the failings, or sins, of others. They may even secretly fantasize about administering harsh punishment and believe, on some dark level, that doing so will finally purge them of their own sins.

As such, dysfunctional Ones typically hide behind religious, legal, cultural, or moral codes to control their own behavior, but they also use these same pure and well-intentioned structures to crucify perceived dissenters. Whatever warmth healthy Ones once had is now gone, and they coolly and calmly rationalize their beliefs to the point of hypocrisy. For example, they may preach equality but typically downgrade anyone not within their fold and abiding by its superior moral codes. And they can be very willing to resort to ruling over someone in order to convert them to the one right way.

Going back in history, you could cite the Franciscans' annihilation of Native Americans as an example of a One religion foisting its beliefs on identified heathens. They virtually imprisoned the Native Americans and forced them to surrender their own very sacred beliefs and accept what those Ones considered the one and only proper religion—Franciscan theology.

The more tightly wound pathological Ones become, the closer they move toward total collapse—it's all or nothing, dark or light, saint or sinner. When they're at the end of their rope and can no longer control their own forbidden impulses, pathological Ones fall sway to abrupt, irrational behavior, breaking their own rules in humiliating ways such as the once highly respected and highly powerful religious leader Jimmy Swaggart proclaiming, "I have sinned" while weeping profusely and begging forgiveness. The more pathological Ones attempt to suppress unwanted emotions or the more they turn their anger inward, the more they sink into depression. The more they preach abstinence, the more they overindulge in alcohol or drug abuse.

According to *The Wisdom of the Enneagram*, a pathological One on a downward slide is dogmatic and inflexible. She constantly rationalizes her own bad behavior. She becomes increasingly depressed, obsessive, compulsive, anxious, and self-destructive. She judges herself and others harshly, often flying into rages over perceived slights or missteps.

When they are losing their battle to maintain self-control, pathological Ones walk a daily tightrope between obsession and compulsion. Many eventually fail themselves, and their moral code, by performing a spontaneous, rebellious, truly unsavory physical act that breaches all of their rules. This means they become the ultimate hypocrite, for example, a priest who molests children, a minister caught with a prostitute, or a leader who betrays a nation.

Because they feel compelled to be pure and virtuous, Ones often develop obsessions with cleanliness or purging, becoming anorexics, bulimics, or so compulsive about cleansing they overuse laxatives or enemas. They can also become that obsessive-compulsive housewife who compulsively scrubs every inch of her floors, cabinets, and walls, especially the darkest corners, either to keep so busy she isn't thinking those nasty thoughts or to wash away the sins inherent in everyday life.

Disintegrating Ones become dangerous when they project their unacceptable thoughts, feelings, or behaviors onto others, making someone or something else the source of all their—and the entire world's—problems.

When the rules, philosophy, or religion they use to order their world has failed to contain their impulses, disintegrated Ones can become dangerously vindictive and cruel. They vehemently believe they are absolutely right, have justice on their side, and are so pure it's virtually their duty to clean up the world. Once they project all the sins of the world onto a person or a group, they feel justified to show no mercy and offer no reprieves in what they see as their noble quest to annihilate the infidels. If you are involved in an intimate relationship with a pathological One, you can become the enemy and the victim of his or her distortion, regardless of whether you've done anything whatsoever to warrant it.

Self-Actualized Ones

The majority of self-actualized Ones, who live just below the level of saint, are also susceptible to self-doubt and fear. But it's a minor, nagging fear that they aren't as good as they should be. Their healthy, internalized superego, or conscience, is their guide, and they both love—and have the inner strength—to live their lives in balanced moderation. They set noble yet achievable goals for themselves and expend the measured concentration and effort required to achieve them.

They are typically passionately committed to truth and justice and not only live their lives according to these high standards but will rigorously defend them. They are honest, trustworthy, rational, and self-disciplined and thus make excellent mediators who can ferret out complicated issues and make impressive moral choices. They don't need to import an external source for validation; their inner compass guides their decisions and their actions. Since they are fully integrated, whole, and living from their essence, they lead by example and have absolutely no inclination, nor the slightest need, to wield a golden hammer.

In direct contradiction to disintegrated Ones, self-actualized Ones exemplify inner-directedness and wisdom. They don't require internalized moral imperatives; they simply reflect man's optimum self. They are highly discerning, accepting souls who believe that right will always trump evil and that all one has to do is allow things to unfold as they are meant to do. Because they have transcended their own limitations, integrated Ones not only see clearly, they are usually able to verbalize their wisdom in a way that others—even those with vastly different world views—are able to hear them.

FACT

Because they worked rigorously to create a moral world, obeyed strictures, and punished themselves, and each other, for transgressions, American Puritans are a prime example of a One society. In history, Joan of Arc, Luther, Calvin, St. Ignatius, St. Paul, and religious fundamentalists, religious leaders, and other moral custodians, such as Elie Wiesel, Ralph Nader, William F. Buckley, Jr., and the fictionalized Mr. Spock are all examples of One enneatypes.

When maximally self-actualized, Ones are willing to sublimate their own needs for a higher good. They value personal, national, and global integrity, stay true to themselves, and encourage others to do the same. They are constantly striving to meet their own high standards and achieve excellence in everything they do. They make great philosophers, lawyers, judges, and teachers—especially legal, philosophical, sociological, or theological teachers. Because they honor justice above all, integrated Ones often appear as the most principled and fair people in the room, and they are authentically the most principled and fair people on the planet.

The Process of Individuation or Self-Actualization

According to Jung, individuation occurs when you successfully separate your personality from that of your parents and become an integrated personality—becoming what or who you were born to be, what you were before you formed an ego or persona, or suppressed negative behaviors in your shadow. The individuation process is a lifelong, ongoing process or quest. Through therapy or active self-development using introspection and conscious choice, you can work toward the unveiling of your shadow, the unraveling of your persona, and the integration of your psyche.

Basically, when merging aspects of Jungian theory with Enneagram theory, one could presuppose that when things in your life are going really well, you are ripe for expansion and are more likely to progress toward individuation and self-actualization by adopting behaviors that support forward movement. On the other hand, when you feel insecure or are under severe stress, you are more likely to regress from the goal of individuation and self-actualization by adopting behaviors that allow you to cope but that do not necessarily help you progress toward health. Again, in some instances, you may uncover traits inherent in your stress point that help you grow during times of extreme stress, e.g., you might both cope and progress toward health by discovering determination, integrity, or industry in your stress point.

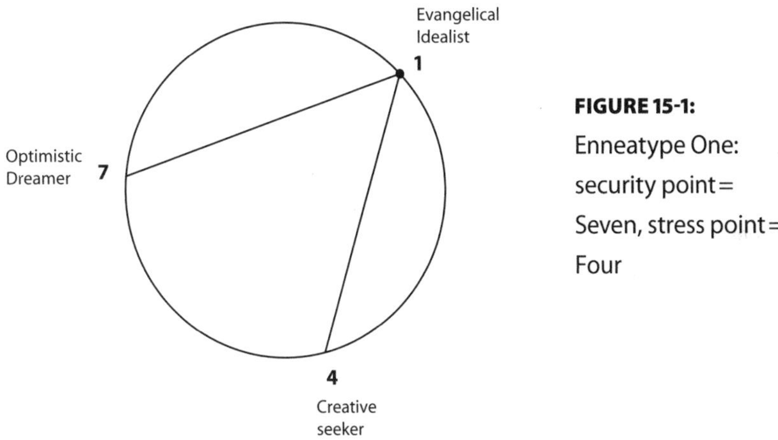

FIGURE 15-1: Enneatype One: security point= Seven, stress point= Four

How Ones Progress

Self-actualizing Ones progress toward individuation by adopting behaviors of a self-actualized Seven—someone capable of accepting imperfection in themselves and others. This helps Ones loosen the moral chains and mellow out, often becoming someone who values and affirms pleasure. Ones progress toward individuation by becoming more relaxed and allowing things to unfold without judgment or manipulation. As they release the need to be perfect, they learn to approach life with enthusiasm rather than obligation and constraint. They go from godlike to goddess, experiencing human emotions and appreciating art, nature, and sensuality.

When Ones connect to Seven, their worlds tend to open up. Rather than rigidly adhering to an internalized moral code, they embrace options and loosen up on thinking there is only one right way. When they connect to Four in a positive way, they are more lenient on themselves and see the merit in being more subjective when forming opinions about themselves and others.

How Ones Regress

When pathological Ones succumb to feeling shameful and guilty, they seek an escape from their tormenting superego and regress by adopting behaviors of a pathological Four, such as conjuring fantasies or developing romantic crushes on unavailable (and therefore safe) men or women. They often delude themselves to distract themselves, but their hypervigilant superego rarely lets them indulge in actual fulfillment. If they adopt other Four traits, like moodiness or melancholy, they often succumb to dramatic excess. They can also become more self-conscious and self-reproachful; and if the downward slide continues, they may resort to self-indulgence and break the strict rules of propriety they so diligently created and so vociferously defended. As the stress increases, they may lapse into deep depression, questioning every idea they have had about life and feeling a sense of despair. Obsessive Ones can become compulsive Fours—hating themselves, blaming themselves, and punishing themselves (instead of others).

When Ones slide down toward the negative side of Seven, they become what some call "trap door Ones," that is, former evangelists who uncharacteristically, and supposedly mysteriously, indulge in sybaritic excess as if they swallowed a Dr. Jekyll (a One)/Mr. Hyde (a Seven) potion and fell through a trap door. When he's an official sinner, the fallen One further regresses toward the negative side of Four and laments his terrible behavior.

Balancing the Opposites

According to Jung's personality theory, the psyche is constantly flowing between two polarities, and your primary task is to achieve a successful balance that more fully expresses your real self and helps you progress toward self-actualization. To achieve individuation, each personality has to acknowledge and work through the limitations of its idealized self and shadow, its strengths and weaknesses, and its motivations and fixations (what keeps it stuck). These primary polarities that a One has to navigate are explored in the following sections.

Shadow and Idealized Self

Every personality forms an inner world that reflects how it feels about itself and an outer world that projects what it want others to know about it. Jung would also refer to these worlds as the *shadow*, or hidden, traits that your psyche squelches and does not want the outer world to see, and the *idealized self*, what your psyche creates and wants the outer world to see.

A One shadow hides rigid black-and-white thinking, intractability, procrastination, perfectionism, compulsivity, and resentfulness. At their worst, Ones can be hypercritical judgmental, cruel, and abusive. In direct opposition to their ego, Ones are ashamed of being inauthentic yet often become hypocritical liars. While an integrated, self-actualized One is virtually a saint, lurking in their shadows are very fallible sinners.

When it comes to an idealized self, Ones are idealistic and discerning with extremely high standards. They are proud of being hyperresponsible, hardworking, and self-reliant. Many Ones love appearing morally superior and gravitate toward being spiritual leaders and humanitarians. They often become teachers of what is correct, for example, Miss Manners telling you how to behave, Martha Stewart telling you how to entertain, and Al Gore telling you how to care for the planet.

Turn-Ons and Turnoffs

According to Jung, your libido is not connected to your sex drive alone, but instead refers to your overall psychic energy or what gives your personality juice. The opposite of what turns you on would be what turns you off. To individuate, Ones need to seek balance between these two polarities.

Ones love a sharply defined set of rules that they can follow to the letter. They pride themselves on doing things right, taking responsibility, and working harder than anyone else. They love being morally superior and capable of keeping their emotions in check.

Ones are definitely turned off when they make a mistake, or when other people make a mistake. They dislike those who don't take responsibility or who don't strive to do their best work. Since they prefer being perfect, they are turned off by their own, or anyone else's, strong emotions. They are turned off when anyone behaves irrationally, and they do not respond well to unwarranted criticism or aggressive people.

Fear and Security

These basic and very essential characteristics determine how Ones approach, live in, and eventually conquer their worlds. Fears stop you short and often cause you to regress, and people rarely progress unless they feel a certain sense of security about themselves or their circumstances.

Ones live in dire fear that they will not meet their own high moral standards and that others will reject them. They have great difficulty being less than perfect or not having a well-defined ideology that keeps them from losing control and behaving badly.

Ones create a sense of security by creating, or accepting, and then living by high moral standards. They need structure and rules to combat a feeling of being out of control, and they gravitate toward narrowly defined philosophies, religions, or other belief systems. By remaining virtuous, they feel above reproach. They feel best when they do things the right way so they bend over backward to achieve perfection.

Motivations and Fixations

The feeling of being motivated or stuck relates to how Ones use or ignore their psychic energy. Knowing their primary motivations and what Ones cling to within their own personality that either helps them progress toward individuation or keeps them stuck in fixations helps you understand how their personality functions.

Ones are deeply motivated by a desire to accomplish self-regeneration. They set very high ideals for themselves and others and then continually and almost compulsively strive to go beyond them. They want to rise above everyone to the point of superhuman or angelic status. They harbor a deep desire to create an ideal self and are constantly working toward improvement and regeneration.

In response to inadequate discipline, One children often develop a severe, judgmental, internal monitoring system that they then use to control their own behavior. They focus on doing everything right so that they can remain above reproach. If their parental figure was a religious fanatic, they may grow up afraid of disappointing God the father or may even develop a God complex, believing they alone are spiritually perfect.

Ones get stuck when they create a dangerous precipice within themselves—by inventing an overpowering, righteous internal critic—that leaves them feeling too anxious and worried to take positive action in their lives. Because Ones are terrified their shadow behavior will overpower them, they spend too much time fighting the devil on their shoulder. They fear any loosening of inhibitions so deny themselves opportunities to relax or to try new behaviors. Eventually, they effectively lose touch with their inner self or soul.

Coping and Failing

This coping-failing dichotomy has to do with the behaviors Ones adopt to cope with their lives, or maintain the status quo, and how those same behaviors can lead to a failure to grow into their personality's full potential.

Ones cope, or maintain the status quo, by maintaining absolute integrity, relying on self more than anyone else, priding themselves on their moral character, feeling superior to others, putting off decisions until they know the right thing to do, striving for perfection in everything they do, and focusing on self-improvement.

Ones fail when they become so dogmatic they have no middle ground and hold themselves to such unachievable expectations that they are doomed to disappoint themselves. Because they so vehemently connect their self-esteem to their moral superiority, they may create and hide an alter ego, or shameful persona, that secretly breaches their strict moral codes.

Falling Apart and Transcending

Each enneatype has a unique way of falling apart. The types each have specific needs they need fulfilled, or mental concepts they can embrace, before they can successfully transcend their ego limitations and become fully integrated and whole.

When Ones fall apart, they worry excessively, shun responsibility, and blame others for all their problems. If they feel provoked, they may fly into a rage that is not appropriate to the situation, or they may suddenly behave in a manner exactly opposite of their usual self. Ones in disarray often create an alter ego that they then use to violate their own precious moral codes—doing shocking and despicable things that go against everything they have always believed in. Eventually, they believe their own fiction—that they are the alter ego, or persona, they created.

Ones transcend, or achieve self actualization, by surrendering their obsession with perfection, remembering that they are perfect the way they are, that we are all on this planet together as one, and that they alone don't have to save the world. Once they love themselves unconditionally, and finally believe that they don't have to do anything special to deserve love, they learn to choose their battles, loosen up, and focus on fun. They learn to cultivate their uniqueness instead of overidentifying with traditions, rules and principles.

Chapter 16

The Wing Subtypes

One of the two points on the Enneagram that lie on either side of your enneatype influences your personality. In other words, your enneatype consists of your main focus and a unique mixture of this core with one of the two types adjacent to it on the Enneagram. The adjacent type that has most influenced your life is called your wing. The wing both complements your basic personality and encompasses important, sometimes contradictory, elements within your personality. It illustrates and shades another side to your self that will increase your understanding of your adult personality in action.

Wings

One of the enneatypes on either side of your core personality type becomes the wing that provides complexity and dimension to your personality. For example, Ones have either a Nine wing or Two wing; Fours have either a Three wing or Five wing; Sevens have either a Six wing or Eight wing; and so on. Understanding the concept of wings and how they function helps explain the how personalities can vary widely within each core personality typology. For example, a Six with a Five wing will be intrinsically different from a Six with a Seven wing.

Wings determine your secondary fears and desires, the motivations that drive you, and the traits or behaviors you develop to form your personality. The proportion of primary and secondary influences can differ significantly. If your wing influences a large portion of your personality, it's frequently called a "heavy" wing. If the wing is present but your core personality still takes center stage, you have a "moderate" wing. If your core fixation completely dominates your secondary personality to the point that it is almost imperceptible, you have a "light" wing. In each case, the core personality predominates the overall personality. For example, a Seven with a light Eight wing will exhibit mostly Seven behaviors, while a Seven with a heavy Eight wing will show strong Eight characteristics in addition to typical Seven behavior; a Seven with a moderate Eight would be somewhere in between.

Twos with a One Wing

Ones internalize a set of moral principles, and they usually behave somewhere in between genuinely loving evangelical idealists and judgmental, critical, perfectionist tyrants. Twos are people pleasers who fluctuate between being true altruists and manipulators who use their ability to determine what someone wants so they can win love. Ones are usually convinced they know the one, true right way; Twos are usually too reliant on others for self-validation. So how do these two combine?

One energy often lends a sense of moral purpose that helps ego-driven or pathological Twos with a One wing lean toward altruism, as opposed to being so focused on getting their immediate needs they ingratiate themselves to a few people whose favors they want.

When it works well, One wing energy brings a cool rationale or a desire for a moral purpose that serves to temper Twos' cloying emotional warmth. They may even circumvent their own needs to adopt important social issues or campaigns.

Unfortunately, in reality, most ego-driven Twos with a One wing live with conflicting impulses—to remain dispassionate and rigidly idealistic (judgmental perfectionist), or to feel sympathy for others and act with kindness (loving altruist). Even when they do feel compassion, the One wing often makes Twos quick on the draw with moral and personal judgments against their loved ones as well as themselves.

FACT

Mother Teresa—whose strong connection to Catholicism combined with her genuine desire and ability to love unconditionally (and universally) gave her life purpose, direction, and energy—is a prime example of a self-actualized Two influenced by a moderate to heavy One wing.

At their worst, Twos with a One wing can be controlling, manipulative, self-righteous, self-destructive, and rigid. Believing they know best, they feel justified in manipulating or attempting to control their loved ones. And they often refuse to believe that they are wrong about anything and will vehemently deny aggressive feelings.

Twos with a Three Wing

Because they are in the same feeling, or relationship, triad, Twos with a Three wing are more compatible than Twos with a One wing, who are in different triads. In this case, both enneatypes in the triad are focused on relationships and have an uncanny ability to observe and interpret other people's emotions. When they are self-actualized, both personalities relate very well to other people. Twos still gauge other people's emotions to create relationships, but the Three wing makes them more confident, charming, and outgoing. They simply are more attractive and more approachable than your average Two.

Rather than being so focused on being seen as lovable, the Three wing often makes Twos focus on being seen as successful. Both types are always highly aware of what others think about them, but the Three wing wants social status and will show off to impress others, often to the point of casually dropping names regardless of if they even know the person being mentioned. This Two wants you to admire him and will create a persona if necessary. Reasonably functioning Twos with a Three wing have enough martyr energy left to control ego inflation, but they often go from feeling guilty when they breach moral standards to being terrified that they will be humiliated or lose social status if they make any public missteps.

Twos with a Three wing often project a charming, poised, confident, and friendly persona that often harbors unbridled ambition to be at the top of their field. The musical galaxy provides examples in the form of Luciano Pavarotti, Barry Manilow, Tommy Tune, Sammy Davis, Jr., and John Denver. These are all very successful performers that exude showmanship and a distinctive, friendly, and engaging personality.

When pathological Twos have a Three wing, the combination can be deadly—to themselves or to someone they once claimed to love. If the Three energy led to the development of a persona that they then feel compelled to maintain, any perceived betrayal or threat of being exposed may make these Twos hostile and aggressive. They can also be all too willing to sink to the lowest depths to get what they want from others. If they feel vulnerable, ongoing frustration may lead to disintegration in the form of pathological obsession, jealousy, and violence.

Threes with a Two Wing

When a Two wing endows a Three personality with genuine warmth and empathy, a Three frequently becomes a genuinely attractive, sociable, charming, and likable person. Rather than having to manufacture these traits to maintain an image, they have integrated these traits. They may have Threes' animated, energetic, and entertaining qualities, but these are usually tempered by a realization that other people are important, that it's good to focus on them occasionally, and that they also deserve to have their needs and desires met.

FACT

Actors and singers illustrate the type—people who dazzle us with their talent and their personality. Combine a superstar persona, charisma, and an uncanny ability to be in tune with what other people love about them and you get Elvis Presley. Even when drugs caused him to lose his grip on reality, people still absolutely adored him, partially because he was a talented performer and partially because he was a people pleaser, generous, and loving to his family and his public.

When a Two wing reinforces negative Three behavior, you get people who crave attention and recognition so vigorously that it's hard for them to maintain their cool when others don't sufficiently appreciate everything they do. They are often openly hostile when someone dares to expose their flaws. They need you to love them and to admire their fabulousness; if you don't, they hate you for it.

Threes with a Four Wing

Threes are all about public persona, climbing over whomever gets in their way to becoming king of hill, master of their game, superstar to the max, or whatever makes them rich. Fours are all about introspection, depth, and finding their true self so they can finally be proved unique and special. Fours are infatuated with their own feelings, particularly melancholy; Threes would rather think about what they feel and manufacture upbeat feelings than brood. Fours are about intensity; Threes are about surface. Threes tend to be extroverted; Fours tend to be introverted.

Thus, a Three with a Four wing endures internal skirmishes on a regular basis, which can manifest in manic-depressive swings. They can't help being image conscious or feeling compelled to work hard to achieve exceptional recognition, but their Four wing tends to make them more subdued and much more in touch with their real emotions. Rather than caring what others think of their accomplishments, they are more concerned about what they feel about their accomplishments.

When it works really well, a Four wing helps a Three value her inner life and present her real, as opposed to a false, self. These Threes still want to excel at what they do, but unlike Threes with a Two wing, they do so quietly because they want to do something meaningful that nourishes them far more than they want to do something solely to impress through money or status.

According to *The Enneagram Movie and Video Guide*, Threes with a Four wing who possess a sensitive artistic sensibility combined with a more introspective, cool, calm, and collected personality include Richard Gere, who embraces eastern religions; former President Jimmy Carter, who founded Habitat for Humanity; intellectually inclined talk show host Dick Cavett; and the late author Truman Capote.

Negative Four energy may cause Threes to swing from a tendency to overindulge in misguided self-reflection and end up doubting themselves at every turn to arrogantly believing that they are smarter than their critics and brandishing their superiority. Four energy sometimes makes Threes vulnerable to emotional instability and low-grade depression.

Fours with a Three Wing

Fours with a Three wing actually fare a little better than Threes with a Four wing. In this case, a Three wing energizes lethargic Fours. All that pent-up creativity gets a boot when it links up with real-life financial goals. Three energy also helps brooding Fours come out of their introspective shell and at least want to feel good about themselves. These Fours are definitely more energetic and often more sophisticated in their tastes—they may even want a high-profile job or luxurious digs to show off.

When they surrender the more typical lack of self-esteem, Fours with a Three wing are able to set concrete goals and transition quickly into Three-type action. A healthy dose of Three motivates them to go beyond dreaming and actually produce works of art that reflect well upon themselves and their desired, self-created image.

Because they can be keenly intuitive, highly creative, dynamic, talented, and ambitious, many Fours with a Three wing look more like Sevens, particularly if they also have a lusty sense of humor and a sparkling dash of pizzazz. But Fours with a Three wing are more in touch with their feelings and willing to weave their emotional context into their creative work than most Sevens.

Even though Three's extroversion tames Fours' tendency to mope or succumb to melancholy, they may swing from one extreme to another. They may behave like the life of the party and then go home feeling very much alone and lonely, or they may be melodramatic and flamboyant one minute and quiet and secretive the next.

Fours with a Five Wing

A Five wing often adds intellectual muscle to Fours' feeling-intensive, hypersensitive modus operandi, bringing complexity and depth to their lives and to their creativity. The blending of a piercing intellect with emotional intensity helps them become confident in their individualistic skin and more capable of utilizing their insights in productive ways. They burn with creative fervor and often produce successful works of art. They also try to think their way out of their emotional doldrums.

On the other hand, Fours with a Five wing may become more conservative, self-contained, subdued, private, and analytical. When they take on more of the analytical bent of Five energy, they are often drawn to solitary professions such as a researcher, using their intellect to be a scientist, or using their fascination with feelings as a psychologist or therapist.

Many Fours with a Five wing are geniuses in their creative field. According to *The Enneagram Movie and Video Guide*, prime examples include Diane Arbus, Marlon Brando, Eric Clapton, Kurt Cobain, Bob Dylan, Sylvia Plath, Arthur Rimbaud, Edgar Allan Poe, and Virginia Woolf. All combined exceptional intelligence with an artistic soul, which resulted in original works of art that captured the world's attention. Unfortunately, many of them fell prey to a Four's susceptibility to a deeply pathological depression that led to suicide.

On the negative side, Fours with a Five wing can become even more introspective and solitary. Sometimes Five energy leads to quirky or idiosyncratic behavior, or a feeling of being so different they feel alienated. This could result in further social withdrawal and longer periods of isolation that, unfortunately, bolster Fours' proclivity for unproductive brooding or feeling sorry for themselves. Fours with a heavy Five wing who spend too much time alone can get lost in nonproductive rumination, depression, and morbidity.

Fives with a Four Wing

A Four wing brings emotional subtext to a typically cool, calm, and collected Five. Without question, they are more sensitive, empathetic, and emotionally supportive. A heavy Four wing means the Fives have easier access to their emotions, which assists them in being either more humanistic and focused on the emotional welfare of others or more self-absorbed and focused on how they feel about what's happening in their own lives.

According to *The Enneagram Movie and Video Guide*, examples of Fives with a Four wing include Tim Burton, David Byrne, Agatha Christie, T. S. Eliot, Albert Einstein, Gary Larson, George Lucas, David Lynch, and Georgia O'Keeffe.

Fives' creativity is also bolstered by having a Four wing. They probably won't be as melodramatic, brooding, or focused on the emotional intensity of their work as Fours, but they may use intellectual constructs to create works or art, such as writing imaginative philosophy, mathematical books, or inventive science fiction novels. They might be very attracted to the Enneagram, for instance, where the cool rationale of psychological concepts as they relate to personality formation incorporates spirituality and intuition.

Fives with a Six Wing

Although Fives remain their detached, intellectual loner selves, a heavy Six wing could make them feel more dependent on other people and perhaps create a burgeoning urge, or at least an occasional desire, to mix with people. It may bring improved people skills, or at least a slight opening up, even if it's only to ask Sixes' typical probing questions.

However, Sixes' tendency to flip from phobic to counterphobic behavior may make Fives more fearful, although they are still more likely to move forward, albeit with skepticism and caution. However, once they form alliances or friendships, Six wings help reticent Fives form trustworthy relationships, and once they've bonded, they are more loyal.

Robin Williams's portrayal of Oliver Sacks in *Awakenings* showed a typical Five with a Six wing behavior. He was a quirky, idiosyncratic doctor who was socially awkward. His Six wing led him to have a questioning mind, and a little counterphobic Six behavior occurred when he went against his profession's conventional wisdom and tried a radical treatment on patients everyone else had written off.

Fives with Six wings may have even stronger analytical skills and be attracted to scientific or mathematical professions, but a negative Six wing can bring fear to the table and cloud the Five's normal ability to think clearly.

Sixes with a Five Wing

Sixes with a Five Wing are more shy, cautious, and withdrawn, which others often mistake as being cold and standoffish. It's really just that Five tendency to need private space, opportunities to observe before engaging, and a need to seek solitude until they can wrap their minds around whatever is bothering them. Like Fives, these Sixes are simply more introverted, intellectual, and attracted to solitary activities such as research or informational gathering. Fives' love of being alone to process and contemplate can benefit phobic Sixes' need for outside approval. Although it could lead to paranoia, most Sixes with Five wings remain loners because they simply like to protect their privacy, acquire knowledge to distinguish and separate themselves, and even shield themselves from too much outside interference.

FACT

According to *The Enneagram Movie and Video Guide*, examples of Sixes with a Five wing include Warren Beatty, Gene Hackman, J. Edgar Hoover, Spike Lee, Richard Nixon, Janet Reno, and Brian Wilson. Movie roles that portray Sixes with a Five wing include Martin Landeau in *Crimes and Misdemeanors*, Sam Neill in *The Piano*, and Anthony Perkins in *Psycho*.

A Five wing helps Sixes perfect a smooth exterior that hides a percolating intelligence and a lot more depth than you would imagine. Negative Five wings can amplify Sixes' phobias or counterphobias, particularly when Sixes spend too much time alone brooding over past hurts. When mixed with paralyzing Six fear, some start believing that danger lies everywhere and may become increasingly antisocial and paranoid.

Sixes with a Seven Wing

A Six with a Seven wing seems almost the complete opposite of a Six with a Five wing. These Sixes are ready to party. Seven energy makes them playful, spontaneous, adventurous, and far more impulsive than your classic fearful Six. These Sixes hold a few more positive thoughts about the world and trust themselves and others enough to take an occasional risk. If they're not careful, however, Seven energy can lead a Six to ruin—overindulgence in alcohol, drugs, or casual sex is not uncommon among this set.

Like Sevens, Sixes with a Seven wing attempt to control their underlying fear with frenetic activity, sometimes reaching manic phases. Many become comedians who write clever jokes and tell funny stories about their foibles to cover their underlying depression.

According to *The Enneagram Movie and Video Guide*, examples of Sixes with a Seven wing include Kim Basinger, Rodney Dangerfield, Judy Davis, Ellen DeGeneres, Carrie Fisher, Diane Keaton, Richard Lewis, Julia Roberts, Susan Sarandon, and Jon Stewart. Movie roles that captured the Six with Seven wing personality include Woody Allen in anything, Billy Crystal in *City Slickers*, Bill Murray in *What About Bob?*, and Meg Ryan in *When Harry Met Sally.*

Negative Seven wing influences create internal confusion that manifests in mood swings, amplified fears, nervous jitters, and blaming others. It's as if Seven energy makes these Sixes covet fame and fortune, but they still lack the confidence to really go for it.

Sevens with a Six Wing

Sevens with a Six wing are a little bit more down-to-earth and interested in sitting still long enough to forge relationships. They care whether you like them or not, and once they've committed to a relationship are more likely to be loyal, faithful, and stick with it through thick and thin. And lucky you, because they are often warm, gracious, and sweet.

Sevens with a Six wing are also light on their feet and full of charm. They seem sweet, vulnerable, and somewhat silly, but it's obvious a clever mind runs the show. They also have charming senses of humor and entertain many with their infinitely endearing stories. A lot of comedians are also Sevens with a Six wing, but they tend to be the ones without a heavy dark side hidden under their jocular persona. Their natural gluttony can be for the desire for information instead of appetite.

FACT

According to *The Enneagram Movie and Video Guide*, examples of Sevens with a Six wing include Dave Barry, Jackie Chan, Chevy Chase, Goldie Hawn, Magic Johnson, Eddie Murphy, Brad Pitt, Martin Short, Lily Tomlin, and Robin Williams. Movie roles that portray Sevens with a Six wing include Ruth Gordon in *Harold And Maude*, Audrey Hepburn in *Breakfast at Tiffany's*, Sidney Poitier in *Lilies of the Field*, and George Clooney in *One Fine Day*.

If they are pathological, Sevens with a Six wing can be interminably sensitive, weepy, fearful, and clinging. It's as if they become easily unglued and spin off in divergent destructive cycles: latching on to negative partners and then abruptly breaking things off, sleeping around very indiscriminately, or drinking or eating too much and then starving themselves. Some develop a proclivity for really mean humor, the kind you see in some cartoonists.

Sevens with an Eight Wing

Sevens with an Eight wing can be marvelously exuberant, cheerful, and friendly. They can be also be assertive, competitive, bold, confrontational, and aggressive. When a lust for intensity and gluttony combine, Sevens with an Eight wing are often prone to chemical addiction. Sevens with a Eight wing mask their fear by meeting it head on. Luckily, they're not intent on mowing you down like Eights, but they can still make your heart quiver if they're directing anger toward you.

Sevens with an Eight wing care more about having a good time than amassing power, but they do like accumulating nice things to spice up their lives. And one needs money to buy fancy clothes, cars, houses, so Sevens with an Eight wing are ambitious and hardworking. It's just that they have another side—a playful side.

According to *The Enneagram Movie and Video Guide*, examples of Sevens with an Eight wing include Michael Caine, George Clooney, Francis Ford Coppola, Cary Grant, Tom Hanks, Jack Nicholson, and Barbra Streisand. Movie roles that depict Sevens with an Eight wing include Jeff Bridges in *Tucker*, Ray Liotta in *Good Fellows*, Jack Nicholson in *Batman*, and Roy Schneider in *All That Jazz*.

Sevens' joie de vivre combined with an Eight's powerful focus makes them multitalented, dynamic, inventive, and fascinating. They can be visionary, full of bright ideas and the energy to bring them to fruition.

If they're pathological, however, they are frequently narcissistic and demanding. The world revolves around them and their immediate needs, which they expect to be fulfilled immediately.

Eights with a Seven Wing

These Eights take on the tendency of Sevens to see a positive outcome. They blend their usual realism with a sentimental idealism. Seven energy tames the lion in Eights and helps them learn to sublimate at least some of their more aggressive feelings.

As Eights they are still business oriented, but a Seven wing makes them energetic, quicker on the draw, and more entrepreneurial or visionary. A Seven wing also helps them be more sociable, often to the point of going overboard at parties.

According to *The Enneagram Movie and Video Guide*, examples of Eights with a Seven wing include Lucille Ball, Richard Burton, Sean Connery, Rush Limbaugh, Ann Richards, Grace Slick, and Donald Trump. Movies roles that depict Eights with a Seven wing include Matt Damon in *Good Will Hunting*, Michael Douglas in *Wall Street*, James Earl Jones in *The Great White Hope*, and Christine Lahti in *Leaving Normal*.

Pathological Eights with Seven wings are highly susceptible to the diseases of excess—alcoholism, drug addiction, shopping addictions. When their anger becomes distorted, they are capable of vicious behavior.

Eights with a Nine Wing

When Eights have a Nine wing they are more in tune with others, which helps them gain a more expansive, all-encompassing view of life. Nines' desire for equanimity tones down the Eight's lust for power, helping them achieve a more balanced personality. They are more relaxed, more inclusive, and even somewhat introverted. Their energy quiets down, creating opportunities for them to be mild-mannered and receptive; they even take other people's views under consideration occasionally.

According to *The Enneagram Movie and Video Guide*, examples of Eights with a Nine wing include Johnny Cash, Fidel Castro, Michael Douglas, John Huston, Evel Knievel, Mao Tse-tung, Golda Meir, Robert Mitchum, and Queen Latifah. Movie roles that depict Eights with a Nine wing include Humphrey Bogart in *Casablanca*, Russell Crowe in *L.A. Confidential*, Judd Hirsch in *Ordinary People*, and Jack Palance in *City Slickers*.

Unfortunately, all that Eight anger doesn't totally disappear. If provoked, the dormant anger that was lying just under their surface spews out, wounding people who don't deserve it. A pathological Eight with a Nine wing can become desensitized, cruel, and chronically abusive.

Nines with an Eight Wing

A healthy Nine with an Eight wing exudes a palpable, albeit quiet, charismatic confidence. They look and feel comfortable in their own skins—a little too good—and are usually very good at maximizing the sort of king-of-the-jungle command they personify. They almost always get what they want—as if it was their destiny to have it all along.

Unfortunately, under the auspices of Eights' aggressive tendencies, Nines' can lose their congenial disposition and become narrow-minded and willful. If they are pathological, at some point their anger will surface—abruptly and out of proportion. They may be so desensitized that they don't notice the damage they've just inflicted, and they often feel sufficiently justified in going for their opponent's throat.

FACT

According to *The Enneagram Movie and Video Guide,* examples of Nines with an Eight wing include Connie Chung, the Dali Lama, Clint Eastwood, Dwight Eisenhower, John Goodman, Woody Harrelson, Gena Rowlands, Gloria Steinman, and Billy Bob Thornton. Movie roles that depict Nines with an Eight wing include Clint Eastwood in *Unforgiven,* Woody Harrelson in *White Men Can't Jump,* Bob Hoskins in *Mona Lisa,* and Ann Margaret in *A New Life.*

On the positive side, they have a touch of Eights' energy, which helps most Nines be more confident, assertive, outgoing, and capable of actual rebellion. However, they are more typically torn between needing peace and quiet and wanting to grab whatever they want, or displaying an urge to merge and wanting to push people away.

Nines with a One Wing

Self-actualized Nines with a One wing have improved focus. They can actually get their ducks in a row, prioritize, and get things done in a timely manner. Positive One energy also helps Nines set firm boundaries based on crystallized views of what is right and what is wrong. They develop their own values instead of blindly accepting what those around them think or feel. Their strong sense of moral imperatives may spur them to tackle social issues or develop missionary zeal for worthwhile causes.

Your more typical ego-driven Nine with a One wing is commonly a lost soul. According to *The Literary Enneagram*, a perfect example would be Harry "Rabbit" Angstom, John Updike's antihero in the Rabbit novels (*Rabbit Run*, *Rabbit Redux*, *Rabbit Is Rich*, *Rabbit at Rest*, plus the novella *Rabbit Remembered*). Rabbit peaked in high school and then spent the rest of his life neither here nor there, never quite able to make up his mind.

However, pathological Nines with a One wing may wield their values as weapons, becoming hypercritical, condescending, and judgmental. Worst of all, they usually treat themselves equally bad. When things fall apart, they may latch onto a zealot and walk around blindly following the wrong path as if they are under a bad spell.

Ones with a Nine Wing

When Ones with strong moral codes have a Nine wing that brings a certain discomfort with actual reality, they often become a bit too cool, calm, and collected and are emotionally disconnected. Self-actualized Ones with a Nine wing know and value the benefits of remaining emotionally detached in terms of being principled, rational, logical, and fair, particularly in the pursuit of ideals. Most ego-driven Ones with a Nine wing tend to simply detach or become apathetic.

Examples of Ones with a Nine wing who became gifted speakers and well-respected—perhaps surprisingly passionate—champions of social, political, or environmental causes because they primarily retain a cool, detached, rational air include Al Gore, Carl Sagan, Ralph Nader, Sandra Day O'Connor, and Margaret Thatcher.

In fact, many ego-driven Ones with a Nine wing can be brilliant thinkers, but they tend to compartmentalize their brains and suppress their hearts, creating disparate behaviors that swing from utmost discipline to laziness, diehard passion (about ideals) to indifference. Their anger, however, reverts to a Nine's more typical passivity, as in primarily covert, and is more often expressed through sharp retorts or bitingly sarcastic comments.

When a heavy Nine wing brings negativity, Ones hide behind emotionally stark black-and-white thinking, no longer pretend to care about other people, and often cope by projecting their dark emotions onto others and then railing against them. They are especially prone to ignore personal and relationship components of the world.

Ones with a Two Wing

Unlike Ones with a Nine wing, who can be emotionally bland, Nines with a Two wing have to cope with pesky warm and fuzzy feelings toward people that butt right up against their usual cool rationale.

Self-actualized Ones with a Two wing extend their moral codes to embrace love of their fellow man and actually stop to consider the very human emotional impact their behavior may have on others. They can be rational and objective as well as warm and empathetic at the same time. In contrast to Ones with a Nine wing, who embrace and fight for ideals, Ones with a Two wing embrace and fight for people. Most Ones with a Two wing meld their ideas about what is right and wrong with a desire to help their fellow humans.

Examples of fiery, action-oriented Ones with a Two wing who take on contentious social values and wage political campaigns—because they are as passionate about people as they are about the ideals or principles involved—include Jane Fonda, Mario Cuomo, Bill Moyers, Vanessa Redgrave, Jerry Brown, and Joan Baez.

This new interest in people leads many ego-driven Ones with a Nine wing to flip from a desire to control themselves to a desire to control those around them. Unlike Ones with a Nine wing, who focus on ideals, dysfunctional Ones with a Two wing focus on how they can force people to adhere to their moral codes. As such, they often appear smug, overconfident, and narrowly defined. If someone questions their moral or behavioral authority, they may fly off the handle. Judge Judy would be a lively example of this.

When Ones with a Two wing are pathological, they can be condescending and intolerant, wielding anger and guilt like a sword. They become intractable in the face of criticism and eventually become increasingly self-righteous and hypocritical, yet are blind to their own faults.

Chapter 17

Twos, Threes, and Fours in Love

When Twos, Threes, and Fours are well-rounded, highly functioning, psychologically healthy people, their particular sensitivity to feelings helps them form solid, functional relationships. In fact, they tend to be more concerned about their relationships than the other types. Even though they may feel things more deeply than other types, they also tend to have more difficulty when it comes to relationships. When Twos, Threes, and Fours lose it, or become pathological, their emotions go haywire, approaching volatile, unmanageable, oppressive, and imprisoning.

How Type Affects Relationships

People need love, and understanding oneself—and others—helps you develop and nourish healthy relationships as well as identify and release negative relationships. Once you know your basic type and its primary wing influences, you can identify patterns within other types that will be compatible in certain situations. Understanding the common or disparate motivations, the underlying strengths and weaknesses, and the best aspects of each type will enable to you understand why people act the way they do and what you can do to help them understand you or, at the very least, your point of view.

While any normal, relatively healthy person can relate well to someone operating on the same basic level—no matter what enneatype that person is—the Enneagram can be very helpful in figuring out what areas within each of your Enneagram styles are most likely to lead to discord down the road. Since it also helps you gain a better perspective on the motivations, fears, and behaviors of each type, it can also be used as a tool for improving your current relationships by increasing your understanding of your family and friends and identifying the points where your personalities mesh and where they combust.

FACT

Two personalities within the same type are likely to share a common point of view and modus operandi, but they may also grow weary of reflecting the negative aspects of their type to each other. Also, even when two people meet at the same points, they may feel a mutual understanding of the issues until one partner gravitates toward another point (during progression or regression) on the Enneagram and disagreements or misunderstanding occur.

Obviously, there are a multitude of complexities. Where you are in terms of functioning—self-actualized, ego-driven, or pathological—as well as the weight of your wing and your security point or your stress point can all affect you and the other person.

The Feeling Triad in Relationships

It all started when they felt rejected by their parents or parental figures and assumed, on some level, that it was their fault. As a result, Twos, Threes, and Fours basically developed feeling complexes. To cope, they surrendered important parts of themselves to create what they thought were more attractive, agreeable personas in hopes their parental figures, and everyone who comes after, would love them more. Unfortunately, feeling rejected resulted in deep emotional wounds that became an ongoing problem. And all three feeling types struggle with the hostility that grew out of feeling rejected by denying it, suppressing it, disowning it, expressing it inappropriately, or turning it against themselves.

All three feeling types have problems with who they are and how they cope with unbridled anger, resentment, or scary feelings, particularly rejection or abandonment. Everyone covers over their real self or essence to some degree, but far more than others, Twos, Threes, and Fours repress or distort huge parts of themselves to accommodate others or to become what they think a potential partner wants.

Twos coped by forming an image of being so completely loving, generous, and thoughtful that everyone would surely love them. Threes coped by forming an image of external success that they thought would guarantee them love. Fours coped by forming an image of being special and hypersensitive that made it hard for anyone to get close to them and thus unable to reject them. And all three types are always comparing themselves to other people and falling short in their own minds.

How Twos Fit in the Triad

Twos are in the heart-centered, feeling, or relationship Triad. Twos aren't particularly sensitive to their own feelings, but they constantly monitor what other people think of them and where they stand in relation to other people.

Right out of the gate, they learned to gauge what their caretakers needed and then provided it in order to win love, attention, or a feeling of safety. Thus, they become both motivated by others' feelings and primarily focused on their relationship to others—as opposed to their inner self.

Since they are also an extroverted type within the feeling triad, they focus their sensitivity to feelings outward, becoming too reliant upon others to provide and validate their own image of themselves or to make them feel worthy of love. Eventually, they are so focused on fulfilling everyone else's needs that they lose touch with their own feelings. They also become dependent upon others to fulfill their unacknowledged needs and may use their ultrasensitivity to what others are thinking and feeling to manipulate them.

Because they didn't feel seen, validated, mirrored, or cared for by their father figure, Twos feel compelled to make themselves lovable, worthy of admiration, and so essential to your well-being that you will never leave them. They may do this by making themselves indispensable and appearing as if they truly meant well—two qualities they think will solidify their esteem in your eyes. To feel comfortable in the outer world, they require constant attention and approval from others. Neurotic or pathological Twos breach emotional boundaries and are codependent in the truest sense of the word.

Twos can be the ultimate givers and the ultimate takers. When self-actualized, these people pleasers give love from their hearts in a truly unconditional way. When dysfunctional, they take whatever they can get in order to fill the vast holes in their souls created when they didn't feel loved or accepted by their parents.

What It's Like to Love a Two

Twos generally look really good and go out of their way to impress you in the beginning stages of romance. Twos base their self-image on being loving and generous to a fault, which means they do their best to squelch any evidence that they have negative feelings, habits, or behaviors. Twos believe that they have to meet your needs to acquire love and will bend over backward to do whatever they think you need or want in order to keep you. They often surrender any sense of their real self to become what they think a powerful, attractive potential mate, or even a friend, wants them to be.

Even if you protest, ego-driven and pathological Twos may feel compelled to sacrifice everything for the people they love. Eventually they can feel like the objects of their affection have taken them for granted, making them feel resentful and uncharacteristically angry. Many Twos lose touch with their feelings and need their loved ones to bolster their esteem. If they can't get the emotional fulfillment they need directly, particularly as they inch toward pathology, they may become manipulative and dramatic—begging for constant attention, requiring excessive praise and flattery (even when it's not deserved), and cleaving themselves to your side.

They may want you to feel flattered that they are so willing to be whatever you want them to be, but later they can resent the sacrifices they made and want to break free from what they then perceive as your need to control them.

What you'll love about Twos:

- They often know how they feel about you and express it.
- They want to love you and make it the focus of their lives.
- They will see your best qualities and talk about you in glowing terms.
- They shower you with attention and always remember important events.
- They often feel your pain and seek ways to make it better.
- They will typically wait on you hand and foot.
- If they have what you want, they usually gladly give it to you.

What will drive you crazy about Twos:

- They often want to know where you are at all times.
- They may get jealous if you even talk to someone else.
- They can become whiny and get mad for little reason.
- They complain constantly that you're neglecting them.
- They need lots of attention, and it's never enough.
- They often see themselves as flawless.
- They tend to scream at you and then deny being angry.
- Instead of asking for what they want, they resort to manipulation.

Once you're in a relationship with them, Twos can become martyrs who will smother you with love and then expect a dramatic display of adoration in return. If you're involved with a dysfunctional, codependent, or pathological Two, ulterior motives and unreasonable expectations commingle. Their love not only has strings attached, it has ropes attached.

Self-actualized Twos can be a dream, but those integrated, evolved Twos are usually far more interested in serving humanity than serving you. Their altruistic nature typically dominates their personality, which means they may fly off to Africa to run a school or spend the majority of their time in church activities.

How Threes Fit in the Triad

Threes are in the central position in the heart-centered, feeling, or relationship Triad. At an early age, Threes had an uncanny ability to know what their parents wanted from them, and they learned to use that information to replicate behavior that induced love or admiration from their primary caretakers. Threes adapted to their early environment by giving their sense of self-worth over to others and by being willing to work for any length of time to succeed. Threes typically don't define their own idea of success but form it in reaction to external markers: smiles and hugs, then later grades, trophies, medals, credentials, and applause.

Eventually Threes surrendered their real feelings to become or behave as the type of person they felt would make the greatest impression or win the greatest accolades. In other words, they valued the appearance of what they could make others think they were far more than what they actually were. They played whatever role would get them what they wanted, even when they had to expend a lot of energy suppressing a strong, nagging feeling that they were phonies.

Threes eventually blur the lines between what they really feel and what they think they should feel to maintain an impressive persona. They lose touch with their genuine feelings, or become so confused they lose the ability to readily identify what they are feeling in the moment.

FACT

Patrick O'Leary, an early Enneagram author, observed that Threes are "like secretaries at the switchboard of life: They put their emotions on hold and get back to work."

In relationships, Threes play the role they think will win your heart. But once they have you, they latch on and their dark side soon emerges. If the Three is relatively integrated, he is authentic and there will be no nasty surprises. However, if he is pathological Three, once he can no longer hold the mask over his face, he is likely to become a sadistic sociopath.

What It's Like to Love a Three

Most ego-driven Threes base their self-esteem on what they can accomplish, how many physical possessions they can accumulate, and how they look to the rest of the world, which means they create an inflated image that requires major upkeep. They become whatever they think will win them what they want, and they do whatever it takes to look successful. As they inch toward pathology, this leads to narcissism and a devouring ego that cannot be satisfied. Their loved ones often become possessions that need to look good and be willing to constantly cater to the Three's excessive needs.

If they want to be with you, like Twos, your average to unhealthy Threes will mold themselves to be whatever you want. They know better than anyone how to be the great pretender. Unfortunately, whenever their carefully crafted persona slips, usually because they feel rejected or they experience failure, everyone discovers that the Three is all show and little substance. Threes on the edge often lose touch with their own ability to be vulnerable and real. Once they set their sites on conquering you, they put on quite a show, formalizing a list of ideas about how to court you—what to say, what to wear, where to take you, how to seduce you—down to the finest detail. They also want you to be a showstopper, someone that others desire because you're a real catch—attractive, smart, rich, successful, sophisticated. Threes need all eyes to be on them, and all eyes to be envious. Because image is all, Threes may also become obsessed with monetary success and often become workaholics that sacrifice their family for the almighty dollar.

Dysfunctional or pathological Threes leap into a false intimacy and become possessive, controlling, and nasty. Their massive underlying (as in hidden) insecurity leads to lies, manipulation, and a need to dominate. Because they are terrified that you'll leave them, they will project their faults onto you and constantly berate you in an attempt to wear your self-esteem into the ground. If you leave them without their permission, they often become violent and bent on revenge.

What you'll love about Threes:

- They fall for you in a big, romantic, wish-fulfilling way.
- They want to give you what you want; they'll be whatever you want.
- They see your best qualities and reinforce them regularly.
- They are typically high-energy, self-motivated go-getters destined for success.
- They set high standards for themselves and work to achieve them.
- They typically want you to feel good about yourself.
- They usually care about being attractive and usually take good care of themselves.
- They have adaptable personalities so you can take them anywhere.

What will drive you crazy about Threes:

- When they see something they want, they will do whatever it takes to get it.
- They often don't turn out to be what you thought they were.
- They can be narcissistic and their inflated ego often demands constant attention.
- They are generally ten times more focused on money and success than family.
- They may see you as a means to an end—you'll make them look good, but they are the only one who gets to shine.
- Once they feel like they have you, their dark side usually emerges.
- If pathological, they can become possessive, controlling, manipulative liars.

- When stressed, they are quite capable of being verbally, emotionally, or physically abusive.

Self-actualized Threes make an ideal mate. They have dug well into their souls to uncover the neuroses that caused all their problems. They are integrated, self-accepting, self-nourishing, and self-directed. They are confident in a good way, as in modest, unassuming, and authentic. They are also very in tune with those they love and have amazing social graces. In other words, they'll charm the pants off you and everyone else.

How Fours Fit in the Triad

Fours are located in the heart-centered, feeling, or affective triad, which means they are relatively comfortable in the realm of emotions and rely upon their sensitivity to feelings to navigate the world. Like Twos and Threes, Fours have their North Star, or locus, in the opinions of others. Because they were often neglected or emotionally abandoned as children, Fours usually require external validation that they are finally lovable. They don't feel lovable, so they often see in others what they feel they lack in themselves, which leads to one of their downfalls—a longing to have what they don't have but see in others.

As the introvert in the triad, Fours focus their attention inward and spend vast amounts of time focusing on whatever is going on in their inner self and digging around in their feelings, particularly the bittersweet or painful ones. Fours suffer from or often create inner angst and typically find ways to express it through a creative outlet that illustrates their unique talent and expresses their rich emotional life so that they will finally feel genuine and lovable.

Like their comrades in the feeling or relationship triad, Fours are focused on their image, but while Twos want to appear kind and loving, and Threes want to appear wealthy and successful, Fours want to appear unique, special, or talented. Unlike Ones, who will repress undesirable feelings, or Threes, who lose touch with their real feelings, Fours are in tune with their deepest emotions and essentially milk them in efforts to transcend them through creative expression. Their ultimate goal is to finally prove that they are truly special.

In relationships, Fours can be extraordinarily romantic—they may even write you a love poem—but they tend to focus more on romantic fantasy than they do on relating to you in the here and now. They can be incredibly sensitive to your pain, but it's ultimately all about their pain and how they can never really get over it.

What It's Like to Love a Four

Unlike Twos and Threes, ego-driven Fours are more introverted and base their self-esteem on how they feel about themselves. They prefer being unique, special, hypersensitive, and dramatic. Because they are often open, intuitive, and receptive; emotional in a passionate way; verbally or artistically expressive; as well as visionary artists and intriguing conversationalists, you are likely to be immediately drawn to Fours. Unfortunately, once you form a romantic attachment, you may find that Fours frequently suppress their best qualities and rather enjoy seeing themselves as flawed and wounded beyond repair. While Twos hide painful feelings, most Fours seem to wallow in them, as if painful feelings or memories are honor badges. And because they need to feel special, Fours often create romantic fantasies in their minds that prevent them from appreciating what is right in front of them.

According to Palmer, "A romantic Four in an empty room can get so caught up in her own reveries about 'what it felt like when he hurt me,' or 'what it will be like when he loves me,' that she can lose touch with how she feels about 'him' in the present moment."

Ego-driven and pathological Fours are easily hurt and will nurture those hurts for a long time, frequently suffering in silence. In other words, many Fours unconsciously exaggerate real feelings to achieve emotional intensity. They may live their entire lives in preparation for the real life that will commence when they meet the ideal lover. Even when mildly neurotic, they tend to focus on the negative aspects of whomever or whatever is present and fantasize about the perfection of whomever or whatever is out of reach.

Because they fear the abandonment that could result from intimacy, Fours often create long-distance or on-off relationships.

Because pathological Fours are hypersensitive and neurotically attached to negative feelings, they often sulk when they are hurt, angry, or disappointed. They will also exaggerate their emotions and create unnecessary drama that becomes wearying. A Four's deep need to feel "different" makes others feel as if the Four feels superior when in reality Fours are insecure, needy, and care too much about what others feel about them. When down, pathological Fours retreat into isolation and depression, making them difficult to be around.

What you'll love about Fours:

- They have a quiet confidence and seem to know who they are.
- They are in touch with their feelings and open up to you right away.
- They are usually sensitive, kind, caring, and actually talk about their feelings.
- They seem to understand you, and you often feel safe around them.
- They are often intelligent, artistic, creative, and interesting to talk to.
- They seem genuine and deeply caring in a philanthropic way.
- They can be the best, most sympathetic friends to those in pain.

What will drive you crazy about Fours:

- They can get so immersed in their feelings they shut you out.
- They brood when angry or hurt and wallow in past hurts.
- They pine over lost loves and often don't seem to be fully present.
- They berate themselves and have a long list of what's wrong with them.
- They may actually seem to enjoy feeling melancholy and acting melodramatic.
- They may succumb to major funks and are often susceptible to deep depressions.
- They usually have difficulty believing that you actually, truly love them.

Pathological Fours would rather uniquely feel their pain than be happy. They are constantly conflicted between compulsively longing for someone and then finding fault with him when he becomes attainable, or desperately wanting to possess a lover and then automatically rejecting him before he abandons her. In fact, terrified they will recreate the original wound, a Four will often reject someone simply to avoid the possibility of being abandoned.

Self-actualized Fours can be superior partners who can weather emotional storms and offer exceptional support and understanding to their partner. Their love for creativity, beauty, ambiance, and romance add spice to a relationship. The healthier they are the more likely they are to be intelligent, charming, fascinating, and passionate.

Chapter 18

Fives, Sixes, and Sevens in Love

When self-actualized, Fives, Sixes, and Sevens are capable of remarkable insights and revolutionary ideas, which makes them fascinating partners, parents, or children. However, because they generally rely on thinking to interpret and navigate the world, they aren't nearly as comfortable in the realm of feelings and occasionally use their brilliance to avoid emotions. And when they lose their grip, Fives, Sixes, and Sevens suffer from clouded thinking that can definitely affect their relationships.

The Thinking Triad in Relationships

All three thinking types suffer from insecurity and anxiety that began when they didn't feel adequately validated or supported as children. Each type learned to use thinking as a way to cope with anxiety, and, unfortunately, it both helps and hinders their relationships.

When suffering from relationship stress, Fives retreat to rehearse, replay, and analyze; Sixes second-guess themselves, scan for danger, and put protective defenses in place; and Sevens think about something else or take impulsive action to prevent thinking.

Fives find the outer world chaotic and frightening. They accumulate a lot of knowledge to buffer themselves from an onslaught of people and retreat to a private world to interminably mull things over. Sixes don't feel safe in their inner or their outer world so counteract their anxiety by latching onto (or rebelling against) a religious, philosophical, or corporate belief system. Sevens get so good at hiding their anxiety that most people think they've got it all—brains, charisma, sex appeal—but they are using frenetic activity to keep anxiety and insecurity at bay. Unlike Fives who go inward to escape anxiety, Sevens go outward to avoid anxiety.

How Fives Fit in the Triad

Fives are one of three types in the head-centered, thinking, or fear-based triad, which means they rely on their heads rather than their hearts or their physical bodies to interpret the world. Fives are most comfortable in the world of ideas and learned at an early age to use their intellectual abilities to make sense of what was happening to and around them. Like the other types (Six and Seven) of the thinking triad, Fives feel threatened when fearful but deal with it by withdrawing or compartmentalizing the fear. Fives rely on their ability to analyze and rethink situations and use their ability to counteract fear by accumulating enough information to get a grip on the situation, or at least to appear smarter than everyone else on the subject.

Fives are the introverted point in the thinking triad, and they exemplify this by withdrawing from whatever or whomever makes them feel afraid. Whenever a normally reclusive Five feels anxious, she will pull back into her shell, retreat to a private space, and analyze what went wrong so that she can either reorder her universe or contemplate a solution. Fives retract from anxiety by seeking solitude.

Fives need orderly, logical lives and feel most secure when they build a substantial base of knowledge. Because Fives tend to be highly intelligent, introverted loners, they are often attracted to the sciences or fields where they can retreat to a research lab or library for hours, days, or preferably weeks at a time. As introverts who prefer the intellectual realm, they strongly prefer learning about life from books over learning about life by becoming involved in messy emotional relationships. In relationships, Fives often appear withdrawn and disinterested when all they really want is a little space to be the outstanding thinkers and observers they are.

What It's Like to Love a Five

Fives are often brilliant, inventive thinkers and scholars who gravitate toward science, math, or some other intellectually challenging profession that accommodates solitude and utilizes their overactive brains. Their quiet, reserved, and centered countenance often makes them very attractive, but Fives can be powerhouses in the intellectual realm and stunted in the emotional realm. They are reluctant to form relationships and are not very good at successfully maintaining them. Fives would rather intellectualize and think through problems than get down to the nitty-gritty, messy emotions involved and battle it out. Fives may also spend so much time reading and improving their knowledge base that they tend to neglect relationships.

Intimacy feels risky to Fives, who will only cautiously enter relationships in which they are permitted sufficient time alone, independence, and autonomy. Anyone who makes demands will be kept at arm's length or avoided altogether. Generally, they choose relationships that they can wrap their mind around and justify intellectually—such as someone who meets some of their physical needs but does not require a deep emotional engagement. They don't like feeling strong emotions, and if spooked they will cower from a blossoming romance or commitment and will run away from conflict. When they are hurt, rather than express their feelings, they retreat to sort it out intellectually and will too easily chalk it up to poor communication.

What you'll love about Fives:

- They can absolutely dazzle you with their brilliance and their commitment to knowledge.
- They have a strong, quiet center that implies exceptional wisdom and confidence.
- They are often unusually rooted, structured, and serene.
- What you see is what you get; there are few surprises.
- They can be real homebodies and make few demands on your time.
- They typically have a storehouse of knowledge, are usually intellectually invigorating, and can participate in multilayered conversations.
- They can be witty and entertaining, like a normally shy and reclusive Johnny Carson when the camera is switched on.

What will drive you crazy about Fives:

- They would rather bury their heads in a book than talk, especially when you're upset.
- They may lord their intelligence over you, constantly correct you, or imply that you are dumb.
- They may think they know better than you or anyone else.
- They often become very fixed in the way they think and live life.
- They typically don't like social occasions and rarely want to do anything adventurous.
- They may suffer from a deeply ingrained fear of never having enough and can be miserly with money and affection.
- Their fantasy life can be more real to them than their life with you.
- They can demand so much privacy that you will feel neglected or even shut out.

Self-actualized Fives are also slow to connect but in a healthy way. When they decide on someone, they make long-term commitments and remain faithful and trustworthy. They may fall short when it comes to being verbally or physically expressive, but they show their undying affection and appreciation in quiet ways.

How Sixes Fit in the Triad

Sixes are in the head-centered, thinking, or fear-based triad and are the most conscious of their fears. Unlike Fives, who are introverts, and Sevens, who are extroverts, Sixes are unable to take effective action because they are literally of two minds about who they can trust, what they want to do, and what they believe in. They decide and then second-guess their decisions.

Many Sixes seek to counteract their fears by finding a strong, idealistic, or at least particularly forceful guru or system of beliefs that will make their decisions for them and help them feel secure and safe in the world. Other Sixes do the exact opposite and rebel against any and all authority. Thus, Sixes are either responding to their fear by being phobic and afraid to confront a scary world on their own, or they are counterphobic, convinced that no one knows anything more than they do and that they should protect themselves by striking first. Their thinking, like their orientation, can get caught somewhere in the middle of two opposing thoughts.

Sixes deal with their ambivalence about feeling safe in the world by overpreparing or vigilantly scanning the environment. When they feel anxious, they either look for someone smarter than them to make a decision, or they rebel against authority figures they no longer trust. Rather than confronting their fear directly, Sixes react to it by seeking a belief system they can stake their safety on or one they can completely reject.

In relationships, Sixes can be the most loyal and loving of mates, but you may have to tolerate their chronic need for reassurance, endure their doubts and fears, and remain calm when they flip into counterphobic attack mode.

What's It's Like to Love a Six

Sixes can be very engaging when you first meet them. They exude energy, and because they desire a long-term relationship and want to attract the best person possible, they are usually physically fit, well put together, cultured, witty, charming, and effusive. That being said, the primary attraction to Sixes is that they are amazingly loyal.

When they are integrated, Sixes are delightful, exceedingly committed, loyal companions. When somewhere in the middle or ego-driven stages, they're intrinsically distrustful, suspicious, a bit paranoid, and hard to pin down—appearing friendly and compliant one day and hostile and reactionary the next. The problem with ego-driven or pathological Sixes is that they lack trust in themselves or in anyone else. As such, they look for authoritative figures to give their lives direction and essentially tell them what to do. They often become so insecure that they won't make a move, or even make a single decision, without someone telling them what to do. Obviously, this quickly becomes a drag on the partner.

Sixes have a sort of dual personality. They rely on outside authority figures to help them feel safe in the world, but this often leads to feeling resentful toward them, feeling like they have had a bellyfull of being told what to do, and rebelling against those same authority figures.

Sixes view the outer world as threatening and cope by desperately seeking security at any price. They constantly scan the surroundings and what's going on with everyone to get the first jump—developing a self-defensive posture that is both off-putting and limiting.

Sixes are programmed to expect the worst, and when they slide toward pathology, their schizoid behavior sets all their worst nightmares in motion. When they are pathological, they live in a constant state of anxiety and are so insecure they need constant attention. They often become hypervigilant, controlling, and paranoid, pushing away the very people who once helped them feel secure.

What you'll love about Sixes:

- They may have a strong belief system that reinforces admirable values.
- They are usually honest, fair, reliable, hardworking, and all-around solid citizens.
- They typically take their time and check you out thoroughly before committing.
- They can be exceedingly dedicated and loyal once committed.
- You can usually depend on them to come through in emergencies.
- They can be exceedingly practical and make educated decisions only after exploring all the options and ferreting out the best one.
- They typically don't make impulsive choices or go off on wild tangents.
- They will fight for what they believe in.

What will drive you crazy about Sixes:

- They often lack enough self-confidence to make up their own minds.
- They are always second-guessing themselves and being contrary.
- They send mixed signals, keeping you off balance.
- They freak out if you break the rules or if they break the rules.
- They can be suspicious about the most insignificant things.
- They are often overprotective and don't seem to trust anyone.
- They can absolutely obsessed with obtaining external security.
- They can be reactive and defensive when in the throes of disagreement.
- They can be judgmental and bitingly sarcastic.

Self-actualized Sixes use their exceptional intellectual abilities to scan the horizon for potential partners who will share their values and commit to a mutually beneficial, long-term relationship. Once they have committed to you, they will never let you down or abandon you when you need them.

How Sevens Fit in the Triad

Sevens are in the head-centered, thinking, or fear-based triad, but unlike Sixes who are conscious of their fears but cannot decide on a clear course of action, or Eights who take their fears head on, Sevens choose impulsive activity in order not to feel their fears. Sevens are the extroverted type within this triad, and they do love activity! More than any other enneatype, Sevens typically move toward people in an attempt to charm and disarm them. They need to have people around them and plenty of activity going on when those nagging fears they dislike so much surface occasionally.

When fear, anxiety, or disagreeable emotions threaten to darken their mood, Sevens tend to engage in constant, even impulsive, activity. They keep themselves so busy that they don't have time to think. Because they are so enthusiastic, energetic, and fun-loving, Sevens attract people like flies, which means they're always able to find someone to hang out with, someone who will both distract them and show them a good time. Sevens are also always looking for people they can show a good time, and they become inveterate entertainers—they just keep dancing those blues away.

While Sixes imagine the worst, Sevens have overactive imaginations that work solely on imagining the best. Even though all three enneatypes in the thinking triad grapple with fear, Sevens are the ones who dress their fearfulness in a completely charming persona. They make use of that extroverted personality to wow everyone with their buoyant attitude, sparkling wit, and unwavering optimism.

In relationships, they are always full of ideas. But just as they flit from idea to idea, they are also prone to flit from relationship to relationship, particularly if someone is asking them to delve into painful feelings or slow down long enough to dwell on negative thoughts.

What's It's Like to Love a Seven

Sevens have impressive mental agility, which they use to dazzle and get ahead. Whatever they do, they do with panache. They are generally so upbeat and optimistic that everyone finds them wildly attractive. They also love and live for good times—they are always up for adventure, full of creative ideas, and spilling over with enthusiasm. A Seven restores your faith in life, good fortune, and possibility. They are the optimists' optimist.

The problem with Sevens is that their hyperactive, imaginative, lightening-fast minds are easily bored, creating a chronic search to find something, or someone, new. Sevens also use positive thinking—or more accurately, abolish all negative thinking—to keep their demons at bay, which means they don't like anything that makes them feel sad, bad, or angry. Sevens are often willing to do whatever it takes to suppress, deny, or sublimate any problems or hurtful feelings by thinking about something else or keeping themselves frenetically busy until you let it drop. They can also be amazingly evasive or noncommittal, and may discount the importance of your feelings.

Ultimately, despite what you think when you first meet a Seven who appears captivating and extremely interested in your stories, Sevens are usually more focused on themselves and what you can bring to them than they are in you. If they listen, which they frequently do not, they tend to listen with their heads instead of their hearts. They will analyze and intellectualize your feelings or concerns when what you wanted was for them to understand and commiserate.

Pathological Sevens often border on narcissism and have lusty appetites that lead to rash decisions and impulsive behavior. With a Seven, you may be in for a wild ride.

What you'll love about Sevens:

- They can be full of vitality, have a great sense of humor, and are sexy.
- They're usually open-minded, spontaneous, playful, and positive.
- They always have great ideas about what to do and where to go.
- They are rarely boring, frequently hilarious, and tell great stories.
- They absolutely believe that your future is bright and know how to promote you.

- They have unique, fun ideas and make every day an adventure.
- They are enthusiastic about life and embrace change.
- They are usually very accomplished, confident, and attractive on many levels.

What will drive you crazy about Sevens:

- They definitely like to keep their options open.
- They tend to make promises they may or may not be able to keep.
- They may get antsy and constantly seek fresh stimulation, that is, someone new.
- They rarely slow down for a long chat or a rest.
- They really don't want anyone feeling sad for any reason.
- They typically would rather leave you than argue with you.
- They usually think far more about their own needs than yours.
- It's all them, all the time; and all action all the time.

Self-actualized Sevens are enthusiastic, accomplished, uninhibited, and just a whole lot of fun. Plus, they really are interested in you and will use their high-energy joie de vivre to liven up your life and help you become the best you can be.

Chapter 19

Eights, Nines, and Ones in Love

Eights, Nines, and Ones all rely on their gut instincts or physical wisdom to navigate the world. When they've got it all together, they are great, responsible, dedicated citizens who are often wise leaders. Unfortunately, when their defense systems fall apart, they charge through the world like bulls in china shops intimidating everyone (Eights), disassociate from their feelings and ignore the world (Nines), or become self-righteous fundamentalists bent on global conformance (Ones).

The Gut or Physical Triad in Relationships

For whatever reason, these three types in early childhood all felt a need to establish firm personal boundaries that either kept out external or internal aggressors or fenced them in. Eights use a frontal attack to aggressively tear down external boundaries; Ones form a punishing superego and then use strict rules and judgmental, pious attitudes to fence themselves into narrow corners and to reject others; and Nines are so afraid of conflict they wall off the outer world and ignore their inner world.

Each of the enneatypes in the physical triad erases their true self and then finds ways to compensate for it. Eights overreact in volume and energy by almost literally shouting, "I am here and I count!" When Ones realize they have surrendered huge parts of their selves, they overidentify with a tradition or principle or system and then push that system on themselves and others. Nines willingly surrender themselves and then become angry that they've done so. But rather than openly claiming their anger, they act out this anger by either passive-aggressively projecting it onto others or by turning it in on themselves through depression.

How Eights Fit in the Triad

Eights are in the physical, gut, or effective triad, which means they rely on their gut instincts, belly wisdom, and action in the physical world to navigate life. Eights are the extroverted enneatype within this triad, which means they expend their energy outward and are more focused than the other two enneatypes on action in the outer world.

FACT

All three enneatypes in this triad have anger issues and tend to operate from and rely upon their gut instincts. They may also exhibit a shared weakness in the thinking department, specifically a tendency, when dysfunctional, to think in black and white.

Eights' thought patterns are distorted by their desire to appear strong. In actuality, all three types in this triad are often out of touch with their real feelings. Eights are too busy exerting externalized anger to identify or claim their inner concern that they might be vulnerable.

Eights act out their anger—they directly express their anger by being forthright and aggressive—because they have an unconscious belief that the world is not quite fair and it is their responsibility to bring justice. They like appearing strong, tough, rude, and crude. Eights like feeling powerful and will spend a lot of energy chasing fame and fortune and suppressing their vulnerable side. They are not afraid to be intimidating, arrogant, and domineering. They love a fight, and they love to win a fight, which means they will pound their fists against their chests in a literal and metaphorical sense. If someone goes up against an Eight, they had best be well prepared for battle. Eights see the world as a battleground—a war—and they will pulverize an opponent without a second's thought because all is fair in war.

Eights are the doers and shakers who are very likely to lead an active and successful life. They have a burning desire to win over or dominate anyone who threatens their sense of security, which can quickly become very sticky in personal relationships.

What It's Like to Love an Eight

Eights typically have a real lust for life that can be intoxicating. They often come on like gangbusters, sweeping you off your feet with romantic gestures and over-the-top courting. They will woo you with champagne and caviar, and they will attempt to give you the best nights of sexual fulfillment you could ever imagine. You will be so attracted to their life force, magnetism, and dynamic, larger-than-life persona that you'll fall under their spell and think you've gone to heaven.

Unfortunately, like all people, Eights are also complicated souls who, if you're lucky, harbor a tender heart under the blustery, controlling, dominating, overbearing personality that ultimately emerges. The problem is that once you surrender to their dominion, particularly if they are ego-driven or pathological, they often claim the right to determine your future.

If you have given your heart to wounded Dominator and find you want it back, a dysfunctional Eight may hunt you down and attempt to put your heart permanently under lock and key. In other words, once you hand your life over to a pathological Eight they often consider you a possession, and they don't handle betrayal well.

Eights can be compared to mafia dons, forceful politicians, top-dollar lawyers, and corporate moguls who wield power for fun. They may earn a lot of money and give you a lavish lifestyle, but they are usually also so obsessed with power that they will spend most of their time and energy in single-minded pursuit of it. As a life partner of an ego-driven, compulsive Eight, you can go along for the ride as long as you don't make many demands and keep your mouth shut. However, if you ruffle their feathers, they are prone to blame you for all their problems and will do their best to make your life miserable.

Pathological Eights unfortunately often become absolute tyrants who will put you in a pumpkin shell, throw away the key, and then batter you with words or fists at their whim. They expect total obedience, and they are capable of being ruthless, vengeful, and violent when they feel betrayed. The worst, most corrupted, most completely disintegrated Eights are megalomaniacs fully capable of mass murder.

Evolved or self-actualized Eights, on the other hand, are larger than life in the best ways. They are incredibly energetic and full of life. They are strong, confident, self-possessed souls who can open their hearts and minds to others. They protect the ones they love and can be gentle, tender, affectionate partners, parents, and friends.

What you'll love about Eights:

- They typically know what they want and go after it with gusto and style.
- They have a commanding presence and always make an impression.
- They are often strong, full of vitality, and always on the go.
- They can be sophisticated, urbane, powerful, and ambitious.

- They may exude courage and promise to always defend you and protect you.
- They usually have lucrative jobs, big houses, and fancy cars.
- They can be very generous and buy expensive presents.
- They love to make you feel like you can do anything.

What will drive you crazy about Eights:

- They are afraid to show any vulnerability and rarely tell you what they really think or feel.
- They rarely let down their guard or show any tenderness.
- They usually think they always know more than anyone else.
- They may resort to bullying you into doing what they want.
- They may try to rule over you with an iron hand.
- They are sometimes intolerant, controlling, manipulative, argumentative, and cruel.
- They can be impulsive, reactionary, and ruthless under stress.
- They appear to love getting angry and often equate it with love.
- If you leave a pathological Eight, he or she may become punitive and even violent.

Self-actualized Eights are virtually heroes. They have the same powerful, magnetic force that other Eights possess, but they use it as a force for good. They are the natural leaders who love people and want to use their ability to inspire others to help them achieve their maximum possibility. They are well worth admiration, but they may also be so busy being a hero that they don't have much time for you.

How Nines Fit in the Triad

Nines are in the central position of the physical triad. They are highly intuitive and rely on their gut instincts but are susceptible to confusion or a lack of grounding. While Eights are extroverted and Ones introverted, Nines frequently blend in the background or merge with others, such as a spouse, a boss, or a close-knit group or team.

Like Eights and Ones, Nines rely on their intensified ability to sniff out or sense what is going on with others. They are focused on fulfilling their own physical and emotional needs and will often use their gut instinct to discern how they can manipulate things in their favor. They all struggle with anger, but unlike Eights, who are aggressive, Nines are typically passive-aggressive. They may take care of their physical selves, but they tend to sublimate or surrender their emotional needs.

Nines find their own anger so threatening that they bury it somewhere deep inside and frequently adopt a pleasing and passive exterior personality. Even when it's clear that they are mad, they deny feeling angry or even negative about anything or anyone. However, when pushed, Nines may eventually explode. But mostly they go through life making their feelings or their needs secondary to whomever they love or need in their lives. While they may look really good in the beginning stages of a relationship, their passivity has real potential to become an albatross around your neck.

What It's Like to Love a Nine

In some ways, Nines seem like the little Buddhas of the Enneagram—they can be virtually unflappable, emotionally detached, and absolutely nonconfrontational. And they are all about peace and love. When you first meet a Nine, you'll likely be enchanted by her easy-going, go-with-the-flow personality. You'll marvel at her laissez-faire attitude and ability to seem so calmly detached from trauma or drama. She'll sit down beside you, wrap a loving arm around you, and listen to every syllable you utter. You'll feel understood, appreciated, nurtured, and admired by what appears to be the most genuinely loving person on the planet.

Once they are embedded in a relationship, Nines tend to bend to your needs, wishes, desires, schedule, lifestyle, and decisions, thereby surrendering huge chunks of themselves.

Many Nines will truly merge into a relationship and submerge their essence, laying aside anything that threatens the union. What you once saw as Buddhalike detachment now feels like a selfish, nonresponsive lack of engagement that can leave you feeling abandoned.

For the sake of peace, Nines seem willing to sell their soul in a heartbeat. They want the perfect union—to be one with you and with the world—and they view conflict as upsetting, so they avoid conflict at all costs. This may sound inviting to some, but unless you want an angry passive/aggressive partner, you may want to steer clear of pathological Nines.

Unfortunately, ego-driven Nines sliding toward disintegration have surrendered so much of themselves that they don't remember their likes or dislikes, wants, or needs. When asked to make a choice, they will stall until they can figure out what you want and then present it as their own idea. As things worsen and they realize that they buried their own potential, they often cope by blaming their partner. Because they are still rarely capable of outright confrontation, they rebel in annoying passive-aggressive ways—denying that they are angry with you but stubbornly digging in their heels, procrastinating, or simply ignoring you when you ask them simple questions. Pathological Nines withdraw so far into their shell that they can ultimately completely disassociate from their feelings.

What you'll love about Nines:

- They are usually friendly from the get-go, warm, sensitive, and sweet.
- They often have a centered, wise, comforting presence that makes you feel safe.
- They genuinely want to know all about you and listen to everything you say.
- They act as if you are the cat's pajamas and make you feel special.
- They'll put your needs above their own, which feels good for a while.
- They are so loving, they look like they'll make great parents.
- They are usually nonjudgmental diplomatic, kind, and highly sociable.
- They create a very peaceful, harmonious life where everything is pleasing.

- They see all sides of an argument and rarely take sides or chastise anyone.

What will drive you crazy about Nines:

- They may have relinquished any desires they might have had.
- They often have no real sense of identity beyond pleasing others.
- They rarely express any preferences and won't make choices, such as what flavor of ice cream they want.
- They regularly refuse to discuss anything remotely negative or painful.
- They will occasionally dig in their heels, clam up, and withdraw without explanation.
- They move at their own very slow pace, and no amount of pleading will help.
- They are usually trying so hard to please everyone that they please no one.
- They may resort to passive aggression to manipulate you.
- They may withdraw for no reason and become nonresponsive for long periods of time.
- They seem to swing from acting as if they live in an enchanted fairyland to retreating from reality entirely.

Self-actualized Nines have developed a strong sense of self that allows them the level of comfort and self-possession needed to form healthy unions. They can be in relationships and yet independent. In fact, the most integrated, evolved Nines are the epitome of how it should function when two people come together and are wholly together and yet separate individuals.

How Ones Fit in the Triad

Ones belong to the physical, or anger, triad, which means they rely primarily on their physical instincts, gut reactions, or belly wisdom to navigate the world. Like the other types within this triad (Eights and Nines), Ones tend to be somewhat flawed in the thinking department. Ego-driven and pathological Ones typically limit the amount of original thinking they do by adopting a religious or moral creed that does their thinking for them.

Ones will often relinquish their own sense of self in order to perfectly conform to an idea, principle, or tradition. Many develop judgmental attitudes and moral strictures to implement and reinforce their imported self—the self they formed to belong to a philosophical, religious, professional, or corporate theology. They erase their own preferences by criticizing themselves according to the norms of the ideal or rules of that tradition or principle.

Like the other members of the anger triad, Ones have a baseline of low-level anger that they usually express through well-intentioned, but sometimes abrasive, criticism of others who they feel don't measure up to their moral standards.

FACT

Like Eights and Nines, Ones erased their own authentic self and adjusted their needs in order to survive. While Eights fight to get their own way and Nines quietly surrender their life without getting their way, Ones typically insist on implementing the rules that they have chosen to follow and then make what they think is their way the only way.

Integrated Ones are altruistic, genuinely loving, evangelists that inspire the world; pathological Ones often become both hypercritical and hypocritical tyrants.

What It's Like to Love a One

Ones play an important role in society as religious or philosophical leaders, and they have a charismatic appeal as very impressive crusaders—for truth, justice, freedom, individual rights, or religious beliefs. However, in one-on-one relationships, Ones create a challenge. When you see them championing a high-minded, principled belief system or worthwhile cause, they appear caring, giving, generous, unselfish, and inspirational. Later, you realize that they often value the cause above themselves or anyone else and will choose the cause over you almost every time.

Neurotic or pathological Ones can become so zealous they sell their own souls to the imagined path of righteousness. This tendency to idealize outward religions, causes, or means of consciousness makes them feel inadequate and view others as in need of redemption. They can become preachy, judgmental, and obsessed.

Ones learn to repress what they consider their dark emotions and use sublimation to rationalize their quest. They often adopt a black-and-white view of the world and act as if they know better than anyone else how one should behave. Their high standards can become oppressive, and the rigid way they view the world soon becomes tiresome. Ego-driven Ones are the "should" people who are always telling others what they should or should not be doing. The fact is they are die-hard perfectionists who deflect the anger they feel toward themselves for falling short of their own high standards by projecting those same standards onto others, and they then berate others when they fail to meet those standards.

Unhealthy Ones often lock themselves—and their friends, family, and coworkers—into adhering to a strict moral code. Instead of being fair, they become intolerant, cruel, controlling, and obnoxious. Even though they become angry with themselves and others for any failure to obey their narrowly defined code of conduct, when they reach the latter stages of disintegration they may do the unthinkable—hypocritically breach all the rules of propriety they spent their lives upholding.

What you'll love about Ones:

- They can be passionate about, and champion, worthwhile causes.
- They are often cool, calm, collected, and steered by strong values.
- Very little seems to ruffle their feathers or cause anger.
- They usually create a smooth and orderly environment.
- They're typically committed to living a very principled life.
- They are very good at considering various opinions and making a fair evaluation.
- They are usually strong, solid citizens, extremely predictable and reliable.
- They often make kind, loving, and dedicated partners and parents.

What will drive you crazy about Ones:

- They may have a rigid belief system, with rigid rules they feel compelled to follow.
- They may suppress their feelings or desires and seem almost robotic.
- They can be harshly judgmental in a strict or puritanical manner.
- They seem to deny themselves joy, exuberance, and lust.
- They frequently turn into perfectionists with high expectations.
- They may punish themselves, and everyone else, for perceived transgressions.
- They seem to be constantly at war with themselves.
- They can become controlling, hypercritical zealots.
- They will refuse to argue but harbor a palpable, cold anger.

Self-actualized Ones are able to cherish, respect, and honor moral values while accepting human fallibility. Integrated Ones are mature souls who are generally more wise, caring, and balanced than any other enneatype. They live their lives according to standards that include fidelity, honesty, and charity, and they inspire others through example rather than imposing expectations.

Chapter 20

The Enneatypes at Home

Since your primary or core personality is formed at home, knowing more about how you might have experienced your parents, as well as how your personality unfolded as a child, will help you gain a more comprehensive picture of your own adult personality. You may be able to easily spot your enneatype among the following descriptions. (If not, the test in Chapter 1 is sure to help you identify your real enneatype.) You may also gain important insights into parenting issues you face as well as another window into understanding and nurturing your children.

The Two Parent

Twos make attentive parents. If they are healthy, they nurture, encourage, and validate their children; if they are pathological, they smother and control their children. If you have a self-actualized Two parent, you are one lucky child. This parent sees your unique qualities and nurtures and supports your development by empowering you. If you have a pathological Two parent, you are not so lucky. This parent may say his or her world revolves around you, but you are probably all too aware that this parent is self-absorbed and needy. A pathological Two parent may undermine your self-confidence and hold onto you tightly, discouraging any signs of independence. These parents usually have rigid rules for behavior and invade your privacy on a regular basis. Some Two parents are so busy fulfilling needs at church, school, or work that they neglect their children. Many Two parents require constant reassurance that they are loving parents—even if they're not.

The Two Child

Two children may seem like model children—well behaved, polite, easygoing, caring, and outgoing. They usually like being around other children and get very attached to their friends. You might notice them being particularly sensitive to everyone else's feelings or needs, always wanting to make someone happy, or wanting to rescue animals and insects They are usually conscientious students who want to please both you and the teacher, and they'll generally abide by the rules.

How to nurture a Two child: Appreciate everything she does for you or others, but rather than reward her or fuss too much, encourage her to develop her own interests and to focus attention on herself. Make sure she knows that expressions of anger will not lead to rejection. Offer her lots of opportunities to make decisions and be patient until she does. To help her develop a strong sense of self, praise her when she does something well.

Some behavioral problems that may indicate possible danger ahead when it comes to raising Two children:

- If anyone criticizes them, they may blow it out of proportion and take it as personal rejection.
- They are so convinced they have to be good children that they may repress any feelings of anger, sadness, or frustration.
- They may feel more anxious than they reveal and have sleeping or eating problems.
- They may feel like they're the boss and order everyone around.
- They may get so used to fading into the background that they get confused about their own likes, dislikes, wants, or needs.
- They may want so desperately to be popular that they feel like they have to do what everybody else is doing to fit in.

Two children are usually highly sensitive, caring children who see a need in their primary family environment that they attempt to fill. They empower themselves by seeing themselves as intrinsic to the well-being of those they love, and their identity gets locked into being the ultimate people pleaser: someone who is willing to sacrifice her own needs for the sake of others. Two children tend to base their whole image of themselves on how well they can serve others and often need help refocusing their energy on themselves so that they develop an integrated sense of self based on who they are, what they need, and what they want for themselves.

The Three Parent

Ego-driven Three parents often have inflated egos that require constant shoring up. They often have carefully crafted personas of being extremely successful and admirable. Yet they give too much credence to how people view them, which means they may put undue pressure on their children to be overachievers, athletic or academic stars, or simply to look better than anyone else. Consciously or unconsciously, Three parents may care more about image than substance—wanting their children to reflect well on them and often entirely miss seeing, validating, or encouraging their children's real talents or essence. Three parents may have a fabulously unique child that they try to mold into a successful image scripted by someone else, often someone they don't even know. These parents may end up burying what is best in their child, or creating a child that never feels good enough.

The Three Child

Three children began life very in tune with the expectations of their parents, so they grow up attempting to fulfill their parents' need to look good by overachieving or excelling at something. They often develop an early drive to develop a strong, assertive, hard-working persona based on what they can do that makes others look up to them. Three children connect what they can achieve to how much their parents, or other authority figures, love them.

They are frequently precocious children who dazzle you with their brilliance, star power, or charisma. They have boundless energy and almost careen off the walls when they are excited, which is often. They can get a bit obsessed about doing well in school and go out of their way to impress their teacher or gain special favors. They excel at challenges and love it when you—and everyone else—applaud or tell them they were the best. They are smooth talkers who can convince their friends to do almost anything. They tend to fuss over their appearance and want to have the latest toys or gadgets.

How to nurture a Three child: Reassure him that you love him for who he is, not what he does or how good his grades are. Encourage him to spend more time just hanging out and having fun. Praise him when he does something out of the goodness of his heart rather than something done to impress. Help him keep his dreams and expectations grounded, and help him ease up on being outwardly directed by developing an inner life—art and drama, for example, would be nourishing.

Some behavioral problems that may indicate possible danger ahead when it comes to raising Three children:

- Their self-esteem is based on their accomplishments.
- They can be overly competitive and get angry if they don't win.
- They are often status conscious at an early age and worry too much about what other kids will think about the way they dress, what they have or don't have, or who they hang out with.
- They may tell lies or exaggerate to make themselves look good.
- They can become overly aggressive and get angry if they don't get what they want.
- They may alter their appearance or their behavior to fit in with a crowd.
- They may have difficulty relaxing, winding down at night, or sleeping.

Rather than developing according to who they are, Three children become identified with an image of an overachiever, a star, or a precocious child destined for success. They develop ego needs that are only satisfied by an external sign that they are the best, the brightest, or the richest person they know. They may become dependent on others to view them as the king of the hill.

The Four Parent

If you had a healthy Four parent, you probably had a great childhood. An integrated, self-actualized Four parent likely provided an inspiring and nourishing home filled with art, beauty, and creativity and would have celebrated your uniqueness and encouraged creative expression. An ego-driven or pathological Four parent, on the other hand, may have been fun occasionally but may also have been self-absorbed, pessimistic, melancholic, or depressed. The pathological Four parent may seem preoccupied and focused more about what happened in the past than on what was occurring in the present or taking action to improve the family's lifestyle. When caught in the throes of their melancholy, Four parents may be so unguarded that the intensity of their emotions leaves the child feeling overwhelmed, nervous, and inadequate when it comes to understanding what is happening or why her parent is so emotional.

The Four Child

Four children have fantastic imaginations and love to play dress-up, particularly if they make up the game or create the story. They can be bright, sensitive, emotional children who can be delightful one minute and maddening the next. They tend to take life seriously and seem older than their age, particularly when they brood or proclaim that life bores them. They can be very shy and spend a lot of time in their room. They may spend too much time daydreaming and have trouble staying focused on what's happening in the real world. They are usually more introverted than most children and will withdraw occasionally just to be alone. The rich imagination of the Fours enables them to appreciate artistic endeavors. The symbolic nature of art gives them a place to express their intense emotions safely.

How to nurture a Four child: Even if her intense feelings seem out of proportion, encourage rather than dismiss the expression of them. Reassure her regularly that you understand and care about how she feels. Keep in mind that she is usually introverted and needs time alone to rejuvenate. Help her stay in the present, and encourage her to focus some of her emotional intensity outward; if she falls into a funk, urge her to choose a course of action and take it.

Some behavioral problems that may indicate possible danger ahead when it comes to raising Four children:

- They may spend too much time brooding, feeling sad or sorry for themselves.
- They may think they're special one minute and the lowest form of life the next.

- They would rather fantasize about their failures and woes than participate in daily life.
- They are often so sensitive they overact when hurt and then nurse past hurts for a long time.
- If you get angry with them, they think it means you don't love them anymore.
- When they do something wrong, they feel like they're complete losers.
- When they get angry, they blame themselves and get depressed instead of openly expressing their anger.
- They sometimes need a lot of emotional pampering.

Four children are usually overly identified with their feelings. If they feel rejected by either parent, they tend to blame themselves and often come to view themselves as flawed, broken, or even unlovable. Many cope by seeing themselves as special, unique, or as someone who feels more deeply than others and is thus separate from them. Unlike Two children who will hide their sadness or pain, Four children often visibly suffer, either by complaining of aches and pains, having stomachaches, or moping around. They are in danger of overidentifying with their sadness, melancholy, or image of themselves as broken in some permanent way. Paradoxically, their image of themselves as defective can make them feel a strong sense of entitlement and lead them to think that their suffering makes them special so they deserve special treatment.

The Five Parent

The chief complaint you may have about Five parents is that they don't seem very interested in you. Many Five parents are naturally reclusive and like to be alone; they might be surprised to hear you complain about their being absent. They often create a world of their own, whether it's spending the majority of their time in a library or science lab conducting research or earning yet another college degree. Fives may have trouble identifying with small children, but often engage with their children when the children become teenagers and can mentally challenge the Five parent. Five parents usually appear very rational and can feel somewhat detached, which can leave a child feeling as if he isn't important enough to be interesting to his parent.

The Five Child

Five children are either naturally reticent or they construct boundaries to ward off what they feel are overbearing parents. Five children are usually intelligent, imaginative, and so self-sufficient and contained that they can be overlooked. They rarely demand attention and often rebuff attention, preferring to retreat to their room to think things over in private.

How to nurture a Five child: Feed his thirst for intellectual stimulation, but provide balance by encouraging physical activity and socializing. Reassure him that there is always enough love, money, or security to meet his needs. Foster his imagination. Model healthy emotional interchanges so that he feels more comfortable with his own emotions. Provide him with a sanctuary and give him the space he needs to think things over, and encourage him to use his wit to lighten things up.

Some behavioral problems that may indicate possible danger ahead when it comes to raising Five children:

- They spend too much time alone and rarely want to socialize with their peers.
- They seem completely detached from their feelings and rarely express anger or frustration.
- They can be very secretive or become agitated and defensive when asked simple questions.
- They complain of being tired and don't want to play with their friends because they are "too tired."
- They hoard their allowances and rarely treat themselves.

- They insist they know more than you do or belittle your intelligence.
- The expression of negative emotions makes them anxious, fearful, or withdrawn.

Five children can also be model children in that they rarely make demands and rarely argue. Instead, they will withdraw into whatever offers them an intellectual outlet for their emotions. While a gregarious parent may unconsciously invade a Five child's boundaries, it is important to encourage the child to engage with family and friends, as well as participate in life beyond the confines of her room. Five children rarely need extra mental stimulation, but they often need to be reminded to play or to openly express their feelings.

The Six Parent

Even though Sixes are usually incredibly devoted and loyal parents, how they parent will depend on which kind of Six parent you have: phobic or counterphobic. A phobic parent is likely to project fear onto his children and give them the impression that the world's one superdangerous place. Hopefully, this Six parent will be evolved enough to limit cautionary tales to a minimum and would teach his children how to scan the environment for helpful rather than dangerous situations or opportunities. If the Six parent is counterphobic, she may live dangerously, break societal rules, and encourage rebellion and dissent. Healthy Six parents would show their children how to use observation and discernment to find people and situations they could trust in and build relationships with.

The Six Child

Because they often have a true flip side to their personality, Six children can be the most complex types in the Enneagram. Six children are often either insecure, nervous and focused on everything that could possibly go wrong, or they are supremely confident that they are right and you are wrong and not afraid to loudly tell you so. They can flip back and forth or linger in one or the other mindset forever.

When they are afraid, Six children may compile a list of safety precautions and drive you crazy with a string of what ifs. Or they may grit their teeth and face the challenge head on, taking risks that will make you squirm. They often manage to confuse themselves by overthinking, but if you make a suggestion and they feel restricted, they may rebel for the sake of rebelling.

How to nurture a Six child: Provide a safe, sane, quiet, and secure environment. Be consistent with expectations and let her know what to expect ahead of time. Get her out of her head and into her body, and encourage her to expand her idea of herself. Help her find balance and become more comfortable with her emotions. Help her quell her anxiety from the inside out, and point out her competencies and achievements so she develops the ability to trust she will make it in the world.

Some behavioral problems that may indicate possible danger ahead when it comes to raising Six children:

- Even the simplest decisions seem to be too much for them.
- They may develop nervous habits like biting their nails or twisting their hair.
- They can be fearful to the point of not wanting to participate in normal activities.
- They may break all the rules and say things to shock or anger you.
- They refuse to do their normal chores and become hostile when asked about them.
- They will often get angry if asked to do things that frighten them.
- They are clearly anxious, fearful, or nervous about what could happen.
- Their anxiety is out of proportion to what is occurring.

Six children felt unsafe in their early environments and coped by watching what happens like a hawk and anticipating worst-case scenarios. They are the worrywarts who will have a hundred reasons why they shouldn't go to summer camp. Or, if they are fighting rather than succumbing to their fears, they may be daredevils who indulge in risky behavior to prove to themselves and others that they aren't afraid. A Six child needs at least one, and preferably two, steadying parents who can help the sensitive Six overcome her fears and truly blossom.

The Seven Parent

Seven parents can be a wild ride, filled with adventure, joviality, and excitement. Although they can be a little self-absorbed, Seven parents are also a lot of fun. They always have fresh ideas and are big on activity. They usually have a cast of interesting characters as friends who will liven up your life. Sevens are also epicures, so their children will probably be exposed to eclectic tastes and learn to enjoy exotic food. The downside to Seven parents is that they don't like complaining or feeling angry or sad, so they often send a blatant message that all negative feelings must be banished. Some Seven parents pay little attention to their children, aren't particularly sensitive to what's going on with them, and can be impatient and demanding.

The Seven Child

Seven children are frequently lively, adventuresome, sociable, dynamic, and talented. They can be truly vivacious, witty, open-minded, and happy. When offered a chance to learn something new, they bring curiosity and enthusiasm to the table, and they are generally comfortable around all kinds of people in all kinds of situations. On the other hand, Seven children may be counteracting feelings of being in unstable environments or having unpredictable parents by keeping themselves too busy to notice or creating a fantasy that portrays their lives as entirely happy. They may also be far more afraid than they ever appear and may use excess activity, food, or drugs to mask it.

How to nurture a Seven child: Encourage his interests, but also encourage him to stick with a few interests rather than abandon them quickly. Let him know it's okay to feel sad and that the expression of sad or angry feelings helps them dissipate while pushing them out of his mind prevents resolution. Teach him how to enjoy his alone time. Plan exciting vacations or miniadventures to keep his lightening-quick mind stimulated. Listen to his stories, and encourage him to channel his energy into good works.

Some behavioral problems that may indicate possible danger ahead when it comes to raising Seven children:

- Even when it's obvious they're hurt, sad, or angry, they often refuse to acknowledge it, talk about, or express it in any way.
- They can become hyperactive when stressed, or use frenetic activity to distract themselves from important feelings.
- They have great difficulty focusing on their schoolwork long enough to complete homework assignments.
- They flit like butterflies from hobby to hobby or passion to passion without giving anything a real chance.
- They seem to crave constant activity or want to be entertained all the time—they rarely take time just to relax or be reflective in any way.
- They make the same bad choices over and over without seeming to grasp the part they play when it turns out badly.
- They are clearly masking pain when overindulging in activity, food, alcohol, or drugs.

Seven children can be very spontaneous, fun loving, adventuresome, and creative. Give them a challenge and they are likely to find a solution that surprises and delights you. They generally feel good about themselves and flourish in school, but they need constant stimulation, challenges, and new experiences. A savvy parent will encourage a Seven child to also claim her sadness, or at least be willing to slow down the pace and focus long enough to figure out if what she is doing is best for her or if she is just trying to distract herself.

The Eight Parent

Self-actualized Eight parents are strong, confident, protective, and nurturing. They model plenty of admirable qualities, including the ability to be assertive and to go after what you want. If they are ego-driven Eights, these parents can be overbearing and controlling. Eights have been little adults for so long they often forget how it feels to be a vulnerable child. Because they are high energy and usually focused on the acquisition of power, Eight parents may not pay enough attention to their children, or they may unload pent-up frustrations by shouting or otherwise intimidating them.

The Eight Child

Eight children often feel as if the world is not a safe place and that everyone is exploited, manipulated, or mistreated. As such, they usually identify with someone they see as particularly forceful or strong enough to counter the dangers. If they have a benevolent yet powerful role model, they are usually gentle souls who rescue and protect the vulnerable, be it smaller children, pets, or even insects. If they have a brutal, aggressive, or belligerent role model, they can become bullies who may still protect others but often through the threat of strong-arm tactics. Eight children are bursting with energy and typically develop a lust for power that energizes them. When feeling hyperactive, they metaphorically bounce off the walls. Eight children often require patience and lessons on restraint. They need consistency and calm, rational responses to their outbursts or attempts to control. They can have extremely rigid ideas about what they want to do and what they absolutely won't do. Underneath this bravado you often find a child who is steeling himself against an unsafe world and fighting back the only way he knows how.

How to nurture an Eight child: Help her feel safe in the world and reassure her that she can count on you for protection and stability. Help her access her softer side and teach her the benefits of benevolence. Listen when she expresses her feelings of being undermined or disrespected. Show her ways to contain her strength by gentle rather than overt assertion, and provide structured activities that engage her curiosity and her mind.

Some behavioral problems that may indicate possible danger ahead when it comes to raising Eight children:

- They rarely show vulnerability or sensitivity to others.
- They can be rebellious, contentious, demanding, and physically intimidating.
- They have great difficulty sitting still long enough to focus on homework and rarely finish expected tasks without an unpleasant power play.
- If they feel ignored or misunderstood, they react by throwing a temper tantrum or exploding in an angry outburst that could be a verbal barrage or a physical lashing out.
- They walk around with a combative attitude and consequently get into physical or verbal fights at school.
- They constantly defy authority and think they know better than school administrators.

Healthy Eight children are bursting with energy, but they channel it in positive ways. Wise parents of Eight children will give them a list of chores they will enjoy doing and can take pride in doing well, and encourage them to participate in physical activities that will keep them busy and burn off unspent energy. Eight children need a safe, stimulating, and stable family environment.

The Nine Parent

Nine parents are usually so good at reading others that they can usually connect with their children on their own level. If they are integrated, Nine parents are able to maintain their own boundaries and encourage their children's interests. If they are ego-driven or pathological, Nine parents tend to merge inappropriately and often fail to establish firm boundaries. Children may soon learn that they can manipulate an unhealthy Nine parent, who is often all too willing to surrender her needs to those of her children. Nine parents may create an easygoing household, but they also fail to teach their children that it's fine to have needs and wants and okay to go about getting them fulfilled. Unfortunately, dysfunctional Nine parents model indecisiveness, passivity, and inertia.

The Nine Child

Next to Seven children, Nine children often appear to be the happiest, or at least the most content, children on the planet. When it comes to sunny dispositions, they are right up there. They are typically very easygoing, pleasant children who prefer peaceful, quiet, orderly, harmonious family life when everyone gets along and no one gets angry or upset. Nine children find it difficult to say anything that they think will make someone unhappy, so they sometimes say things they don't really feel or think just to keep that sacred peace. Eventually, they lose bits and pieces of themselves and may have difficulty forming a solid image of who they are. If they never express anger or frustration, they may reach a breaking point when it all spills out unexpectedly and explosively. Nine children can become so passive and low energy they move slowly through life as if weights were attached to their feet.

How to nurture a Nine child: Keep the focus on him—what he wants to do, what he likes, and what he feels—and let him know he is important and that what he wants or needs is important. Teach him how to express disappointment, hurt, or anger constructively before it reaches a critical level. Let him be in the limelight more often. Make sure he doesn't hide in corners and speaks up for himself when it's needed, and let him know he can say whatever he wants and you won't stop loving him.

Some behavioral problems that may indicate possible danger ahead when it comes to raising Nine children:

- They show little initiative and little interest in stimulating activities.
- They have trouble making even simple decisions.
- They can be extremely stubborn and resistant to new ideas.
- They look sad or upset yet keep a smile plastered on their face.
- They prefer to sit back and watch what happens rather than actively participate.

Nine children may need help narrowing down choices or clarifying what they want or need. While they are, in fact, sweet, you may want to encourage them to add a little spice to their personality.

The One Parent

Self-actualized One parents are ideal in a multitude of ways—they are committed to each other, to the marriage, to the children, and to their values. They treat their children with respect and have reasonable expectations for them. They are able to help their children form original ideas yet feel comfortable within their community. Ego-driven One parents, on the other hand, can be perfectionists who have very high expectations and impose them on their children. They may control the child's every move, giving them the impression they can't do anything right on their own or, worse yet, that there is something inherently wrong with them. Pathological One parents can be exceedingly rigid, controlling, and hypercritical. They may have a belief system that they force upon the children, and they may punish the children if they breach any of the rules, even if the rules don't make any real sense. They may use guilt as a way to keep their children in line.

The One Child

One children are usually well behaved, self-sufficient, orderly, organized, principled, and do things without their parents even having to ask. They are usually bright children who have a game plan for their lives and pretty much keep themselves on course. However, they can also be nervous, anxious, timid, rigid, and regimented. They typically internalize the rules and regulations of their parents' religion or ideology and punish themselves if they do something wrong. They may set very high standards for themselves and drive themselves, and everyone around them, crazy trying to achieve them. They may take everything too seriously, setting impossible standards. It's important to help One children lighten up and act like the children they are. You can spot the One children that are working too hard—they are desperately trying to avoid both external and internal criticism, that is, they have an obsessive need to appear as if everything they do or say is perfect.

How to nurture a One child: Teach her to lighten up, encourage her playfulness, and reassure her that it's okay to step over a few lines or screw up once in a while. Help her express herself through art or music. Reassure her that everyone stumbles once in a while. Teach her the art of moderation; praise her for things she does well, and try not to criticize her (she does enough of that to herself). Take the focus off competition and encourage her to do things just because they're fun. And help her learn to make decisions based on what she really wants instead of what she thinks she should want.

Some behavioral problems that may indicate possible danger ahead when it comes to raising One children:

- They may punish themselves if they make even a simple mistake.
- They often have rigid ways of doing things that they refuse to alter.
- They criticize other children for petty reasons.
- They order other children around, and occasionally do the same to their parents.
- They think they are the only ones who know how to do something right.
- They put down their parents for failing to meet an arbitrary standard.
- They latch onto a belief system and rigidly adhere to its principles.
- They have difficulty letting their hair down, being silly, or simply having fun.
- They can be extremely serious at a young age.

One children usually have a narrow view of themselves and really benefit from encouragement to broaden their horizons. The last thing they need is highly structured lives or to be criticized—they'll do enough of that on their own. Instead, a One child needs to loosen up, allow herself to make mistakes, give herself a little elbowroom when it comes to strictures, and find opportunities to think outside of the box.

Appendix A

Enneagram Resources

You should supplement this presentation of Enneagram concepts with additional reading. The following list gives a brief description of each book or resource in terms of what they have to offer. You will find additional resources in Appendix B.

Overall Interpretation of Enneagram Theory*

Don Riso's book, *Personality Types: Using the Enneagram for Self-Discovery*, and Helen Palmer's book, *The Enneagram: Understanding Yourself and the Others in Your Life*, were both published in the 1980s and are widely considered classics that have been reprinted many times. They each have a distinct way of presenting Enneagram concepts that will help serious students of the Enneagram broaden their understanding of the system and how it works overall as well as the specifics of each enneatype. Both have long been internationally recognized authorities on the Enneagram.

Don Richard Riso and Russ Hudson

Don Richard Riso and his partner, Russ Hudson, emphasize the use of modern psychological tools and principles to interpret and work with the Enneagram. Most Enneagram teachers recognize at least three ranges of health within each type—healthy, average, and unhealthy—but Riso and Hudson codified a far more detailed and comprehensive concept of nine levels of development: three within each of the three primary ones (healthy, average, and unhealthy) within each enneatype. Any serious student of the Enneagram will gain a more wholly comprehensive understanding of each enneatype by reading Riso and Hudson's books on personality types, as well as their other excellent books on the subject, all of which are exceptionally well researched and informative. Anyone interested in learning more about the Enneagram of Personality should begin here:

Riso, Don Richard, and Russ Hudson. *Personality Types: Using the Enneagram for Self-Discovery* (New York: Houghton Mifflin Company, 1996).

———. *Understanding the Enneagram: The Practical Guide to Personality Types*, (New York: Houghton Mifflin Company, 1996).

———. *The Wisdom of the Enneagram: The Complete Guide to Psychological and Spiritual Growth for the Nine Personality Types* (New York: Bantam Books, a division of Random House, 2000).

www.enneagraminstitute.com—everything you could possibly need is here, including the Riso-Hudson Enneagram Type Indicator (RHETI), considered by many to be the most comprehensive personality test for determining your Eneatype.

Helen Palmer

As one of its earliest proponents, and also one of the most highly respected international scholars, teachers, and authors, Helen Palmer is considered a grande dame of the Enneagram. Her books on the Enneagram are classics, and she teaches classes on an ongoing basis all over the world. Palmer writes about "spiritual passions" and types people based on fundamental sins: anger, pride, envy, avarice, gluttony, lust, sloth, fear, and deceit—sort of the seven deadly sins plus two. She called these sins or weaknesses "capital tendencies" and postulated that each personality is dominated by one of the nine capital tendencies.

Palmer, Helen. *The Enneagram: Understanding Yourself and the Others in Your Life* (New York: HarperSanFrancisco, 1988.).

———. *The Enneagram in Love & Work: Understanding Your Intimate & Business Relationships* (New York: Harper SanFrancisco, 1995).

www.enneagram.com—check out the courses available!

David Daniels, M.D., and Virginia Price, Ph.D.

The Essential Enneagram: The Definitive Personality Test and Self Discovery Guide was originally published as *The Stanford Enneagram Discovery Inventory and Guide*. This book contains an excellent test—developed from the authors' many years in research and clinical observation—for discovering your type as well as abbreviated yet very clear descriptions of each type, clarifications about possible misidentification, and suggestions on what to do when you know your type and want to expand your consciousness. The $10 price tag equals the cost of taking an online test. The following resources are recommended:

Daniels, David, M.D., and Virginia Price, Ph.D. *The Essential Enneagram: The Definitive Personality Test and Self Discovery Guide* (New York: HarperCollins Publishers, 2000).

www.enneagramworldwide.com—this site has a wealth of information and classes. Founded by Helen Palmer and David Daniels.

The Enneagram at Work

Even though this book didn't focus on the use of the Enneagram in the workplace, the information in the following two books is extremely helpful in understanding multiple layers of the nine enneatypes and how they manifest in the world. If using the Enneagram as a resource at work is your goal, then by all means snap up these books!

Goldberg, Michael J. *The 9 Ways of Working: How to Use the Enneagram to Discover Your Natural Strengths and Work More Effectively* (New York: Marlowe & Company, Avalon Publishing Group, 1999).

Lapid-Bogda, Ginger. *Bringing Out the Best in Yourself at Work: How to Use the Enneagram System for Success* (New York: McGraw-Hill Books, 2004).

Bast, Mary, and Clarence Thomson. *Out of the Box: Coaching Field Guide* (Louisburg, KS: Ninestar Publishing, 2006).

www.enneagramcentral.com—Thomson offers the free Enneagram test used in this book, along with free newsletters and learning programs.

www.breakoutofthebox.com—Mary Bast provides coaching material and her personal specialty: poetry to exemplify enneatypes.

The Enneagram in Therapy

An intelligent guide to working with the concepts of the Enneagram in therapy. Bartlett's book is particularly helpful in understanding the fixations of the various types, particularly in how they present themselves and how to find little windows into their worlds. It's an excellent resource for coaches and counselors, or anyone who aspires to become one.

Bartlett, Carolyn. *The Enneagram Field Guide: Notes on Using the Enneagram in Counseling, Therapy, and Personal Growth* (Portland, OR: The Enneagram Consortium, 2003).

Spiritual Aspects of the Enneagram

Sandra Maitri has a comprehensive knowledge of the Enneagram that she uses to weave information on the spiritual dimensions of the Enneagram into her two beautifully written books. Both books focus on the Holy Ideas, or as she explains, "nine different enlightened perspectives . . . a particular perception of reality, a vantage point from which it (reality) is seen, experienced, and understood . . . views of reality freed from the prejudices of personality," from which the fixations, or Enneagram of Personality emerge. Maitri's books substantially increase your depth of understanding about the Enneagram as a whole and each enneatype in particular. The following are recommend:

Maitri, Sandra. *The Spiritual Dimension of the Enneagram: Nine Faces of the Soul*, (New York: Penguin Putnam, Inc., 2000).

———. *The Enneagram of Passions and Virtues: Finding the Way Home* (New York: Jeremy P. Tarcher/Penguin, the Penguin Group, 2005).

Clarence Thomson calls upon his other discipline, theology, to explain how an Enneagram style is essentially a trance, and provides parables that illustrate how Jesus and other spiritual masters used parables as a trance-shattering literary form.

Thomson, Clarence. *Parables and the Enneagram* (Portland, OR, Metamorphous Press, 2001).

Blomgren, Karen and Clarence Thomson. *Not Only Angels Have Wings*, (a CD of poetry set to music by Blomgren that serves as entertaining and educational tool).

Movie and Literary Enneatypes

According to the technical editor of this book, Clarence Thomson, "Thomas Condon is a featured speaker at every IEA conference and is consistently asked by local IEA chapters to teach them." His book provides clear and concise information on Enneatype basics, and then illustrates each with fabulous examples from real life and the movies that he jokingly refers to as his "multi-million-dollar audio-visual aids." Not only is it a fun read for anyone, it contains a lot of extremely insightful information. Thus, the following is highly recommended:

Condon, Thomas. *The Enneagram Movie and Video Guide: How to See Personality Styles in the Movies* (Portland, OR: Metamorphous Press, 1999).

www.thechangeworks.com—this is only place to find an accurate and impressive list of famous people's enneatypes. It provides an enormous amount of helpful information.

Also according to Thomson, Judith Searle's *The Literary Enneagram* "has made her nationally popular, and her book is superb." This book is absolutely invaluable in understanding the nine enneatypes, and the use of literary characters to illustrate the behaviors and characteristics of each enneatype is great. Even if you're more interested in enneatypes than literary examples, this book will definitely bring immense clarity and help all the information you are assimilating fall into place. So the following is highly recommended:

Searle, Judith. *The Literary Enneagram: Characters from the Inside Out* (Portland, OR: Metamorphous Press, 2001).

Psychological Perspective

The following books are invaluable in understanding the psychological connections to the Enneagram of Personality. One is a primer on Jungian theory that is easy to read and extremely informative. As other critics of the Jungian connection have noted, not all of Jung's theories correspond or have a direct link to the Enneagram, but Jung himself admitted that his theories were evolving and permeable.

The other book is a classic on personality types derived from the *Diagnostic and Statistical Manual of Mental Disorders, Fourth Edition* (*DSM-IV*), which is widely used by therapists and counselors. Again, there is not a straight correlation, and there are many overlaps, but descriptions of these personality types very much capture aspects of each of the enneatypes. If you're interested in a deeper understanding of human personality, try:

Pascal, Eugene, Ph.L. *Jung to Live By: A Guide to the Practical Application of Jungian Principles for Everyday Life* (New York: Time Warner Book Group, 1992).

Oldham, John M. M.D., and Lois B. Morris. *New Personality Self-Portrait: Why You Think, Work, Love, and Act the Way You Do* (New York: A Bantam Book, 1995).

Other books on Jungian theory:

McGuire, William, and C. G. Hull, R.F.C. *Jung Speaking: Interviews and Encounters* (Princeton, NJ: Princeton University Press, 1977).

Snowden, Ruth, *Teach Yourself Jung* (New York: McGraw-Hill, 2006).

Staub De Laszlo, Violet, ed. *The Basic Writings of C. G. Jung* (New York: The Modern Library, 1959).

Additional books worth a look:

Wagner, Jerome, Ph.D. *An Introduction to the Enneagram: Personality Styles, and Where You Fit* (New York:

MJF Books, Fine Communications, 1996). This book provides valuable information in an easy-to-understand way and can be quite helpful in understanding basic concepts and classic behaviors of each enneatype.

Fensin, Alan, and George Ryan. *Your Secret Self: A Quick and Easy Question-and-Answer Guide That Reveals the True You!* (New York: Avon Books, 1993). This book also has a short test and provides information in short, staccato bursts that are easy to absorb.

Additional Reading

While they do convey pertinent information, the following books are just plain fun, perfect for guessing-type parlor games but also so right-on that you will spot yourself and your loved ones fairly easy.

Baron, Renee, and Elizabeth Wagele. *Are You My Type, Am I Yours? Relationships Made Easy Through the Enneagram*, (New York: HarperSanFrancisco, 1995).

———. *The Enneagram Made Easy: Discover the 9 Types of People*, (New York, NY: HarperSanFrancisco, HarperCollins, 1994).

Wagele, Elizabeth. *The Enneagram of Parenting: The 9 Types of Children and How to Raise Them Successfully* (New York: HarperSanFrancisco, 1997).

Additional Web Sites

This is the site where this book's technical reviewer, Clarence Thomson, shares his knowledge. Definitely check this one out!

www.enneagramcentral.com

This International Enneagram Association Web site is definitely worth reading.

www.internationalenneagram.org

*Please note that the "technical" books on the Enneagram that reference original material from Oscar Ichazo and Claudio Naranjo, M. D., are extremely expensive and/or extremely technical. Many people find them difficult to understand and/or limited in their perspective. As such, they have not been included here. For the majority of people who are interested in the Enneagram as a way to increase self-understanding, the contemporary books and the many workshops available are far more helpful.

Appendix B

Bibliography

Addison, Rabbi Howard A. *Cast in God's Image: Discover Your Personality Type Using the Enneagram and Kabbalah* (Woodstock, VT: Jewish Lights Publishing, LongHill Partners, Inc., 2001).

Baron, Renee, and Elizabeth Wagele. *Are You My Type, Am I Yours? Relationships Made Easy Through the Enneagram* (New York: HarperCollins, 1995).

———. *The Enneagram Made Easy: Discover the 9 Types of People* (New York: HarperCollins, 1994).

Bartlett, Carolyn. *The Enneagram Field Guide: Notes on Using the Enneagram in Counseling, Therapy, and Personal Growth* (Portland, OR: The Enneagram Consortium, 2003).

Chernick Fauvre, Katherine, and David Chernick Fauvre. *Enneagram Instinctual Subtypes* (self-published workbook, 1995).

———. *The Enneagram and Psychotherapy* (self-published two-disc CD).

Condon, Thomas. *The Enneagram Movie and Video Guide: How to See Personality Styles in the Movies* (Portland, OR: Metamorphous Press, 1999).

Daniels, David, M.D., and Virginia Price, Ph.D. *The Essential Enneagram: The Definitive Personality Test and Self-Discovery Guide* (New York: HarperCollins Publishers, 2000).

Fensin, Alan, and George Ryan. *Your Secret Self: A Quick and Easy Question-and-Answer Guide That Reveals the True You!* (New York: Avon Books, 1993).

Frings Keyes, Margaret. *The Enneagram Relationship Workbook: A Self and Partnership Assessment Guide* (Muir Beach, CA: Molysdatur Publications, 1992).

Goldberg, Michael J. *The 9 Ways of Working: How to Use the Enneagram to Discover Your Natural Strengths and Work More Effectively* (New York: Marlowe & Company, Avalon Publishing Group, 1999).

Horsley, Mary. *The Enneagram for the Spirit: How to Make Peace with Your Personality and Understand Others* (New York: Barron's Educational Series, Inc., 2005).

Hurley, Kathleen, and Theodore Dobson. *Enneagram for the 21st Century: The Modern Seeker's Guide to Fulfilling Relationships and Spiritual Vitality* (Lakewood, CO: WindWalker Press, 1999).

———. *My Best Self: Using the Enneagram to Free the Soul* (New York: HarperCollins Publishers, 1993).

———. *What's My Type? Use the Enneagram System of 9 Personality Types to Identify the Secret Promise of Your Personality Type, Break Out of Your Self-defeating Patterns, Transform Your Weaknesses into Unimagined Strengths* (New York: HarperCollins Publishers, 1991).

Ichazo, Oscar. *Interviews with Oscar Ichazo* (New York: Arica Institute Press, 1982).

Lapid-Bogda, Ginger. *Bringing Out the Best in Yourself at Work: How to Use the Enneagram System for Success* (New York: McGraw-Hill Books, 2004).

Maitri, Sandra. *The Spiritual Dimension of the Enneagram: Nine Faces of the Soul* (New York: Penguin Putnam, Inc., 2000).

———. *The Enneagram of Passions and Virtues: Finding the Way Home* (New York: Jeremy P. Tarcher/Penguin, the Penguin Group, 2005).

McGuire, William, and C. G. Hull, R.F.C. *Jung Speaking: Interviews and Encounters* (Princeton, NJ: Princeton University Press, 1977).

Naranjo, Claudio, M.D. *Character and Neurosis: An Integrated View* (Nevada City, CA: Gateway Publications, 1990).

———. *Enneatypes in Psychotherapy: Selected Transcripts of the First Symposium on the Personality Enneagrams* (Prescott, AZ:, Hohm Press, 1995).

Oldham, John M., M.D., and Lois B. Morris. *New Personality Self-Portrait: Why You Think, Work, Love, and Act the Way You Do* (New York: A Bantam Book, 1995).

Palmer, Helen. *The Enneagram: Understanding Yourself and the Others in Your Life* (New York: HarperCollins Publishers, 1988).

———. *The Enneagram in Love & Work: Understanding Your Intimate & Business Relationships* (New York: HarperCollins Publishers, 1995).

Pascal, Eugene, Ph.L. *Jung to Live By: A Guide to the Practical Application of Jungian Principles for Everyday Life* (New York: Time Warner Book Group, 1992).

Riso, Don Richard, and Russ Hudson. *Personality Types: Using the Enneagram for Self-Discovery* (New York: Houghton Mifflin Company, 1996).

———. *The Wisdom of the Enneagram: The Complete Guide to Psychological and Spiritual Growth for the Nine Personality Types* (New York: Bantam Books, 2000).

———. *Understanding the Enneagram: The Practical Guide to Personality Types*, (New York: Houghton Mifflin Company, 1996).

Rohr, Richard, et al. *Experiencing the Enneagram* (New York: The Crossroad Publishing Company, English translation, 1992).

Searle, Judith. *The Literary Enneagram: Characters from the Inside Out* (Portland, OR: Metamorphous Press, 2001).

Snowden, Ruth. *Teach Yourself Jung* (New York: McGraw-Hill, 2006).

Staub De Laszlo, Violet, ed. *The Basic Writings of C. G. Jung* (New York: The Modern Library, 1959).

Thomson, Clarence. *Parables and the Enneagram* (Portland, OR: Metamorphous Press, 2002).

Wagele, Elizabeth. *The Enneagram of Parenting: The 9 Types of Children and How to Raise Them Successfully* (New York: HarperSanFrancisco, 1997).

Wagner, Jerome, Ph.D. *An Introduction to the Enneagram: Personality Styles, and Where You Fit* (New York: MJF Books, Fine Communications, 1996).

Zannos, Susan. *Human Types: Essence and the Enneagram* (York Beach, ME: Samuel Weiser, Inc., 1997).

Index

THE EVERYTHING® SERIES!

BUSINESS & PERSONAL FINANCE

Everything® Accounting Book
Everything® Budgeting Book, 2nd Ed.
Everything® Business Planning Book
Everything® Coaching and Mentoring Book, 2nd Ed.
Everything® Fundraising Book
Everything® Get Out of Debt Book
Everything® Grant Writing Book, 2nd Ed.
Everything® Guide to Buying Foreclosures
Everything® Guide to Fundraising, $15.95
Everything® Guide to Mortgages
Everything® Guide to Personal Finance for Single Mothers
Everything® Home-Based Business Book, 2nd Ed.
Everything® Homebuying Book, 3rd Ed., $15.95
Everything® Homeselling Book, 2nd Ed.
Everything® Human Resource Management Book
Everything® Improve Your Credit Book
Everything® Investing Book, 2nd Ed.
Everything® Landlording Book
Everything® Leadership Book, 2nd Ed.
Everything® Managing People Book, 2nd Ed.
Everything® Negotiating Book
Everything® Online Auctions Book
Everything® Online Business Book
Everything® Personal Finance Book
Everything® Personal Finance in Your 20s & 30s Book, 2nd Ed.
Everything® Personal Finance in Your 40s & 50s Book, $15.95
Everything® Project Management Book, 2nd Ed.
Everything® Real Estate Investing Book
Everything® Retirement Planning Book
Everything® Robert's Rules Book, $7.95
Everything® Selling Book
Everything® Start Your Own Business Book, 2nd Ed.
Everything® Wills & Estate Planning Book

COOKING

Everything® Barbecue Cookbook
Everything® Bartender's Book, 2nd Ed., $9.95
Everything® Calorie Counting Cookbook
Everything® Cheese Book
Everything® Chinese Cookbook
Everything® Classic Recipes Book
Everything® Cocktail Parties & Drinks Book
Everything® College Cookbook
Everything® Cooking for Baby and Toddler Book
Everything® Diabetes Cookbook
Everything® Easy Gourmet Cookbook
Everything® Fondue Cookbook
Everything® Food Allergy Cookbook, $15.95
Everything® Fondue Party Book
Everything® Gluten-Free Cookbook
Everything® Glycemic Index Cookbook
Everything® Grilling Cookbook
Everything® Healthy Cooking for Parties Book, $15.95
Everything® Holiday Cookbook
Everything® Indian Cookbook
Everything® Lactose-Free Cookbook
Everything® Low-Cholesterol Cookbook
Everything® Low-Fat High-Flavor Cookbook, 2nd Ed., $15.95
Everything® Low-Salt Cookbook
Everything® Meals for a Month Cookbook
Everything® Meals on a Budget Cookbook
Everything® Mediterranean Cookbook
Everything® Mexican Cookbook
Everything® No Trans Fat Cookbook
Everything® One-Pot Cookbook, 2nd Ed., $15.95
Everything® Organic Cooking for Baby & Toddler Book, $15.95
Everything® Pizza Cookbook
Everything® Quick Meals Cookbook, 2nd Ed., $15.95
Everything® Slow Cooker Cookbook
Everything® Slow Cooking for a Crowd Cookbook
Everything® Soup Cookbook
Everything® Stir-Fry Cookbook
Everything® Sugar-Free Cookbook
Everything® Tapas and Small Plates Cookbook
Everything® Tex-Mex Cookbook
Everything® Thai Cookbook
Everything® Vegetarian Cookbook
Everything® Whole-Grain, High-Fiber Cookbook
Everything® Wild Game Cookbook
Everything® Wine Book, 2nd Ed.

GAMES

Everything® 15-Minute Sudoku Book, $9.95
Everything® 30-Minute Sudoku Book, $9.95
Everything® Bible Crosswords Book, $9.95
Everything® Blackjack Strategy Book
Everything® Brain Strain Book, $9.95
Everything® Bridge Book
Everything® Card Games Book
Everything® Card Tricks Book, $9.95
Everything® Casino Gambling Book, 2nd Ed.
Everything® Chess Basics Book
Everything® Christmas Crosswords Book, $9.95
Everything® Craps Strategy Book
Everything® Crossword and Puzzle Book
Everything® Crosswords and Puzzles for Quote Lovers Book, $9.95
Everything® Crossword Challenge Book
Everything® Crosswords for the Beach Book, $9.95
Everything® Cryptic Crosswords Book, $9.95
Everything® Cryptograms Book, $9.95
Everything® Easy Crosswords Book
Everything® Easy Kakuro Book, $9.95
Everything® Easy Large-Print Crosswords Book
Everything® Games Book, 2nd Ed.
Everything® Giant Book of Crosswords
Everything® Giant Sudoku Book, $9.95
Everything® Giant Word Search Book
Everything® Kakuro Challenge Book, $9.95
Everything® Large-Print Crossword Challenge Book
Everything® Large-Print Crosswords Book
Everything® Large-Print Travel Crosswords Book
Everything® Lateral Thinking Puzzles Book, $9.95
Everything® Literary Crosswords Book, $9.95
Everything® Mazes Book
Everything® Memory Booster Puzzles Book, $9.95
Everything® Movie Crosswords Book, $9.95
Everything® Music Crosswords Book, $9.95
Everything® Online Poker Book
Everything® Pencil Puzzles Book, $9.95
Everything® Poker Strategy Book
Everything® Pool & Billiards Book
Everything® Puzzles for Commuters Book, $9.95
Everything® Puzzles for Dog Lovers Book, $9.95
Everything® Sports Crosswords Book, $9.95
Everything® Test Your IQ Book, $9.95
Everything® Texas Hold 'Em Book, $9.95
Everything® Travel Crosswords Book, $9.95
Everything® Travel Mazes Book, $9.95
Everything® Travel Word Search Book, $9.95
Everything® TV Crosswords Book, $9.95
Everything® Word Games Challenge Book
Everything® Word Scramble Book
Everything® Word Search Book

HEALTH

Everything® Alzheimer's Book
Everything® Diabetes Book
Everything® First Aid Book, $9.95
Everything® Green Living Book
Everything® Health Guide to Addiction and Recovery
Everything® Health Guide to Adult Bipolar Disorder
Everything® Health Guide to Arthritis
Everything® Health Guide to Controlling Anxiety
Everything® Health Guide to Depression
Everything® Health Guide to Diabetes, 2nd Ed.
Everything® Health Guide to Fibromyalgia
Everything® Health Guide to Menopause, 2nd Ed.
Everything® Health Guide to Migraines
Everything® Health Guide to Multiple Sclerosis
Everything® Health Guide to OCD
Everything® Health Guide to PMS
Everything® Health Guide to Postpartum Care
Everything® Health Guide to Thyroid Disease
Everything® Hypnosis Book
Everything® Low Cholesterol Book
Everything® Menopause Book
Everything® Nutrition Book
Everything® Reflexology Book
Everything® Stress Management Book
Everything® Superfoods Book, $15.95

HISTORY

Everything® American Government Book
Everything® American History Book, 2nd Ed.
Everything® American Revolution Book, $15.95
Everything® Civil War Book
Everything® Freemasons Book
Everything® Irish History & Heritage Book
Everything® World War II Book, 2nd Ed.

HOBBIES

Everything® Candlemaking Book
Everything® Cartooning Book
Everything® Coin Collecting Book
Everything® Digital Photography Book, 2nd Ed.

Everything® Drawing Book
Everything® Family Tree Book, 2nd Ed.
Everything® Guide to Online Genealogy, $15.95
Everything® Knitting Book
Everything® Knots Book
Everything® Photography Book
Everything® Quilting Book
Everything® Sewing Book
Everything® Soapmaking Book, 2nd Ed.
Everything® Woodworking Book

HOME IMPROVEMENT

Everything® Feng Shui Book
Everything® Feng Shui Decluttering Book, $9.95
Everything® Fix-It Book
Everything® Green Living Book
Everything® Home Decorating Book
Everything® Home Storage Solutions Book
Everything® Homebuilding Book
Everything® Organize Your Home Book, 2nd Ed.

KIDS' BOOKS

All titles are $7.95

Everything® Fairy Tales Book, $14.95
Everything® Kids' Animal Puzzle & Activity Book
Everything® Kids' Astronomy Book
Everything® Kids' Baseball Book, 5th Ed.
Everything® Kids' Bible Trivia Book
Everything® Kids' Bugs Book
Everything® Kids' Cars and Trucks Puzzle and Activity Book
Everything® Kids' Christmas Puzzle & Activity Book
Everything® Kids' Connect the Dots Puzzle and Activity Book
Everything® Kids' Cookbook, 2nd Ed.
Everything® Kids' Crazy Puzzles Book
Everything® Kids' Dinosaurs Book
Everything® Kids' Dragons Puzzle and Activity Book
Everything® Kids' Environment Book $7.95
Everything® Kids' Fairies Puzzle and Activity Book
Everything® Kids' First Spanish Puzzle and Activity Book
Everything® Kids' Football Book
Everything® Kids' Geography Book
Everything® Kids' Gross Cookbook
Everything® Kids' Gross Hidden Pictures Book
Everything® Kids' Gross Jokes Book
Everything® Kids' Gross Mazes Book
Everything® Kids' Gross Puzzle & Activity Book
Everything® Kids' Halloween Puzzle & Activity Book
Everything® Kids' Hanukkah Puzzle and Activity Book
Everything® Kids' Hidden Pictures Book
Everything® Kids' Horses Book
Everything® Kids' Joke Book
Everything® Kids' Knock Knock Book
Everything® Kids' Learning French Book
Everything® Kids' Learning Spanish Book
Everything® Kids' Magical Science Experiments Book
Everything® Kids' Math Puzzles Book
Everything® Kids' Mazes Book
Everything® Kids' Money Book, 2nd Ed.
Everything® Kids' Mummies, Pharaoh's, and Pyramids Puzzle and Activity Book
Everything® Kids' Nature Book
Everything® Kids' Pirates Puzzle and Activity Book
Everything® Kids' Presidents Book
Everything® Kids' Princess Puzzle and Activity Book
Everything® Kids' Puzzle Book
Everything® Kids' Racecars Puzzle and Activity Book
Everything® Kids' Riddles & Brain Teasers Book
Everything® Kids' Science Experiments Book
Everything® Kids' Sharks Book
Everything® Kids' Soccer Book
Everything® Kids' Spelling Book
Everything® Kids' Spies Puzzle and Activity Book
Everything® Kids' States Book
Everything® Kids' Travel Activity Book
Everything® Kids' Word Search Puzzle and Activity Book

LANGUAGE

Everything® Conversational Japanese Book with CD, $19.95
Everything® French Grammar Book
Everything® French Phrase Book, $9.95
Everything® French Verb Book, $9.95
Everything® German Phrase Book, $9.95
Everything® German Practice Book with CD, $19.95
Everything® Inglés Book
Everything® Intermediate Spanish Book with CD, $19.95
Everything® Italian Phrase Book, $9.95
Everything® Italian Practice Book with CD, $19.95
Everything® Learning Brazilian Portuguese Book with CD, $19.95
Everything® Learning French Book with CD, 2nd Ed., $19.95
Everything® Learning German Book
Everything® Learning Italian Book
Everything® Learning Latin Book
Everything® Learning Russian Book with CD, $19.95
Everything® Learning Spanish Book
Everything® Learning Spanish Book with CD, 2nd Ed., $19.95
Everything® Russian Practice Book with CD, $19.95
Everything® Sign Language Book, $15.95
Everything® Spanish Grammar Book
Everything® Spanish Phrase Book, $9.95
Everything® Spanish Practice Book with CD, $19.95
Everything® Spanish Verb Book, $9.95
Everything® Speaking Mandarin Chinese Book with CD, $19.95

MUSIC

Everything® Bass Guitar Book with CD, $19.95
Everything® Drums Book with CD, $19.95
Everything® Guitar Book with CD, 2nd Ed., $19.95
Everything® Guitar Chords Book with CD, $19.95
Everything® Guitar Scales Book with CD, $19.95
Everything® Harmonica Book with CD, $15.95
Everything® Home Recording Book
Everything® Music Theory Book with CD, $19.95
Everything® Reading Music Book with CD, $19.95
Everything® Rock & Blues Guitar Book with CD, $19.95
Everything® Rock & Blues Piano Book with CD, $19.95
Everything® Rock Drums Book with CD, $19.95
Everything® Singing Book with CD, $19.95
Everything® Songwriting Book

NEW AGE

Everything® Astrology Book, 2nd Ed.
Everything® Birthday Personology Book
Everything® Celtic Wisdom Book, $15.95
Everything® Dreams Book, 2nd Ed.
Everything® Law of Attraction Book, $15.95
Everything® Love Signs Book, $9.95
Everything® Love Spells Book, $9.95
Everything® Palmistry Book
Everything® Psychic Book
Everything® Reiki Book
Everything® Sex Signs Book, $9.95
Everything® Spells & Charms Book, 2nd Ed.
Everything® Tarot Book, 2nd Ed.
Everything® Toltec Wisdom Book
Everything® Wicca & Witchcraft Book, 2nd Ed.

PARENTING

Everything® Baby Names Book, 2nd Ed.
Everything® Baby Shower Book, 2nd Ed.
Everything® Baby Sign Language Book with DVD
Everything® Baby's First Year Book
Everything® Birthing Book
Everything® Breastfeeding Book
Everything® Father-to-Be Book
Everything® Father's First Year Book
Everything® Get Ready for Baby Book, 2nd Ed.
Everything® Get Your Baby to Sleep Book, $9.95
Everything® Getting Pregnant Book
Everything® Guide to Pregnancy Over 35
Everything® Guide to Raising a One-Year-Old
Everything® Guide to Raising a Two-Year-Old
Everything® Guide to Raising Adolescent Boys
Everything® Guide to Raising Adolescent Girls
Everything® Mother's First Year Book
Everything® Parent's Guide to Childhood Illnesses
Everything® Parent's Guide to Children and Divorce
Everything® Parent's Guide to Children with ADD/ADHD
Everything® Parent's Guide to Children with Asperger's Syndrome
Everything® Parent's Guide to Children with Anxiety
Everything® Parent's Guide to Children with Asthma
Everything® Parent's Guide to Children with Autism
Everything® Parent's Guide to Children with Bipolar Disorder
Everything® Parent's Guide to Children with Depression
Everything® Parent's Guide to Children with Dyslexia
Everything® Parent's Guide to Children with Juvenile Diabetes
Everything® Parent's Guide to Children with OCD
Everything® Parent's Guide to Positive Discipline
Everything® Parent's Guide to Raising Boys
Everything® Parent's Guide to Raising Girls
Everything® Parent's Guide to Raising Siblings
Everything® Parent's Guide to Raising Your Adopted Child
Everything® Parent's Guide to Sensory Integration Disorder
Everything® Parent's Guide to Tantrums
Everything® Parent's Guide to the Strong-Willed Child
Everything® Parenting a Teenager Book
Everything® Potty Training Book, $9.95
Everything® Pregnancy Book, 3rd Ed.
Everything® Pregnancy Fitness Book
Everything® Pregnancy Nutrition Book
Everything® Pregnancy Organizer, 2nd Ed., $16.95
Everything® Toddler Activities Book
Everything® Toddler Book
Everything® Tween Book
Everything® Twins, Triplets, and More Book

PETS

Everything® Aquarium Book
Everything® Boxer Book
Everything® Cat Book, 2nd Ed.
Everything® Chihuahua Book
Everything® Cooking for Dogs Book
Everything® Dachshund Book
Everything® Dog Book, 2nd Ed.
Everything® Dog Grooming Book